GETTYSBURG

PRAISE FOR *GETTYSBURG*

'Here is a splendid first book to read about Gettysburg. Adam I. P. Smith places the battle within its broader wartime context, clearly narrates its tactical ebb and flow, and, most valuably, assesses its powerful influence on popular understanding of the nation's most disruptive and transformational moment.'

Gary W. Gallagher, John L. Nau III Professor of
History Emeritus, University of Virginia

'In this lucid, learned book, Adam I.P. Smith has captured the emotional power of Gettysburg as both a place and an idea. The epic clash symbolized the triumph of freedom for Unionists and the allure of "what ifs" for Confederates. Over time, Gettysburg became a test of Americans' capacity for forgiveness and a testament to the "endurance of the ideal of heroic warfare." Smith deftly conveys the drama and contingency of the battle itself and of the battle of the imagination, over Civil War memory, that still rages on.'

Elizabeth R. Varon, author of *Longstreet: The Confederate
General Who Defied the South*

'In eloquent prose, Smith weaves stories large and small into a sweeping narrative that explains why Gettysburg has loomed so large in the national imagination since those fateful days in July 1863. This volume is destined to become the first place anyone turns to understand the coming, fighting, aftermath, and memory of America's most well-known battle and town.'

Caroline E. Janney, author of *Ends of War: The Unfinished
Fight of Lee's Army after Appomattox*

GREAT BATTLES

GETTYSBURG

ADAM I. P. SMITH

Great Clarendon Street, Oxford, OX2 6DP,
United Kingdom

Oxford University Press is a department of the University of Oxford.
It furthers the University's objective of excellence in research, scholarship,
and education by publishing worldwide. Oxford is a registered trade mark of
Oxford University Press in the UK and in certain other countries

© Adam I. P. Smith 2025

The moral rights of the author have been asserted

All rights reserved. No part of this publication may be reproduced, stored in
a retrieval system, or transmitted, in any form or by any means, without the
prior permission in writing of Oxford University Press, or as expressly permitted
by law, by licence or under terms agreed with the appropriate reprographics
rights organization. Enquiries concerning reproduction outside the scope of the
above should be sent to the Rights Department, Oxford University Press, at the
address above

You must not circulate this work in any other form
and you must impose this same condition on any acquirer

Published in the United States of America by Oxford University Press
198 Madison Avenue, New York, NY 10016, United States of America

British Library Cataloguing in Publication Data
Data available

Library of Congress Control Number: 2024940454

ISBN 978–0–19–967127–4

Printed and bound by
CPI Group (UK) Ltd, Croydon, CR0 4YY

Links to third party websites are provided by Oxford in good faith and
for information only. Oxford disclaims any responsibility for the materials
contained in any third party website referenced in this work.

The manufacturer's authorised representative in the EU for product safety is
Oxford University Press España S.A. of El Parque Empresarial San Fernando de Henares,
Avenida de Castilla, 2 – 28830 Madrid (www.oup.es/en or product.safety@oup.com).
OUP España S.A. also acts as importer into Spain of products made by the manufacturer.

For Caroline

FOREWORD

The phrase 'great battle' carries four immediate connotations. The first relates to time. The standard narrative, whether applied to Marathon or Waterloo, Salamis or Trafalgar, assumes that the events occurred on a single day – or at most over two or three days. Secondly, a battle has to be on a scale large enough not to be deemed a skirmish. Fighting may characterise war but fighting itself does not constitute a battle. If the forces involved are too small or the commitment to engage by one or both sides too slight, then what happens is not a great battle. At least one side, and possibly both, must want to fight. Third, a battle occurs in a defined, and in some cases a confined, space. On land it is sometimes so geographically limited that it takes its name from an otherwise little-known geographical feature, such as Bunker Hill, or an obscure village or hamlet. At sea, its name may be more capacious but as often it gains precision by adopting the name of the nearest landfall. Lastly, a 'great battle' implies that the consequences are commensurate with the commitment; in other words, that the result proves decisive.

The infrequency with which all these four conditions have been met helps explain why 'great battles' have been rare. Great battles need to be infrequent or they lose their cachet Calling some forms of combat battles may be no more than a rhetorical device, coined for effect, or, more pragmatically, to give shape to otherwise seemingly inchoate episodes. Since the nineteenth century the word battle has been applied to events that are not concentrated in time and space. Persistent fighting in all seasons and all weathers combined with technological innovation and full social and economic mobilisation to make outcomes more cumulative than singular. In the Second World War, the 'battle' of the Atlantic was decisive, both in the economic war and in enabling the D Day landings, but it was not clearly defined in time or space. It lasted nearly four years and, although largely restricted to the North Atlantic, still embraced an expanse of sea larger than any major continent.

At sea especially, battle in a traditional sense was rarely decisive. As the British naval theorist. Julian Corbett, observed in 1911, man lives upon the land, and so 'it scarcely needs saying that it is almost impossible that a war can be decided by naval action alone'. The Greeks may have checked the Persians at Salamis in 480 BC but they did not topple the Persian empire. The Christian victory over the Turks at Lepanto in 1572 was similarly a great defensive success, which checked the Ottoman advance into the Mediterranean but not into continental Europe. On 21 October 1805 Nelson 'decisively' defeated the French and Spanish fleets at Trafalgar but war with France continued for another decade. In the short term too, while Nelson's victory ended the danger of a French invasion of Britain, it did not end Napoleon's freedom of manoeuvre within Europe. Just over six weeks after Trafalgar the French emperor won possibly his greatest victory, defeating the armies of Austria and Russia at Austerlitz on 2 December 1805. However, even in land warfare 'decisiveness' can be a relative, rather than an absolute, term. At Austerlitz Napoleon smashed the continental alliance which threatened him in the short term but he did not prevent its resuscitation in 1813. Nor did he win the economic and commercial war waged by Britain and underpinned by its maritime power.

In Corbett's day, the ability of warships to cope with adverse weather conditions enabled by the invention of steam power and the end of sail ought to have made naval battle more possible, but it did not necessarily do so, partly because improved navigation and advanced technology opened up more of the world's oceans and so created greater space in which an opponent could hide. Since the beginning of the twentieth century, war at sea has been increasingly fought under and over the surface, as well as on it. In the Second

World War 'great battles' were fought in the Pacific simultaneously at sea and in the air with devastating effects - at Pearl Harbor in December 1941, the Coral Sea in May 1942 and Midway in the following month. Each was conducted at scale and was limited in time, if less so in space. Each was more clearly a 'great battle' in the classical definition than the whole of the battle of the Atlantic, but the war against Japan was also won by sustained economic warfare conducted by submarines and by island-hopping amphibious assaults. The Second World War did not end in a climactic battle like Waterloo in 1815. That final defeat of Napoleon, for many then and since, embodies the concept of decisiveness, not least because it introduced nearly a century of comparative European peace, but its outcome too rested as much on the exhaustion of France, and of its enemies, after two decades of conflict as it did on the results of a single day on a confined battlefield, however sanguinary the fighting.

For those who practise war in the twenty-first century the idea of a 'great battle' can seem no more than the echo of a remote past. The names on regimental colours or the events commemorated at mess dinners bear little relationship to patrolling in dusty villages or waging 'wars amongst the people'. Contemporary military doctrine downplays the idea of victory, arguing that wars end by negotiation not by the smashing of an enemy army or navy. Indeed it erodes the very division between war and peace, and with it the aspiration to fight a culminating 'great battle'.

And yet to take battle out of war is to redefine war, possibly to the point where some would argue that it ceases to be war. Carl von Clausewitz, who experienced two 'great battles' at first hand—Jena-Auerstedt in 1806 and Borodino in 1812 wrote in *On War* that major battle is 'concentrated war', and 'the centre of gravity of the entire campaign'. Clausewitz's remarks related to the theory of strategy. He recognized that in practice armies might avoid battles, but even then the efficacy of their actions relied on the latent threat of fighting. Winston Churchill saw the importance of battles in different terms, not for their place within war but for their impact on historical and national narratives. His forebear, the Duke of Marlborough, fought four major battles and named his palace after the most famous of them, Blenheim, fought in 1704. Battles, Churchill wrote in his life of Marlborough, are 'the principal milestones in secular history'. For him, 'Great battles, won or lost, change the entire course of events, create new standards of values, new moods, new atmospheres, in armies and nations, to which all must conform'.

Clausewitz's experience of war was shaped by Napoleon. Like Marlborough, the French emperor sought to bring his enemies to battle. However, each lived within a century of the other, and they fought their wars in the same continent and even on occasion on adjacent ground. Winston Churchill's own experience of war, which spanned the late nineteenth-century colonial conflicts of the British Empire as well as two world wars, became increasingly distanced from the sorts of battle he and Clausewitz described. In 1898 Churchill rode in a cavalry charge in a battle which crushed the Madhist forces of the Sudan in a single day. Four years later the British commander at Omdurman, Lord Kitchener, brought the South African War to a conclusion after a two-year guerrilla conflict in which no climactic battle occurred. Both Churchill and Kitchener served as British Cabinet ministers in the First World War, a conflict in which battles lasted weeks, and even months, and which, despite their scale and duration, did not produce clear-cut outcomes. The 'battle' of Verdun ran for all but one month of 1916 and that of the Somme for five months. The potentially decisive naval action at Jutland spanned a more traditional twenty-four-hour timetable but was not conclusive and was not replicated during the war.

Clausewitz would have called these twentieth-century 'battles' campaigns, or even seen them as wars in their own right. The determination to seek battle and to venerate its effects may therefore be culturally determined, the product of time and place, rather than an inherent attribute of war. The ancient historian Victor Davis Hanson has argued that seeking battle is a 'western way of war' derived from classical Greece. Seemingly supportive of his argument are the

FOREWORD

writings of Sun Tzu, who flourished in the warring states period in China between two and five centuries before the birth of Christ, and who pointed out that the most effective way of waging war was to avoid the risks and dangers of actual fighting. Hanson has provoked strong criticism: those who argue that wars can be won without battles are not only to be found in Asia. Eighteenth-century European commanders, deploying armies in close-order formations in order to deliver concentrated fires, realized that the destructive consequences of battle for their own troops could be self-defeating. After the First World War, Basil Liddell Hart developed a theory of strategy which he called 'the indirect approach', and suggested that manoeuvre might substitute for hard fighting, even if its success still relied on the inherent threat of battle.

The winners of battles have been celebrated as heroes, and nations have used their triumphs to establish their founding myths. It is precisely for these reasons that their legacies have outlived their direct political consequences. Commemorated in painting, verse, and music, marked by monumental memorials, and used as the way points for the periodization of history, they have enjoyed cultural afterlives. These are evident in many capitals, in place names and statues, not least in Paris and London. The French tourist who finds himself in a London taxi travelling from Trafalgar Square to Waterloo Station should reflect on his or her own domestic peregrinations from the Rue de Rivoli to the Gare d'Austerlitz. Today's Mongolia venerates the memory of Genghis Khan while Greece and Macedonia scrap over the rights to Alexander the Great.

This series of books on 'great battles' tips its hat to both Clausewitz and Churchill. Each of its volumes situates the battle which it discusses in the context of the war in which it occurred, but each then goes on to discuss its legacy, its historical interpretation and reinterpretation, its place in national memory and commemoration, and its manifestations in art and culture. These are not easy books to write. The victors were more often celebrated than the defeated; the effect of loss on the battlefield could be cultural oblivion. However, that point is not

xi

universally true: the British have done more over time to mark their defeats at Gallipoli in 1915 and Dunkirk in 1940 than their conquerors on both occasions. For the history of war to thrive and be productive it needs to embrace the view from 'the other side of the hill', to use the Duke of Wellington's words. The battle the British call Omdurman is for the Sudanese the battle of Kerreri; the Germans called Waterloo 'la Belle Alliance' and Jutland Skagerrak. Indeed, the naming of battles could itself be a sign not only of geographical precision or imprecision (Kerreri is more accurate but as a hill, rather than a town, it is harder to find on a small-scale map), but also of cultural choice. In 1914 the German general staff opted to name their defeat of the Russians in East Prussia not Allenstein (as geography suggested) but Tannenberg, in order to claim revenge for the defeat of the Teutonic Knights in 1410.

Military history, more than many other forms of history, is bound up with national stories. All too frequently it fails to be comparative, to recognize that war is a 'clash of wills' (to quote Clausewitz once more), and so omits to address both parties to the fight. Cultural difference and even more linguistic ignorance can prevent the historian considering a battle in the round; so too can the availability of sources. Levels of literacy matter here, but so does cultural survival. Often these pressures can be congruent but they can also be divergent. Britain enjoys much higher levels of literacy than Afghanistan, but in 2002 the memory of the two countries' three wars flourished in the latter, thanks to an oral tradition, much more robustly than in the former, for whom literacy had created distance. And the historian who addresses cultural legacy is likely to face a much more challenging task the further in the past the battle occurred. The opportunity for invention and reinvention is simply greater the longer the lapse of time since the key event.

All historians of war must, nonetheless, never forget that, however rich and splendid the cultural legacy of a great battle, it was won and lost by fighting, by killing and being killed. The battle of Waterloo has left as abundant a footprint as any, but the general who harvested most of its glory reflected on it in terms which have general applicability and carry across time in their capacity to capture a universal truth. Wellington wrote to Lady Shelley in its immediate aftermath: 'I hope to God I have fought my last battle. It is a bad thing to be always fighting. While in the thick of it I am much too occupied to feel anything; but it is wretched just after. It is quite impossible to think of glory. Both mind and feelings are exhausted. I am wretched even at the moment of victory, and I always say that, next to a battle lost, the greatest misery is a battle gained.'

Readers of this series should never forget the immediate suffering caused by battle, as well as the courage required to engage in it: the physical courage of the warrior, the soldier, sailor or airman, and the moral courage of the commander, ready to hazard all on its uncertain outcomes.

HEW STRACHAN

applicability and carry across time in their capacity to capture a universal truth. Wellington wrote to Lady Shelley in its immediate aftermath: 'I hope to God I have fought my last battle. It is a bad thing to be always fighting. While in the thick of it I am much too occupied to feel anything; but it is wretched just after. It is quite impossible to think of glory. Both mind and feelings are exhausted. I am wretched even at the moment of victory, and I always say that, next to a battle lost, the greatest misery is a battle gained.'

Readers of this series should never forget the immediate suffering caused by battle, as well as the courage required to engage in it: the physical courage of the warrior, the soldier, sailor or airman, and the moral courage of the commander, ready to hazard all on its uncertain outcomes.

HEW STRACHAN

ACKNOWLEDGMENTS

I spent happy days in the archives in Gettysburg and many months working through primary sources online, and am grateful to all the archivists and institutions who have made historical research in this field so accessible. I also, of course, owe a profound debt to the many scholars who have labored before me to understand the place of Gettysburg in American memory. It is also a great pleasure to be able to thank two brilliant graduate students, Matthew Griffin and Theo Fawcett, for their research assistance. Despite Matt and Theo's help, the book took longer to complete than I'd anticipated, in part because shortly after signing the contract, I took an all-consuming new role as the Director of the Rothermere American Institute in Oxford. I'm very grateful to the brilliant team who now work alongside me in the RAI—Katy Long, Uta Balbier, Hannah Greiving, Richard Purkiss, Dan Rowe, and Bethan Davies—whose good humor and immense competence have enabled me to take the time I needed over the last two years to finish this book.

I am indebted to friends and colleagues including Robert Cook for his shrewd and deeply knowledgeable reading of the whole manuscript and to Rachel Shelden, Michael Woods, Frank Towers, Erik Alexander, and Matt Mason for their brilliant feedback on individual chapters. I gave papers on aspects of this work at the Universities of Durham, Northumbria, Plymouth, and Oxford and was honored to deliver the Peter J. Parish memorial lecture at the BrANCH (British Association of Nineteenth-Century American Historians) conference in September 2023. At all these occasions, audience members asked questions that shaped my thinking. I also want to thank Matthew Cotton, Cathryn Steele, Emma Slaughter, copy-editor Michael Janes,

ACKNOWLEDGMENTS

and series editor Huw Strachan at OUP for their patience as well as their professionalism. I wrote most of this book on visits to the Gladstone Library in Harwarden. Just thinking about their beautiful silent reading rooms with the scent of the Grand Old Man's leatherbound books makes me wistful and I am grateful to the staff and trustees of the library for creating such a wonderful space for writers.

But most of all I would like to thank my wife Caroline, and my daughters Rosie, Eleanor, and Lucy without whose love and relentless teasing I would not, even now, have completed this project.

ADAM SMITH
Oxford
July 2024

CONTENTS

List of Figures	xix
List of Maps	xxi
Introduction	1
1. The Many Roads to Gettysburg	15
2. The Confederate Invasion, June–July 1863	47
3. The Battle, July 1–2	68
4. High Tide and Retreat, July 3 and Afterward	107
5. Aftermath, 1863–1865	134
6. Coming to Terms with Victory and Defeat, *c.*1865–1880	157
7. Gettysburg as the Nation's "Turning Point," *c.*1880–1933	186
8. Gettysburg and the Meaning of America, *c.*1930–1990	221
Epilogue: Gettysburg and American History	248
Notes	263
Further Reading	289
Picture and Map Acknowledgments	291
Index	293

LIST OF FIGURES

2.1. "Pennsylvanian Gratitude" *Harper's Weekly*, 1863   57

3.1. A sketch of the fighting in Devil's Den   93

4.1. Sketch by Edwin Forbes, a staff artist for *Frank Leslie's Illustrated*, of Union soldiers relaxing after the battle, entitled "Behind the breastworks on the right, July 4, 1863."   124

5.1. Photograph by James F. Gibson for Brady's Studio of bloated corpses lying on the battlefield several days after the battle   138

6.1. Peter F. Rothermel, *The Battle of Gettysburg: Pickett's Charge* (1870)   159

7.1. John Bachelder's "isometric map" of the Gettysburg battlefield, showing topography and troop positions   193

7.2. The "High Water Mark of the Rebellion" Monument, situated near the spot on Cemetery Ridge where Confederate attackers briefly broke through Union lines on July 3   198

7.3. The meeting at the stone wall at the Bloody Angle between veterans of the Philadelphia Brigade and Pickett's Division on July 4, 1887   205

7.4. The Fiftieth Anniversary Reunion, 1913: Union and Confederate veterans shake hands at the Bloody Angle, the point on the Union line where the attacking Confederates briefly broke through on July 3   211

7.5. Photograph of a dead Confederate sharpshooter in Devil's Den   213

LIST OF FIGURES

8.1. Postcard of the Eternal Light Peace Memorial at
Gettysburg showing the gas flame, which was intended
to burn in perpetuity, but which was turned off
permanently in 1974 during the oil crisis   223
8.2. President Eisenhower and Field Marshall Montgomery
tour the Gettysburg battlefield in 1957   233

LIST OF MAPS

2.1. Map of Lee's advance into Pennsylvania, June 3–July 3, 1863   53

3.1. Overview of the first day of the battle, July 1, 1863   71

3.2. Lee's plan for the second day's attacks   81

3.3. Overview of the second day of the battle   92

4.1. Overview of the fighting on July 3, 1863   119

Introduction

As soon as the guns had fallen silent on July 3, 1863, Gettysburg became a place of the imagination. The three-day battle fought across the gentle ridges around the small Pennsylvania town was the bloodiest encounter of the American Civil War. Farmers and bounty hunters uncovered human remains in the fields for years afterward. Even today, you can still find bullets.

But it was not only the scale of the violence that bestowed upon this battle a sacred place in American national mythology.[1] The stories told about Gettysburg are the stories of America itself, more intensely so than other hallowed places in the American story, including even the places where the Revolution was fought, or the Constitution was written. The essence of the Gettysburg myth is that here the fate of the republic was determined; here that America was re-consecrated.

Gettysburg has been a vacation resort, a war grave, and a public park, and, more than that, it has become a shrine. Over a century and a half, pilgrims have come to Gettysburg in their millions to remember the dead but also to feel connected to some essential quality of the American experiment. Even those who came to have a good day out were also constructing memories and meaning.

If, like countless visitors before, you stand on Cemetery Ridge, perhaps in the fading light of a summer evening, you will see a blue-tinged range of hills on the western horizon. In front of you, the fields slope gently away toward a road and then rise again to a wooded ridge about a mile in front. In 1964, the writer Norman Cousins went to Gettysburg to interview former president Dwight Eisenhower, who had retired to a farm on the battlefield. "It is difficult," Cousins wrote, "for the mind to sustain the thought that these quiet fields were once the setting for one of the most violent encounters in history. The blood in the earth runs deep at Gettysburg, but the eye sees only an enchanted land."[2] Blood and soil: the vital nationalist ingredients of sacred ground. The land is enchanted not just by the beauty of the countryside but by the enchantments of meaning imposed on the field by those who fought there and those who have come after.

Why Gettysburg and not some other battle at some other time? When and why did this happen? The simple answer to the *when* question is Independence Day, July 4, 1863. It was then that it became clear that the battle was over, and the Union Army of the Potomac was victorious. The Confederate Army of Northern Virginia had run out of options after the repulse of Pickett's Charge on July 3. This was the massive frontal assault on the Union line by around twelve thousand soldiers under the command of three Confederate generals, one of whom was George Pickett. It is a familiar story and one which echoes that of so many other "heroic" failed attacks against well-entrenched defenders, from the charge of the Light Brigade at Balaklava to the ranks of British soldiers advancing toward German machine guns on the first day of the Somme. Having suffered around 30 percent casualties, any hope of advancing on Baltimore or Washington extinguished, Lee's army began the hazardous business of retreating south, across the flood-swollen Potomac River and back into Virginia. In the following decades, veterans relitigated every tactical and strategic decision in print, in testimony to Congressional hearings and in valedictory speeches.

The main aim of this book is to offer some answers to the *why* question. In the Gettysburg Address, Abraham Lincoln summed up American exceptionalism: the idea that the United States had a Providential mission to preserve free government everywhere on earth. Similarly, there is also a Gettysburg exceptionalism: the idea that the bloody struggle in those Pennsylvania fields was both different from all other battles while also of universal significance. Gettysburg was the only big battle of the Civil War fought on free soil. (Antietam, in

September 1862, was fought in a loyal state, but one in which slavery remained legal.) People's perception at the time in both North and South was that this mattered greatly. It was one thing for the Union Army to invade the South; it was quite another for the rebels to strike into the heart of the free North. Gettysburg became the turning point of turning points, the moment when all was lost and all won. It was the Civil War in miniature: a glorious, storied, tragic tale that was small enough to comprehend but large enough to be inspirational. For all its complexity, understanding Gettysburg was easier than understanding the whole war—or so it seemed. Many people labored to define what Gettysburg meant, from the town boosters who wanted tourist dollars, the veterans in blue and gray (who often warred among themselves more than with their erstwhile enemies), to self-appointed custodians of the battlefield such as the various agencies of the Federal government and generations of historians, journalists, and battlefield guides. The story of how and why Gettysburg has come to matter so much—why it has become an American "shrine"—is a story of many hands, and it has kept rolling on from that Independence Day in 1863 down to the latest generation.

* * *

So much for the battle of the imagination. What of the real-life events? It is a challenge to attempt even the most basic summary of what happened between the first and third of July 1863. One of the most familiar themes in the Gettysburg literature is, paradoxically, its unknowability. It is undoubtedly true that, as Carol Reardon points out, there is contradictory evidence about even such apparently "knowable" facts, such as how long the Confederate artillery bombardment on July 3 lasted. Was it ten minutes or four hours? Confident primary sources can be found to support either.[3] Although hundreds of soldiers left written accounts of their experience at Gettysburg, their recollections are necessarily partial. One rebel soldier confessed after the war to his former commanding officer that "I was very much like the French Soldier of whom you sometimes told us, who never saw anything while the battle was going on except the rump of his fat file leader."[4] The military historian Richard Holmes has argued that for combatants under extreme stress, rightly thinking that each breath could be their last, the human brain "records clips of experience, often in erratic sequence."[5] And even if soldiers could cognitively process what was happening around them, the undulating landscape and the smoke from artillery fire all constrained their vision. Lieutenant Frank Haskell, an aide to a Union general, who wrote one of the most fluent and apparently complete witness accounts, emphasized how difficult it was for anyone—even someone who was there, never mind those who were not—to really know what was going on. "A full account of the battle *as it was* will never, can never be made," he wrote. "Who could sketch the changes, the constant shifting of the bloody panorama? It is not possible."[6]

Politics compounded the fog of war. Veterans feuded over which commanders should take credit or blame. Later, they fought over the design and placement of the monuments that sprouted like spring flowers across the battlefield. The Civil War generation cared deeply about inscribing the correct version of history on the landscape, identifying the precise spot at which storied events occurred. One modern historian has been driven to conclude that "our knowledge of Gettysburg [is] a collection of changing and varying opinions manipulated intentionally or unwittingly by thousands of veterans and historians alike."[7] As the military historian Clare Makepeace pointed out, individuals recall episodes in their past differently depending on what happened next. That is especially true of soldiers who survive wars. Indeed, as Makepeace also says, drawing on research by psychologists, "the principal function of a memory may not even be to record the past, but to enable an individual to generate meaning in life in the present."[8]

Nevertheless, with those caveats in mind, here are the barest bones of the story. In June 1863, Robert E. Lee's Army of Northern Virginia advanced into Pennsylvania. It was the first time in the war that an entire rebel army had invaded a free state. (Lee had marched into

Maryland the previous September and fought a major battle at Antietam, but, although it had not seceded from the Union, Maryland was still a slaveholding state, and no one, before the war, would have regarded it as anything other than Southern.) On July 1, two Confederate brigades arrived in the South-Central Pennsylvania town of Gettysburg from the northwest, where they were surprised to be met by stiff resistance from Union cavalry. Both armies rushed units to the scene. After heavy fighting, the rebels drove the Union forces out of the town and onto the higher ground of Cemetery Hill, in normal times a fifteen-minute walk up a gentle gradient. Overnight, Union reinforcements arrived and, making the most of the topography, extended the defensive line southward for about a mile along a ridge. Eventually, the Union line was in a shape often referred to as a "fishhook," curling from Culp's Hill and Cemetery Hill in the north toward the rocky mound of Little Round Top at the southern end. The Confederates meanwhile took up their position along Seminary Ridge, which ran north–south in parallel to Cemetery Ride. The stage was therefore set for a set piece battle between armies that eyed each other across two-thirds of a mile of farmland.

The next day, July 2, Lee ordered assaults on the Union's right and left flanks. There were some successes—especially in an area where the Union line formed a salient—but, despite heavy losses, the Confederates did not break the Union lines as Lee had hoped. It was on July 2 that some of the most famous episodes of the battle took place, including the desperate Union defense of Little Round Top, which anchored the Union's left flank.

On the third day, July 3, at around 1 pm, the rebels launched a massive artillery bombardment designed to soften Union defenses, after which came the infantry assault on the Federal center that has gone down in history as Pickett's Charge, one of the great military disasters of modern history. Confederate soldiers advanced slowly up the gentle slope toward the low line of stones where Union troops waited. As they clambered over fences, with only the occasional dip in the land to obscure them from the sight of the defenders, artillery and rifle fire ripped into them. A few hundred attackers breached the Union line, but they were soon overwhelmed. One Union general described Pickett's Charge as "that famous scene which made the battle of Gettysburg more dramatic than any other event of the Civil War, and which more nearly approximates the conception of what a battle is in the imagination of persons who have never seen one."[9] The mid-twentieth century's best-selling Civil War historian, Bruce Catton, wrote of Pickett's Charge in an elegiac tone: "There it was, for the last time in this war, perhaps for the last time anywhere, the grand pageantry and color of war in the old style: beautiful and majestic and terrible."[10]

It sometimes seems, however, that what happened at Gettysburg is less important than what did not. There are many "what-ifs": if Jeb Stuart's cavalry had provided better intelligence, Lee might have avoided a full-scale engagement on such unpromising terrain; if the overly cautious General Richard Ewell had ordered an assault on the reeling Union troops gathering on Culp's Hill on the evening of the first day, perhaps the Union Army would never have secured so strong a defensive position; if Longstreet had organized the assault on the second day with less tardiness, perhaps the rebels could have secured Little Round Top before it was properly defended; or possibly if A. P. Hill's and Ewell's Corps had supported Longstreet more energetically, the second day's attacks might have broken the Union lines. In 1953, the science fiction writer Ward Moore published *Bring the Jubilee*, a novel set in an alternative universe in which the Confederacy had won the "War of Southron Independence," as it became known, simply by occupying Little Round Top before Union troops did so. (In Moore's novel the protagonist travels back in time and changes the course of history to our own by accidentally delaying the Confederate advance.)[11]

And then there's the final "what-if": if only Pickett had not charged. Or if he did charge, if only it had succeeded—if he had been better supported, or if the rebel artillery had wrought more destruction on Union defenses, or (as Winston Churchill imagined in a 1931 exercise in counterfactual history), if Stuart's cavalry had attacked from the rear causing panic in the Union's left flank—in other words, if the Yankees had not somehow spoiled the script by holding firm.[12]

The most hallowed places on the battlefield are those where the battle seemed to turn, such as the copse of trees and the "Bloody Angle," which marked the focus of Pickett's charge. In recent decades, those legendary spots have been rivaled in popularity by the hitherto little-visited monument to the 20th Maine. This is due to the influence of Michael Shaara's novel *The Killer Angels* (1974) and the film *Gettysburg* (1993), based on Shaara's book, which turned the colonel of that Maine regiment, Joshua Lawrence Chamberlain, into the man who saved the Union by holding the extreme left flank against superior numbers. Chamberlain was a gifted writer and a decent officer, but his responsibility for the outcome on Little Round Top has often been exaggerated. Today, the licensed battlefield guides dampen visitors' often overblown assumptions about Chamberlain's role. Still, the image of Chamberlain ordering a bayonet counter-charge down the slope of Little Round Top, like the futile heroism of Pickett's charge or the foot-dragging of Longstreet, has become what Gettysburg "means" to millions of people. Through these moments and these heroic characters, the battle has become a lived experience for millions who were not there.

Chamberlain was one of the thousands of veterans on both sides who labored to secure Gettysburg's place not just as the preeminent battle of the Civil War but as one of the decisive moments in world history. "The theater and the play were well matched," proclaimed John C. Black, the colonel of the 37th Illinois Infantry Regiment, as he surveyed the battlefield in 1885. "On those commanding heights, and sheltered by those now silent groves, stretched out in grim and deadly opposition the gathered hosts of kindred yet warring men. Here, as at Marathon, as at Cannae, as at Waterloo, destiny brought two great causes together and bade them struggle for the mastery of the world and the guidance of the future."[13] Like the Major-General in *The Pirates of Penzance*, who boasted that he could "quote the fights historical from

Marathon to Waterloo in order categorical," Black was no doubt consciously or unconsciously influenced by the best-selling 1851 book *Fifteen Decisive Battles of the World: From Marathon to Waterloo*, by Sir Edward Creasy, which explained world history through these great military turning points. Sure enough, when a new edition of Creasy's book was published in 1899 in New York, it included an additional chapter on the 1863 struggle in Pennsylvania written by John Gilmer Speed, a former *New York World* editor. Gettysburg had achieved immortality as one of the "fights historical." "Confederate hope was not utterly destroyed" by defeat at Gettysburg, wrote Gilmer; but, had it gone the other way, "Union hope would have been destroyed." And therefore "Gettysburg was one of the great decisive battles of the world."[14]

It is intoxicating, that fantasy of alternative endings. Our imaginations are fired by the idea of a single turning point so profound that the destiny of nations lies in the balance. The Southern novelist William Faulkner captured the yearning especially well:

> For every Southern boy fourteen years old, not once but whenever he wants it, there is the instant when it's still not yet two o'clock on that July afternoon in 1863; the brigades are in position behind the rail fence, the guns are laid and ready in the woods, and the furled flags are already loosened to break out and Pickett himself with his long oiled ringlets and his hat in one hand probably and his sword in the other looking up the hill waiting for Longstreet to give the word and it's all in the balance, it hasn't happened yet, it hasn't even begun yet, it not only hasn't begun yet but there is still time for it not to begin against that position and in those circumstances which made more men than Garnett and Kemper and Armistead and Wilcox look grave yet it's going to begin, we all know that, we have come too far with too much at stake and that moment doesn't need even a fourteen year old boy to think *This time. Maybe this time* with all this much to lose and all this much to gain: Pennsylvania, Maryland, the world, the golden dome of Washington itself to crown with desperate and unbelievable victory the desperate gamble.[15]

This famous passage may be overwrought, but it captures something essential about the public memory of Gettysburg. We all know "it's going to begin" not just because with the benefit of hindsight we know it *did*, but because having gotten to that stage—with the furled flags loosened—the actors were trapped in a logical sequence of events of their own making.

The "might-have-beens" at Gettysburg are made more, not less, compelling by the simultaneous, if paradoxical, sense that fate was almost—*almost*—inescapable. If Gettysburg is the ultimate fantasy "turning point" of the American Civil War, it is one in which the chances of an alternative outcome were tantalisingly small. Could Lee really have acted any differently on July 3, given Meade's decision to remain on the field after resisting Confederate assaults on July 2? And could Lee have really done anything other than ordering those assaults on July 2—notwithstanding the unpromising terrain—with an army that was in high spirits and had (once again) just sent Union troops scattering in semi-disorder? Could Lee have avoided a full-scale engagement on July 1, once first contact had been made? One could go back further—did Lee have better alternatives than taking his army into Pennsylvania? If the answer to these questions is "probably not," then, in retrospect, the rebel armies were trapped in circumstances in which their chances of victory were vanishingly small. With hindsight, perhaps the battle's outcome was foreordained by the end of the first day, when the Union Army, having been ignominiously driven through the town, found itself, as much by luck as by design, in an enviable defensive position.

This is the essence of the "Lost Cause" myth: the idea that the war was nobly fought by brave Southern men against odds that were, if not impossible, then almost so. And it is a feeling captured in the idea that the battle marked the "high-water mark" of the rebellion. As the millions of visitors to the Gettysburg battlefield over the years know, the "high-water mark" is also a literal place—the portion of Cemetery Ridge near the angle in a low stone boundary wall where Confederate soldiers in General Lewis Armistead's brigade of Pickett's Division breached the Union defenses, only to be captured or killed. The term "high-water mark" was coined by John Bachelder, an eccentric and indefatigable early historian of Gettysburg, of whom we will hear more later. "It was here," Bachelder wrote, in the first tourist guide to the battlefield, "that one of the most gallant charges recorded in history terminated: here that the tide of success of the Confederacy turned; from this spot the defeated troops fell back, and never again made a successful stand. This was indeed 'the high-water mark of the rebellion!'"[16] Tides, of course, always turn: the water always recedes even if it doesn't look as if it will.

The allure of the "if only" Faulknerian fantasy proved so alluring that the losing side has probably received more attention over the years than the victors. They have certainly been far more thoroughly romanticized. For most of the last century and a half, the image of Gettysburg as the "high-water mark" of the rebellion, with all the neo-Confederate romance that idea conjures, has overshadowed the Lincolnian image of Gettysburg as the site of a "new birth of freedom." If Gettysburg was where the "tide" of the Confederacy began to ebb, then it was where the nation was saved. Little wonder the battle's tale, told and retold in a thousand voices, has become the stuff of legend.

At the dedication of the National Cemetery at Gettysburg in November 1863, the renowned orator Edward Everett concluded his two-hour address with the prediction that, wheresoever the accounts of the war were read, "down to the latest syllable of recorded time," there will be "no brighter page than that which records THE BATTLE OF GETTYSBURG."[17] So far, at least, his prediction has been borne out. No other Civil War battle matches Gettysburg's status in the national consciousness. Gettysburg has been the site of demonstrations by Civil Rights leaders and present-day white supremacists, a place of pilgrimage for history buffs and the ultimate stage set for re-enactors. About no other clash of arms have so many Americans cared so much.

It is impossible to delineate precisely how much this is due to the battle itself and how much to the battle's chief early interpreter, Abraham Lincoln, whose brief "address" followed Everett's great oration at the ceremonies to consecrate the new burial place for the

Union dead. In just nine elegantly constructed sentences, Lincoln set out a compelling rationale for the cause for which the fallen soldiers of the Union had given their "last full measure of devotion." That cause, Lincoln said, was to give the nation a "new birth of freedom" and, more than that, to ensure that "government of the people, by the people, for the people, shall not perish from the earth." The stakes could not have been higher: if the Civil War was a conflict to determine whether government based on the proposition of "equality" could exist, and if this battle was the greatest battle of the war, then it mattered to the "whole family of man" (as Lincoln put it in another speech) that the tide was turned back. For Lincoln, the Union's effort to suppress the slaveholder's insurgency was part of a global Manichean struggle between democracy and autocracy—slaveholders were the American manifestation of mankind's dark impulse to dominate. Russia had a Tsar; the US had spawned the Slave Power. In substance, there was nothing that Lincoln said at Gettysburg that he hadn't said before, but the way he said it ensured that his speech—and therefore the battle—belonged to the ages.

1865 was as significant a caesura in the historical experience for white and Black Southerners as was 1945 for mainland Europe. But in another sense, the war matters not because it created a new world but because it ratified the status quo: reaffirming the American Union as the indispensable carrier of liberty. In global terms, it was the thwarting of what most Northerners saw as the rebellion against the best government on earth—the closure of a diabolical alternative path—that mattered.

So, why did Gettysburg become the ultimate representation of the war and, in a larger, Lincolnian sense, of the Manichean struggle between liberty and despotism? Some of the answer lies in Gettysburg's "what-if" quality. For it to matter that the stakes were high, it must be possible to imagine an alternative ending. This points us to the key to Gettysburg's cultural significance as the most legible moment when the war might have gone either way. If, for the South, Pickett's charge was the high-water mark of their cause, for

Northerners, accepting the same logic, this was the moment, above all, when all could have been lost.

J. R. R. Tolkien argued that fairy stories could provide moral or emotional consolation because of their very particular type of happy ending: a sudden turn of events which prevents the protagonist from meeting some terrible and very plausible fate.[18] He coined the neologism "eucatastrophe"—a good catastrophe. Good or bad, it is in the imagined contingency of battle that the drama resides. Gettysburg was the battle in which the contending forces of the 1860s seemed, in retrospect, to have been most similar. They were armies of white men fighting for noble and, with retrospective paradox, apparently compatible ends. Although by July 1863, the Emancipation Proclamation had come into effect, Black troops did not play a role in the battle, and if one ignored the enslavement of Pennsylvanians by Confederate armies (a willful memory lapse that was near universal among white people), it was possible to relegate the issue of slavery to some distant arena, as if it had no direct bearing on the fight. Gettysburg was also removed in time and place from the more problematic memory of the relentless and bloody bloody-mindedness of Grant's overland campaign in 1864. And so, this battle—like no other—could easily be remembered as the last and greatest of the romantic clashes between two well-balanced sides, testing the martial virtues of courage and valor as if it had been the field of Marathon or Waterloo.

* * *

Is it an exaggeration to claim, as many have done, that Gettysburg was the most important battle of the Civil War? Probably. In a war that sprawled across a continent and was to continue for almost two years afterward, it is a stretch to claim this battle as the singular turning point. Military historians typically argue that the Union Army's capture, after a long siege, of the river town of Vicksburg, Mississippi, on July 4—the day after the battle in Pennsylvania concluded—was a more serious blow to the rebellion. The fall of Vicksburg gave the United States control of the Mississippi river, cutting off Texas and the rebel-held areas of Louisiana and Arkansas from the rest of the Confederacy. Gettysburg's prominence is grist to the mill for military historians who chafe at how far the eastern theater of war attracts a disproportionate amount of attention compared to the battles in the west.

Yet Gettysburg did matter for much the reason that the battle's postbellum boosters said it did: had the Union Army been defeated, the political consequences would have been dire, in a way that would not have been the case had Grant failed to break through at Vicksburg. It is true that we cannot understand the strategic weakness of the Confederacy if we are too distracted by General Lee's dashing campaigns in Virginia, Maryland, and Pennsylvania. But it is also true that, after Gettysburg, Lee could never again be seen as invincible. Never again did his army march on Northern soil. Never again did Northerners en masse feel vulnerable to invasion. The insurgency continued but never again posed the same military threat to the national state.

In any case, Gettysburg will matter so long as it remains the largest battle ever fought in North America. Of the seventy-five thousand Confederates, twenty-two thousand six hundred (30 percent) were killed or injured. The toll of general officers was appalling: six dead, eight wounded, and three captured. Just as significantly, the Southern field grade officers suffered high casualties, and their absence would be felt for the duration of the war. Of the eighty-three thousand three hundred Union troops at Gettysburg, seventeen thousand seven hundred (21 percent) were killed or wounded.

This book explains why a battle came to be fought here, why it ended how it did, and what it has meant ever since. I do not claim to be comprehensive, but I have sketched out the main topographical features of the Gettysburg story. Chapters 1 to 3 explain the origins of the war, why the contending armies came to be at Gettysburg and provide an outline of the fighting over the three days. In doing so, I outline some of the major areas of controversy, not only about the wisdom of command decisions but also about what actually happened—although there are, as I will argue, aspects of the battle that remain forever unknowable despite the mountain of writing on the subject. On Confederate leadership (or the failures thereof), I should declare up front that I think that in the end, neither the lack of cohesion nor Lee's apparent overconfidence were in themselves fatal. On this vexed question, I find myself in broad agreement with General Pickett, who, when asked by reporters why the Confederacy lost, is often quoted as having replied, "I've always thought the Yankees had something to do with it." (Though fittingly, for a battle so encrusted with myths, there is no good evidence that he ever said such a thing.)[19] Chapter 4 explains the immediate impact of the battle on those who experienced it, in the armies, in the town, and further afield. Chapter 5 covers Lincoln's visit to Gettysburg and assesses what his address meant and how it has mattered. Chapters 6 and 7 explain how Northerners and Southerners fought over the meaning of the battle (not least among themselves) during the decades when veterans worked to inscribe their meanings on the battlefield itself through monuments and markers. The final chapter and the Epilogue discuss the importance of Gettysburg in American culture in the decades since the 1930s, years during which the Ku Klux Klan rallied there, and Civil Rights leaders prayed there.

This is the story of a battle that has acquired meanings far beyond the purely military. Gettysburg is the most famous small town in America and the most American small town. As a place and an event, it has become a repository of the values and ideals different groups of Americans have wished to place upon it. Accounts of the battle often begin with the observation that these two vast armies clashed there because all the roads in the region converged in the center of the town. Similarly, it so often seems that all investigations into what the United States is and has been led, and still lead, in one way or another, through Gettysburg.

1

The Many Roads to Gettysburg

There were many roads to Gettysburg, but all began with slavery. White people debated whether the Civil War was "really" about the enslavement of human beings on American soil, but African Americans knew it was. In Pennsylvania, Black people faced multiple layers of discrimination, but they still knew from personal experience that there was a stark and terrifying difference between a society in which it was legal to own human property and one in which it was not.

When the invading army crossed the Potomac onto Pennsylvanian soil in mid-June 1863, they came as kidnappers as well as marauders. For two weeks, rebel raiding parties unleashed a reign of terror on Black communities in Franklin County and surrounding areas, searching houses and barns for terrified women and children, shackling them and marching them south before returning for more. "Boys capturing negroes and horses," noted a Confederate cavalry commander in his diary on June 16.[1]

In Chambersburg, some twenty-five miles to the west of Gettysburg, a young white woman, Rachel Cormany, first became aware of the Confederate advance when she saw Black men, women, and children fleeing past her house "as fast as they could on any and all kinds of horses, their eyes fairly protruding with fear" and crying that the enemy was on their heels. As a white woman, Cormany was confident that she would not be "disturbed" even if the rebels did come, but it soon became clear that her Black neighbors were right to run. The next morning, General Albert Jenkins' cavalry arrived, hunting down any Black people they could find and "driving them" south down the Chambersburg pike into Virginia "by droves...just like we would drive cattle." For the next two days, the rebels "were carrying away mens clothing & darkeys." Cormany saw no men captured, only women and children. The men had already fled, Cormany surmised, mistakenly "thinking their women and children would not be disturbed." One woman was pleading with her "driver" for her children, "but all the sympathy she received from him was a rough 'March along'—at which she would quicken her pace again." It is "a query," wrote Rachel Cormany, "what they want with those babies—whole families were taken."[2] Another Chambersburg resident, an elderly shopkeeper called William Heyser, saw two hundred and fifty Black people taken prisoner and marched out of town on June 18.[3]

Meanwhile, on the other side of South Mountain, in the town of Gettysburg, the Black population of around two hundred people evacuated in a hurry. Local farmer Basil Biggs evacuated to Philadelphia for a month with his family, returning after the battle to find his livestock seized but his house largely intact, having been used as a Confederate hospital. Two other fleeing Black families—the Palms and the Brians—owned much of the land southwest of the town along Cemetery Ridge, where the battle would be fought. Most Black residents, however, had no property and escaped with no destination in mind and only the belongings they could carry. Most of the hundreds of thousands of refugees in the war were from the South, but in the summer of 1863 this part of the free state of Pennsylvania became a war zone, and the Biggs, Palms, and Brians became unwilling members of this exodus. White residents were mostly unsympathetic. "The Darkies made such a racket up and down by our house that we could not sleep," recalled one neighbor.[4]

We will never know for sure how many civilians were captured by Lee's army as they moved through Pennsylvania in 1863, but an informed estimate suggests it may have been at least a thousand.[5]

Many of these were free-born people who had never been south of the Mason-Dixon line before: Rachel Cormany reported that she saw "some of the colored people who were raised here taken along" chained together in an improvised slave coffle. Along with the people, foraging parties seized 50,000 head of cattle, 35,000 sheep, thousands of hogs, and at least 20,000 horses—many of which were put to immediate use in the army.[6]

General Lee issued a General Order stating that he "earnestly exhorts the troops to abstain with scrupulous care from unnecessary or wanton injury to private property."[7] But Confederates called the Black people they captured "contraband"—implying that they were tools of war, a cynical term coined by a Union commander in 1861 to justify not returning escaped slaves to their rebel masters. White Southerners regarded the Emancipation Proclamation as, among other things, an outrageous attempt to "steal" Southern property, and many in Lee's army no doubt thought that capturing African Americans was merely a small gesture of retaliation.[8] Lee's General Orders may have sought to rein in the worst excesses of his raiding parties. Still, there is no doubt that the commanders of the invading Confederate Army sanctioned, if not directed, the slave raiding. When General Longstreet instructed General Pickett to bring up his division to rejoin the First Corps en route to Gettysburg, he added, almost as an aside, "the captured contrabands had better be brought along with you for further disposition."[9] And so, even as he marshaled his forces to confront the Union Army, Longstreet did not overlook the need to keep seized African Americans under the army's control. As an institution emanating from Southern white society, the Confederate Army was structured to control enslaved people. As well as enslaving Pennsylvanians, the army brought enslaved African Americans with them as cooks and laborers. Some, naturally, took the opportunity to escape. As one Chambersburg resident drily observed to a Confederate quartermaster, "your negroes run to us a little more willingly than our horses run to you."[10]

The Confederacy's raison d'être was the defense of slavery. The eleven slave states which seceded did so directly and expressly to protect their system of slave labor. The ordinances of secession they passed in the winter of 1860–1861 did not obfuscate on this point. And once the war began, Southern leaders aspired to unite as many of the slave states as possible in their new republic, which, as Vice President Alexander Stephens of Georgia put it, had as its "cornerstone" the "great truth, that the negro is not equal to the white man; that slavery—subordination to the superior race—is his natural and normal condition. This, our new government, is the first, in the history of the world, based upon this great physical, philosophical, and moral truth."[11] More than half of the officers in Lee's army and almost a third of the rank-and-file were slaveholders or were the sons of men who were.[12] But even the others overwhelmingly assumed that enslavement of people of African descent was both natural and, at least in a biracial society, essential.

Robert E. Lee's family were slaveholders, too. As elite Virginians, it would have been strange had they not been. Yet, for a century after the war, romantic defenders of the Lost Cause who built a personality cult around Lee claimed that he was, in some sense, anti-slavery. There is no evidence to support this claim. On the contrary, when running his family's Arlington estate, Lee broke up every family on the estate bar one by hiring out or selling enslaved people and ran a regime based on violence just as other slaveholders did. He held, in fact, views that were entirely conventional for white Southerners of his generation: that Black people were better off enslaved in America than they would be back in Africa, that slavery was a burden for whites, but that in the fullness of time, when God so decreed that its purposes had been fulfilled, slavery would come to a natural end. "Their emancipation," Lee wrote, "will sooner result from the mild & melting influence of Christianity, than the storms & tempests of fiery Controversy."[13]

* * *

In the final analysis, there was a battle at Gettysburg because of the intractability of the problem of slavery. More specifically, because of the peculiar relationship between slavery and the government of the United States created by the Constitutional Convention held at

Philadelphia in 1787. It is sometimes imagined that the national divisions over slavery only emerged in the decade or two leading up to the outbreak of war in 1861, but this is not true. On the eve of the American Revolution, slavery was legal everywhere in the British colonies. By 1787, when the new Constitution was drafted, slavery had either been abolished entirely or was being phased out in New England and the mid-Atlantic states, but it had never been very important to the economy in those places, and the numbers of Black people were small. The Southern states, in contrast, had large populations of enslaved people, and their economies—driven principally by the production of tobacco, sugar, and cotton—were heavily dependent on slavery. At the time of the Constitutional Convention, nearly three hundred thousand Virginians were enslaved, almost 40 percent of the state's total population. There were only a third as many slaves in South Carolina, but they constituted an even higher percentage of the population. The slave populations of Maryland, Georgia, and North Carolina were not far behind in proportional terms. Furthermore, within those slave states, there were individual counties where the enslaved population was more than three-quarters of the whole. Of the fifty-five delegates who met to draw up a plan for a national government, just under half were slaveholders. At the same time, a handful—including Alexander Hamilton of New York and Benjamin Franklin from Pennsylvania—were outspoken in their opposition to slavery.

Most delegates agreed with the principle that a more credible central government was desirable—to create a single market and better guarantee national security—but Southerners worried that in a polity divided between free and slave states, the Federal government would pose a threat to their human property. The Constitution therefore contained several specific measures to reassure slaveholders. One was that the central government would help recapture fugitives who escaped to a free state. Another was that enslaved people would be counted (at a discounted rate of three-fifths of the population) in calculating how many representatives each state could send to

Congress and how many Electoral College votes for President they would have. The first of these provisions was the constitutional basis for the Fugitive Slave Acts of 1793 and 1850, which overrode state criminal law and, in effect, turned the Federal government into an agent and jailer for slaveholders. The second provision meant that the South was guaranteed additional representation in the Federal government, which to some extent cushioned them from the growing disparity in population size between free and slave states as the decades wore on.

In short, the Constitution ensured that in the United States, unlike in Britain, Brazil, Spain, or France, or (in relation to other forms of unfree labor like serfdom) Russia or Prussia, the central government could not abolish slavery even if it wished to do so. Furthermore, armed with constitutional provisions that insulated them from any meaningful threat of legislative abolition, slaveholders in the United States, unlike those elsewhere, could not easily be bought off. As slave labor fueled the wealth of the cotton kingdoms of the South, American slaveholders had the self-confidence not just to delay abolition for as long as possible, as may have been the case in other countries, but to resist the anti-slavery movement completely.

But if the constitutional order locked slavery into the makeup of the United States from the beginning, this was the non-negotiable price that Northerners had to pay to get Southerners to agree to a stronger Union. They thought it a price well worth paying, especially given the urgency of creating a viable national state that could raise an army and a navy against the multiple security threats from native Americans and European powers that the new United States faced in its early years. The more optimistic anti-slavery campaigners of the Revolutionary generation could hope that slavery would fade away in the South as it was doing in the North; perhaps a moral revolution combined with a pragmatic assessment of slavery's lack of economic viability would lead Southerners to end the institution voluntarily. The American Colonization Society aimed to facilitate this process by identifying locations in Africa or perhaps in the Caribbean to which the freed

Black population might be removed since few whites imagined that a biracial free society could work.

None of this, of course, happened. On the contrary, far from proving a hindrance to the South's prosperity, slavery was the engine of the United States' rapid economic growth. By the 1830s, the South—or "the cotton states" as they were now sometimes known—were the world's leading supplier of raw material to the burgeoning textile factories of the industrialized world. Southern agriculture was modern, mechanized, globalized, efficient—and slave-based. Consequently, the slave population grew and any possibility that Southern states would abolish so fundamental a component of their prosperity vanished.

Territorial expansion enabled slave-based agriculture in the United States to increase production prodigiously. Had the United States remained clustered along the Atlantic seaboard, confined by the borders agreed in the 1783 Treaty of Paris, it is possible that what Abraham Lincoln would later call a nation "half slave and half free" could have endured for longer than it did: with the relative size and power of each section kept constant, ways and means might have been found to mitigate tension between the interests of slave and free states. What happened instead was that the United States almost doubled its territorial size with the acquisition of French Louisiana in 1803 and then almost doubled again in the aftermath of the war with Mexico in the 1840s. Together with other smaller-scale acquisitions (such as taking Florida from Spain and securing Oregon in an agreement with Great Britain), the United States had, by 1850, come to resemble its present-day continental shape. This territorial dynamism was at a huge cost to the people and environment subdued by advancing American power, but it also ratcheted up the internal contradictions between free and slave societies to the point where they became unsustainable.

The Louisiana Purchase ignited a controversy over what measures could be taken, if any, by Congress to restrict or protect slavery in these new territories in the period before they were admitted to statehood. This mattered since slaveholders would not risk their property by moving into a territory unless they could be sure that the local courts and law enforcement would uphold the right to property in man. Conversely, where slavery *was* protected, that area would become unattractive to free white settlers who would not be able to compete for land or wages. Territorial expansion seemed a zero-sum game: new territory had to be open *either* to slaveholders *or* to non-slaveholding white settlers.

The temporary resolution was an apparently simple one. The new territories of the West were divided between a Northern and a Southern sphere of influence, each with a different legal regime and political economy. This was not an unusual situation in international relations but a highly unusual one *within* a nation-state. This nineteenth-century American version of the Iron Curtain was ratified in 1820 in a series of congressional measures known as the Missouri Compromise which specified that slavery would be prohibited in any future settlement north of the line of latitude 36°30' but allowed south of it. Whether this rigid division of the country would have maintained sectional peace indefinitely is a moot question because just eighteen years later, in 1848, the US extracted from the defeated Mexican government a massive territorial concession—adding much of present-day California, New Mexico, Utah, Arizona, and Nevada to the US—which re-opened once again the question of slavery's extension. Not for the first or last time in world history, military victory laid the basis for future war.

Invading Mexico to annex millions of acres of land was the policy of the dominant Democratic Party, the world's first mass political party, which brought together urban immigrants and western farmers on a populist and nationalist platform. Territorial expansion was the Democrats' solution to the economic depression triggered by the 1837 financial crisis. Land-hungry settlers would have new fields of opportunity in the West, easing the overcrowding and unemployment in the eastern cities. Although the Southern wing of the Democratic Party made clear that they expected Mexican lands to be open to slavery, Democrats in the North emphasized the benefits to propertyless white men and downplayed the problem of slavery in national life. The nationalist tradition to which Democrats adhered presented the

United States as a sanctuary of freedom in a world still under the sway of tyranny: it followed that as the boundaries of this exceptional nation expanded, so too did the empire of freedom. Yet it did not require hindsight to see that a successful war would open the Pandora's box of slavery extension: members of the opposition Whig Party, including the young Illinois congressman Abraham Lincoln, predicted as much. Lincoln was every bit as driven by nationalism as his Democratic opponents, but unlike them, he saw slavery as a profound contradiction: the wicked fairy's natal curse on the new nation.

By the 1850s, it was far harder to resolve the problem of whether slavery should expand than it might have been in the 1810s. Much had changed in forty years, not least the international environment. Among the European powers, only the crumbling Spanish empire had resisted abolition, while Britain, preeminent economically and militarily, had redefined itself as a global anti-slavery power. Four decades of transatlantic anti-slavery activity had reinforced the anti-slavery presumptions of many Northerners. And just as every action has an equal and opposite reaction, when Northern anti-slavery campaigners demanded that slavery be barred from the West, Southerners demanded "equal access" to the national domain. Harriet Beecher Stowe's sensational novel *Uncle Tom's Cabin* (1852) catalyzed the anti-slavery sentiment of the North just as a new, more forceful Fugitive Slave Act came into effect. The Act was a massive expansion of the Federal government's coercive power within free states. By its terms, *any* Northerner could be impressed by a Federal agent into a slave patrol to help round up an alleged runaway. Black people arrested under the new act were denied jury trials or the protection of local laws. Draconian as it was, the 1850 Act was fully authorized by the Constitution's fugitive slave clause. Yet this new evidence that slaveholders had the Federal government on their side caused outrage in the North.

Just as the delegates at Philadelphia in 1787 intended, the protection for slavery provided by the Constitution gave Southerners a powerful incentive to maintain the Union. Especially in the early years,

Southern politicians were usually strongly nationalist, a sentiment not unconnected to Southerners' domination of the Federal government for most of the seventy-two years between the ratification of the Constitution and secession. Throughout that time, only two presidents—John Adams (1797–1801) and his son John Quincy Adams (1825–1829)—expressed even the most tepid anti-slavery views; all the others were either slaveholders or allied with slaveholders. Southern control of the executive branch ensured a predominance of pro-slavery justices on the Supreme Court, and the "three-fifths clause" mitigated the possibility of an anti-slavery majority in the House of Representatives. In retrospect, however, the Fugitive Slave Act of 1850 was the high-water mark of slaveholder influence in Washington.

Southerners may have had the Constitution on their side, but with Northern public opinion against them—and with immigration ensuring that the population of the free states increased far more rapidly than that of the slave states—they still felt persecuted. Their fear was that whatever the Constitution said, the Federal government's power, which hitherto had protected slavery, might one day be its nemesis. This led to a schizophrenic attitude to Federalism on the part of Southern politicians. On the one hand, they actively sought to *increase* the power of the Federal government to protect slavery. On the other hand, they talked of "states' rights" and were quick to object to what they saw as an over-extension of Federal power in the interests of the North (such as when tariffs were increased on imported goods to protect Northern industry). That they sometimes used "states' rights" rhetoric in the run-up to war created the impression that Southerners sought to leave the Union in 1861 in protest at how overbearing the government was becoming. That is an impression Southerners at the time were eager to foster, not least because it echoed the complaints of the eighteenth-century colonists about the over-extended power of the government of George III. The Confederate "Revolution of 1861" thus appeared to be a re-enactment of the Revolution of 1776.

In the twentieth and twenty-first centuries, "states' rights" became the default answer of many white Americans when asked why the South left the Union. The truth, however, was very close to the opposite: Southerners were driven to secession only because their demands for ever *greater* coercive powers for the Federal government to protect slavery were successfully resisted by the free states, where roughly two-thirds of the population of the US now resided. A significant driver of the increasing support for secession in the South was anti-slavery resistance to the central government's coercive power. During the 1850s, it was *Northern*, not Southern, states which passed laws attempting to nullify Federal law—or at least one Federal law in particular: the 1850 Fugitive Slave Act. In a proclamation issued on Christmas Eve, 1860, the government of South Carolina justified independence on the grounds that the North had betrayed both the spirit and the letter of the Constitution, and a prime piece of evidence was Northern states' resistance to the Fugitive Slave Act. The South Carolinians listed the free states which had "enacted laws which either nullify the Acts of Congress or render useless any attempt to execute them. In many of these States the fugitive is discharged from service or labor claimed, and in none of them has the State Government complied with the stipulation made in the Constitution."[14]

Southern secessionists had good reason to be fearful. They were right to worry that their slave property would be insecure if the Federal government's power to act as an agent of slaveholders was successfully challenged by "states' rights" Northerners. They were right, too, to worry about the long-term implications of having as a chief executive in the White House, a man whose political appeal was premised on the idea that slavery was wrong.

This was why the election of Abraham Lincoln in November 1860 was the catalyst for war. Lincoln's party, the Republicans, had support only in the free states. The party's platform committed them to oppose the extension of slavery into US territories, notwithstanding the Supreme Court's 1857 *Dred Scott* decision which had ruled that the Federal government could not constitutionally ban slavery from any territory since it breached the property rights of slaveholders. In most respects, Lincoln was an essentially conservative man. He went into politics in the 1830s to support public infrastructure projects and a healthy banking system which would provide the credit needed to stimulate small-scale capitalist economic development. Yet slavery was the antithesis of his vision for national development and offensive to his sense of natural justice. Lincoln held the racist assumptions that one would expect of someone born in his time and place, and he did not react to slavery as a pressing human outrage as abolitionists did. Yet there is nothing in the record to contradict his 1864 assertion that he had always felt that "if slavery is not wrong, nothing is wrong." In about 1850, one of Lincoln's legal colleagues predicted that "the time would soon come...when we must be Democrats or Abolitionists." A middle path would no longer be possible. "When that time comes," replied Lincoln, "my mind is made up."[15]

As an increasingly well-known Republican Party leader, Lincoln played a role through the 1850s in convincing Northerners that Southerners were corrupting the republic in their effort not just to defend slavery but to expand it. By 1858, he had become convinced that the slave interest was on an unstoppable collision course with the free society of the North. Quoting Jesus's words from the Gospels, he warned that a "house divided against itself cannot stand," that the nation could not sustain itself "half slave and half free," and that it would inevitably become all one thing or all the other. This speech by the man who was, two years later, to become the Republican Party's presidential candidate was, not unreasonably, interpreted by white Southerners as a call to arms to his fellow Northerners. Born into relative poverty and now a prosperous lawyer in Springfield, Illinois, Lincoln's principal motivation was to defend the free labor society in which he had succeeded and which he believed only the American Union could guarantee. But he had come to the view that slavery—or at least the "Slave Power" which wielded disproportionate influence in national politics—was an existential threat to that world.

Even so, the Republican Party did not propose that slavery should or could be abolished. Because it was protected by the Constitution, making slavery illegal through legislative means was not an option for anyone who wanted to operate in the political mainstream. To maintain their political viability, Republicans went to great lengths to distance themselves from radical abolitionism. The Republican-supporting *New York Times* insisted that the party had no "more love of the negro—any greater disposition to make sacrifices for his sake, or to waive their own rights and interests for the promotion of his welfare, than the rest of mankind, North and South."[16] Instead, Republican leaders argued that the greatest threat to order and national stability came not from slavery's opponents but its increasingly authoritarian defenders. But in the end, there was no mistaking the Republican Party's intention to put slavery—as Lincoln put it—"on the road to ultimate extinction," a place that he claimed, with political skill if historical imprecision, was where "the Founders had placed it."[17] This was the sort of sentiment the South Carolina legislature had in mind when it justified its secession ordinance by warning that "a geographical line has been drawn across the Union, and all the States north of that line have united in the election of a man to the high office of President of the United States, whose opinions and purposes are hostile to slavery."[18]

The precise circumstances in which this standoff became a military conflict had enormous implications for how each side understood the war. There were four months between Lincoln's election in November 1860 and when he took office in March 1861. In that time, seven slave states (South Carolina, Georgia, Florida, Alabama, Louisiana, Mississippi, and Texas) announced they had left the Union, set up an independent Confederacy of their own with the capital in Montgomery, Alabama, and began seizing Federal property.

The lame-duck president James Buchanan, a Pennsylvanian Democrat with close ties to the South, prevaricated about how the Federal government should respond and has understandably been given bad press by historians for his weak leadership. In fairness, however, the crisis he faced was probably not one that even the deftest chief executive could have defused. Even if it was generally agreed in the North that the Union should not be broken up (and some voices urged that the "erring sisters" be allowed to "go in peace"), what could realistically be done by a government with such limited military or other power? A peace convention was held, and proposals were made for a new constitutional amendment to clarify any possible ambiguity about whether slavery could ever be abolished within the Union, but the secessionists were no longer interested in keeping the Union together on any terms. The seemingly insoluble dilemma for the Federal government was that if peaceful negotiation failed, only coercion remained, and surely a republic based on the consent of the governed could not force its people to accept sovereign authority in the style of the Austrian government subjugating nationalist revolts. What made the dilemma even more challenging was that eight slave states had *not* seceded but might be provoked to do so if the Federal government appeared to be making the crisis a conflict over slavery. In Virginia—the most populous of the slave states still in the Union and one with great symbolic importance since it had been the home of many of the Founding Fathers, including Washington—a convention had convened to consider secession but was adopting a "wait and see" attitude.

Buchanan was hideously ill-equipped personally or politically to deal with the crisis, but he was hardly alone in his bewilderment. One well-placed local politician in Ohio reported that Democrats in his district were "without exception in favor of the preservation of the Union," but they are "also almost as unanimous in their opinion that coercion is not only impolitic but suicidal." Suicidal, that is, to the nature of republican government since those rebellious states may be defeated in battle, but they "will not stay whipped, and it will require an army of three or four hundred thousand men to keep them in subjugation."[19] Even before a shot had been fired, these Northern Democrats feared that the incoming Republican party would try to use the secession crisis to launch an "abolition war." To Republicans like the president-elect, however, the secessionist leaders were disingenuous when they claimed to be acting defensively in response to his election; their real goal was to expand slavery. The South, Lincoln pointed out in January 1861, "now have the Constitution, under which we have lived over seventy years, and acts of Congress of their own framing, with no prospect of their being changed." The threat to break up the Union was an attempt at extortion, an effort to force the majority in the free states to "surrender" to the slaveholders' desire for ever greater control. "If we surrender, it is the end of us, and of the government. They will repeat the experiment upon us *ad libitum*. A year will not pass, till we shall have to take Cuba as a condition upon which they will stay in the Union."[20]

In this context, Lincoln's inaugural address, on March 4, 1861, assumed vastly more importance than any of his predecessors' addresses. Every word was analyzed for indications of how the new president would deal with the seven states that had declared themselves no longer subject to US jurisdiction. In a closely argued speech, Lincoln assured the slave states of the safety of their property within the Union—the guarantees of the Founders could not be violated. And then he made a case for the indissolubility of the Union on which the entire Union war effort was soon to be premised. Secession, Lincoln argued, was by definition an unconstitutional act since one party could not lawfully dissolve a compact without the agreement of the others. It followed that "acts of violence, within any State or States, against the authority of the United States, are insurrectionary or revolutionary." Secession, furthermore, was the "essence of anarchy" since it was a rejection by the minority of the right of the majority to prevail. Since unanimity was impossible, and the permanent rule of the minority was intolerable, the basis of American republican government, Lincoln said, was that "a majority, held in restraint by constitutional checks, and limitations, and always changing easily, with deliberate changes of popular opinions and sentiments, is the only true sovereign of a free people." Whoever would reject this notion of a restrained majority rule, conditioned by constant

GREAT BATTLES

responsiveness to public sentiment, had no palatable alternatives: "anarchy, or despotism in some form, is all that is left."[21]

Several critical elements of the Union's military strategy in the coming war followed logically from Lincoln's premises in this speech. First, and most fundamentally, he never recognized the legitimacy of the Confederate government—instead there were only rebels who must be wooed or subdued. Although it took on many other dimensions, in this essential sense, the Union military effort was always akin to a giant police action, with the Confederates in the role of rioters. And secondly, Lincoln laid the groundwork for resolving the impossible dilemma of either coercing the South or letting them go: instead, he set the South up as the aggressors and framed any military response by the North as defensive. As president, he vowed, he would do no more than use the power confided in him "to hold, occupy, and possess the property and places belonging to the government, and to collect the duties and imposts; but beyond what may be necessary for these objects, there will be no invasion, no using of force against or among the people anywhere." The Federal government, he told Southerners "will not assail you. You can have no conflict without being yourselves the aggressors."

A few weeks later, in the early hours of April 12, 1861, rebels played into Lincoln's hands by performing their assigned role as the aggressors. On the order of the Confederate government, a battery of more than four thousand guns and mortars opened fire on Fort Sumter, a US military post on an island in Charleston Harbor still garrisoned by Federal troops. The previous day the commander of the small detachment at Sumter, Major Robert Anderson, a native of slaveholding Kentucky, had politely declined a final demand from the Confederates to surrender. Fort Sumter was one of the last remaining pieces of Federal property still in US hands in a seceded state. By the time it was attacked, according to the calculations of historian Joseph Harsh, the rebels had already forcibly taken nineteen other forts, sixteen ships, eight arsenals, one mint (in New Orleans), and "numerous" customs houses and post offices.[22] Mostly, though not always, they did this without firing a shot. But Sumter had become symbolic of the standoff between Federal authority and the rebel states, a test case of Lincoln's pledge to hold Federal property. In the weeks preceding this dramatic denouement, the Buchanan and then the Lincoln administration had fretted over whether to surrender the Fort to avoid a conflict, to reinforce it with arms or men, or—the middle path that in the end was chosen—to send food by sea from Washington since the garrison could not now be resupplied from Charleston. Lincoln announced that an unarmed supply ship was coming, but the rebel guns fired first.

Throughout the free states, the news of the attack on Fort Sumter was met with widespread outrage, fueled by the press and politicians. The South had fired the first shot and had done so literally, as well as figuratively, on the American flag. "Coercion" had been controversial because it implied an invasion of sovereign states. But now, Lincoln called for seventy-five thousand volunteer militiamen to resist a violent rebellion. In practical terms, the likely military plans of the newly mobilized troops might be the same, but the rationale was transformed. After Sumter, even James Buchanan now supported military mobilization: "To talk about peace and compromise, when we know that the Confederate States would accept of nothing less than a recognition of their independence is absurd," wrote the former president from his home near Lancaster, Pennsylvania, just ten miles from the path of invading Confederate troops in the summer of 1863.[23] Within days of the attack on Sumter, hundreds of thousands of men clamored to fight in what most people assumed would be a short war. The challenge facing Northern state and Federal governments was now logistical rather than ideological: how to organize, pay, arm, train, transport, and deploy a vast crowd of amateur soldiers. Almost half of the Union Army were teenagers, packed with adrenaline. They were boys, really, these newly minted soldiers.

On the face of it, the Northern reaction to Sumter amply vindicated the one member of the Confederate cabinet who warned against firing the first shot: Secretary of War Robert Toombs, who reputedly told Confederate President Jefferson Davis that to use force in this way would "lose us every friend at the North. You will only strike a hornet's nest.... Legions now quiet will swarm out and sting us to death. It is unnecessary. It puts us in the wrong."[24] Even when the Confederate war was going well, a suspicion lingered in the South that they may have been rash in precipitating war as they did. In the summer of 1863, one rebel soldier in Chambersburg informed an indignant Rachel Cormany that, had it not been for Fort Sumter, Pennsylvania—with its economic ties to the slave states—would have seceded. But if the firing on Fort Sumter provoked a surge of military enthusiasm in the North, Lincoln's consequent call for volunteers galvanized the South. Crucially it was also the catalyst that pushed four more slave states— Arkansas, North Carolina, Tennessee, and Virginia—to secede. The Virginian Robert E. Lee, then a colonel in the United States Army, was among those serving officers who faced the dilemma of whether to resign or face the prospect of being ordered to lead an invasion of their home states. Lee's daughter later wrote that it was "the severest struggle of his life." His family estate at Arlington was "in the shadow" of the US Capitol across the river in Washington, his daughter noted, and their family had up until now always resisted the hot-headed secessionism of radical Southern politicians. Yet Lee appalled his commander—another Virginian, Winfield Scott—by resigning a commission he had held for thirty-five years. He was not alone, though more than half of field officers from seceded states stayed loyal to the Union.[25]

* * *

Gettysburg, the seat of Adams County, had around two thousand four hundred residents in 1861. They made their living from farming, tanneries, and carriage-building workshops. Nearby were lumber and flour mills, and lime kilns. Modernity had reached the town two years earlier with the arrival of the railroad. Another line was being built but was still unfinished by the time of the battle. Of course, Gettysburg was in a free state but was less than ten miles from the Mason-Dixon line. Gettysburg carriages were sold throughout the

Shenandoah Valley and further south; it was reputed that Confederate Secretary of War Robert Toombs had bought one. Young men in Gettysburg (white men anyway) were as likely to seek work on farms in Virginia as anywhere. Lincoln had barely carried the county in the 1860 election even though it was the home of Thaddeus Stevens, a radical anti-slavery Republican who ran a sheet iron and copper works nearby. And yet, even in a town with so many links to the South, anyone who had doubts about the war kept their head down and their voice silent in the weeks after the firing on Fort Sumter.

In Gettysburg, as in hundreds of similar towns across the free states, public meetings were held to pledge loyalty to the Union "irrespective of party difference." One resolved "that humiliating as is the present distracted and perilous condition of the country, and however variant may be our views as to the causes which have contributed to the present condition of affairs, in the face of the perils now threatening the republic, it is the duty of every good citizen to forget party feeling and partisan distinctions, and to unite in a common effort to maintain the honor, the integrity and existence of our National Union."[26] A 120-foot-high "liberty pole" was erected in the town square ("the diamond" as locals called it), and a newly recruited company dubbed the "Gettysburg Blues" paraded around it and were cheered off into the railroad cars for a train to Hanover junction, and thence to Baltimore, by "an immense concourse of people."[27] Tillie Pierce, an observant thirteen-year-old, wryly commented in her diary that the troops were "'armed to the teeth' with old, rusty guns and swords, pitchforks, shovels and pick-axes."[28] Ministers in the town's eight churches hung large American flags behind the pulpits and preached the importance of defending the nation. One resident later recalled: "Some half-balanced man or woman would prepare some wild project to demonstrate patriotism, and one would be apt to awake suspicion as a traitor, or even a spy, if he opposed it."[29]

The coming of war found countless people stranded in what suddenly seemed the wrong place. Among them were a dozen young men who had been born and raised in Gettysburg but who in 1856 had moved fifty miles to Shepherdstown, Virginia (now West Virginia), when C. W. Hoffman's carriage factory relocated there. Most returned home in a hurry when Virginia seceded in May 1861, but not all. Among those who stayed were Jerry Shepler, Wesley Culp, and at least one of C. W. Hoffman's sons, Robert. All three enlisted in Company B of the 2nd Virginia Infantry.[30]

In 1861, only a few pessimists on either side imagined anything like the scale of destruction that was to come. Those Gettysburg boys who joined up in Virginia could hardly have imagined that they would find themselves back in their old hometown as part of an invading army two years later. Indeed, if it is a general historical truth that no one expects to fight the kind of war they end up fighting, this was especially true of America in the 1860s. The war of the rebellion, as Northerners called it, was meant to be a three-month affair. It was fought by amateurs who entered the ranks of their states' militias thinking that victory would go to those with the most honor and pluck. The obsession of Civil War newspaper reporters with bayonet charges—not least on the second and third days of the Battle of Gettysburg—would be comical if it did not concern so tragic a subject. Enemy positions, it seemed, were invariably "carried at the point of a bayonet." Bayonet charges were described as "splendid," "gallant," "noble," "magnificent," or as "sublimest moment in the physical history of man."[31] At the Battle of Corinth in 1862, the New York *Tribune* reported that the rebels had been unmoving in the face of "grape and canister" but had "quailed at the bayonet."[32] This heroic attitude to warfare fed a widespread dismissal of the idea of "strategy," imagined as creeping, cowardly maneuvering and the direct opposite of "hard fighting."

It is ironic that in a culture so inimical to military expertise, it was the professional officers of the pre-war regular US Army who disproportionately held leadership positions on both sides and most profoundly shaped how the war was fought. The US officer cadre lacked the aristocratic demarcations of European armies (though some Virginia families gave it a good shot), but they had a strong sense of themselves as expert practitioners of the art of war. The writing of Civil War generals is scattered with technical terms like "enfilading fire" (which happens when a unit is positioned so that the enemy can fire at it from the side, along its longest axis), or an "echelon" formation (with each line set behind and to the side of the next). This kind of terminology had a pleasingly chivalrous ring to it, but it also reflected the self-conscious professionalism of officers who saw themselves as expert practitioners in the art of war and for whom the beau ideal of a military leader was Napoleon.

The United States had nothing on the scale of the military training available in Europe at the time, but it did have the United States Military Academy at West Point in New York, and a majority of the senior officers at Gettysburg had studied there, including, among the commanders at Gettysburg, Robert E. Lee and James Longstreet at the head of the Army of Northern Virginia and George Meade, Oliver O. Howard, and John Sedgwick of the Army of the Potomac.[33] Historians have debated whether the West Point curriculum helps explain why Civil War generals made the strategic decisions they did. In part, perhaps, because of the influence, albeit indirect, of the Swiss writer and military aide to Napoleon Antoine-Henri Jomini, the language used by Civil War officers reveals that military thought in the 1860s was still very much shaped by lessons gleaned from the Napoleonic wars.[34] Commanders sought to skillfully maneuver troops to concentrate on key enemy positions while protecting their own communication and supply lines, reflecting the wisdom of the European military establishment of the day. Taking the tactical offensive and moving with speed were assumed to be virtues.

As it turned out, however, not even a West Point training prepared men for this war. No one—including foreign observers—truly grasped the nature of the strategic and logistical problems each side would face. Even an ambitious young West Point graduate like George B. McClellan, who had the additional advantage of having served as an observer in the Crimean War, revealed how poorly antebellum experience had prepared him for this moment when he wrote to General-in-Chief Winfield Scott just after the war began predicting that he could end the rebellion by capturing Richmond with a force of eighty thousand three-month volunteers. Scott's own strategy—dubbed the "Anaconda Plan" because it relied on slowly strangling the Confederacy by establishing a military cordon around it—at least showed an awareness of the scale of the challenge. Still, his vision of a limited war that would minimize bloodshed proved far removed from the struggle that was to follow.[35] The military historian Carol Reardon has concluded that "beyond securing Washington from attack, Scott hardly knew where to start."[36]

Both sides struggled to formulate a consistent and practical military strategy to achieve their political objectives. Military planners at the start of the war were hampered not just by the lack of precedent but also by the absence of a general staff—and even, unbelievably, by the absence of good maps. The goal of the United States was the destruction of the Confederacy. But this simple aim was so daunting in practice that it resolved very little, and Northern politicians disagreed bitterly over how it might be accomplished and at what cost.

The Confederacy's political aim was to establish political independence, but this was also a deceptively simple objective that resolved very little. Did it mean the South should fight a strategically and tactically defensive war? In a speech in Montgomery, Alabama, on 29 April 1861, President Jefferson Davis appeared to suggest as much: "We seek no conquest, no aggrandizement," he said. "All we ask is to be let alone." It was undoubtedly true that Confederates did not aim for the total destruction of the United States in the way that the United States aimed for the total destruction of the Confederacy. But it was not entirely true that the Confederacy sought no "aggrandizement": they always wanted to incorporate Missouri, Maryland, and Kentucky—three of the four slave states which had not seceded (the fourth, Delaware, seems to have been too small to worry much about), while dreams of a Caribbean slave empire never died. And even setting aside expansionist fantasies, the objective of defending territorial integrity was less clear than it appeared. Since in the real world, it never seemed likely that enemy soldiers could be kept out of all three-quarters of a million square miles of Confederate territory, how much, if any, of that territory could be conceded, albeit temporarily, to win the war? Sometimes Jefferson Davis seemed to favor the kind of Fabian strategy that the rebels in the Revolutionary War had pursued: "There are no vital points on the preservation of which the continued existence of the Confederacy depends," he maintained in 1864. "Not the fall of Richmond, nor Wilmington, nor Charleston, nor Savannah, nor of all combined, can save the enemy from the constant and exhaustive drain of blood and treasure which must continue until he shall discover that no peace is attainable unless based on the recognition of our indefeasible rights."[37] Maybe that was theoretically true, but it would have been politically unviable: Southern public opinion demanded battles and victories and conceding large swathes of territory would have undermined the credibility of the Confederate government.

It is a question that historians have debated ever since Appomattox: did the South, outnumbered as it was, bleed itself to death through its willingness to take the tactical offensive?[38] General Lee's plausible view was that the longer the war continued, the lower the South's chances of winning. The North, after all, clearly had a significant advantage over the Confederacy in terms of manpower and industrial capacity. The North's economy expanded during the war, while the South experienced massive economic challenges, including bread shortages, by the summer of 1863.[39] A purely defensive strategy would, in such circumstances, simply allow the Union to work out ways of maximizing its advantages. Instead, Lee sought to accomplish the Confederacy's political objective—independence—through a strategic offensive aimed at the Union's weak point: its will to fight. He took command of the Army of Northern Virginia in May 1862 at a moment of real peril for the South, when the Army of the Potomac, led by General George B. McClellan, had almost reached Richmond. Within just four months, Lee had driven the Army of the Potomac out of Virginia and hoped to inflict on it a decisive defeat that would trigger the collapse of Northern support for the war.[40] Thanks in part to a horrendous security breach (a Union soldier found a copy of Lee's battle plans by the roadside!), the battle that took place at Antietam Creek, near Sharpsburg, Maryland, in September 1862 was not the victory for which he had hoped. But Lee remained confident that the strategy was the right one: inflict victories so visible that Northerners would doubt the wisdom of their war effort.

* * *

This aim is the fundamental explanation for why Lee's army was in Pennsylvania in July 1863 and why Lee took the offensive when he was there. Had the Army of Northern Virginia won at Gettysburg, he hoped the Northern anti-war movement would grow. Lee would have marched on to the "golden dome of Washington" (as Faulkner's character put it) not to occupy it permanently but to open the way for a negotiated settlement. (The US Capitol's "golden dome" was—incidentally but perhaps tellingly—a pure flight of Faulknerian fancy: the dome was still being built during the war, and the capitol was shrouded in scaffolding.) Post-war novelists and Southern Lost Cause writers fantasized about precisely this outcome. And even though things did not go to plan in the summer of 1863, Lee never doubted that his core strategic assumption had been correct. "If I could do so, I would again cross the Potomac and invade Pennsylvania," he was reported as saying near the end of the war. "I believe this to be our true policy."[41]

Lee had begun preparations for a possible invasion of the North shortly after his victory at Fredericksburg in December 1862. In February, he asked the army's highly skilled cartographer, Jedediah Hotchkiss, to map out the road network of central Pennsylvania all the way to Philadelphia. Lee also asked Confederate authorities to repair the Virginia Central railroad to draw critical supplies for any advance into Maryland and beyond. At Fredericksburg, Confederates had the advantage of a rock-solid defensive position from which to repulse a botched attempt by the Union Army to cross the Rappahannock

River. But at Chancellorsville, with forces only half the size of the enemy, Lee had wrested the initiative, divided his forces, and gone on the offensive. It was Lee's most brilliant victory. If a portion of the Army of Virginia could accomplish so much, what might the whole army do? "There never were such men in an army before," Lee wrote of his army in May 1863. "They will go anywhere and do anything if properly led."[42]

*   *   *

Meanwhile, the Union Army of the Potomac had spent a year being bested by Lee. A new commander, "fighting" Joe Hooker, proved no more successful than his predecessor McClellan at creating a sense of esprit de corps. The commander blamed his senior officers for the defeat at Chancellorsville on May 6, and they blamed him, while congressmen and newspaper editors fuelled the bickering and recriminations.[43] President Lincoln followed news of General Grant's progress in Mississippi with great hope, but after Chancellorsville, his expectations in the east were low. On May 14, he told Hooker to repair his army and keep Lee "out of mischief."[44] The spirits of the rank and file of the Army of the Potomac remained more resilient than might have been expected. Unlike after the devastating defeat at Fredericksburg, when as many as one in ten men were listed as absent without leave, there was no mass desertion after Chancellorsville. But the army was shrinking, nonetheless. By early July, thirty-four regiments of two-year enlistees and a further twenty-six regiments of militia who had enlisted for nine-months after the army's defeat in the Peninsular campaign the previous year, were due to go home.[45] In part to meet this challenge, Congress introduced conscription, enraging millions of Northerners who thought that an "abolitionized" radical administration was abusing the exigencies of war to trample on the liberty of white men in order to lift up Black people. Even as the Battle of Gettysburg was raging, draft dodgers in Western Pennsylvania were fighting pitched battles with Provost Marshals, and, in New York City, just days after the battle ended, three days of anti-draft rioting left hundreds dead.

And then there was the divisive issue of the administration's emancipation policy. On January 1, 1863, President Lincoln issued the Emancipation Proclamation declaring that enslaved people in rebel-held areas were free and paving the way for the enlistment of African Americans in the Union Army. In the immediate term, the Proclamation made little difference to the experience of Union troops in the occupied portions of the Confederacy. They had been a de facto army of liberation for enslaved people since at least the summer of 1862. But the military abolition policy destroyed any vestiges of the early cross-party support for the Lincoln administration. It raised the stakes even higher for the army in 1863. If Lincoln were correct, the new emancipation policy would speed the end of the rebellion. That claim was now being tested. Perhaps it would be the case—as the Northern opponents of emancipation argued—that the Emancipation Proclamation would simply reinforce the Confederates' will to fight. If so, it would be utterly counter-productive.

Therefore, for both sides, the campaign of 1863 seemed to be the final throw of the dice. At last, the endgame seemed imminent. In the Virginia theatre, through luck, superior morale and confident leadership, Lee's army displayed an élan that delighted the South and intimidated the North. But even this apparent success was not what it seemed. The cost of victory at Chancellorsville in the first days of May was horrendously high and brought no strategic gains. "Our people were wild with delight," after the victory at Chancellorsville, recalled Lee eighteen months years later. "I, on the contrary, was more depressed than after Fredericksburg." The South lost at least thirteen thousand men, and the most prominent casualty was Lee's right-hand man, General Thomas J. "Stonewall" Jackson, killed by friendly fire. "I do not know how to replace him," confessed Lee. "Any victory would be dear at such a cost."[46] Fundamentally, what Lee understood was that even a brilliant victory like Chancellorsville did nothing to alter the underlying strategic problem, which was that the enemy was still

on Virginian soil and "could easily replace the men he had lost" while the Confederacy's army grew steadily smaller and weaker.[47] Lee's lieutenant, James Longstreet, concurred that the Army of Northern Virginia's dazzling feats between May 1862 and May 1863 were "fruitless." Even victories such as Chancellorsville "were consuming us, and would eventually destroy us."[48]

And relatively speaking, the situation in Virginia was the bright spot. When Confederate leaders looked over the vast canvas of war, from the Atlantic coast across the Blue Ridge Mountains into Tennessee and Mississippi and on into Arkansas, and when they considered the US incursions along the Atlantic and Gulf coasts and the occupation of New Orleans and the Lower Mississippi Valley, the military situation looked perilous. In particular, in addition to Northern Virginia, there were two places where Union forces were concentrated and threatened to take the offensive. One was in central Tennessee, where a Confederate Army of around forty-five thousand men led by General Braxton Bragg faced off against a larger Union force under the command of William S. Rosecrans. After a brutal and inconclusive battle at Stones River at the very start of the year, there had been little fighting (other than the in-fighting among Bragg's hornet's nest of senior officers). Still, it was surely only a matter of time before Rosecrans' forces renewed their attempt to capture Chattanooga and then—perhaps—invaded Georgia. And indeed, on June 24, Union forces in Tennessee resumed their forward push.

Even more pressing was the situation in Mississippi, where Union troops led by Major General Ulysses S. Grant had been maneuvering for months to capture the river town of Vicksburg. If Vicksburg fell— along with Port Hudson, Louisiana, which was being approached by another Union column moving up the river from New Orleans—the whole length of the Mississippi River would be back under the control of the United States, and the westernmost states would be severed from the rest of the Confederacy. By early May, Grant's army had crossed to the east bank of the Mississippi and was moving on Jackson, the state capital, intending to surround the Confederate defenders in Vicksburg. "Hour of trial is on us," Mississippi Governor Pettus telegraphed Jefferson Davis on May 7. "We look to you for assistance. Let it be speedy."[49] By May 18, Grant had trapped Confederate forces under John C. Pemberton in Vicksburg and—as Lee realized when he heard the reports of the siege—the writing was on the wall.

The crisis in Mississippi forced urgent questions on Confederate leaders. In theory, as the West Point-trained Jefferson Davis knew as well as his generals, the Confederacy benefited from being able to exploit interior lines to redeploy units as they were needed. The reality was not so straightforward. There were huge logistical difficulties involved in moving troops hundreds of miles along the fragmented southern railroad network or rutted roads; the government in Richmond had slow and often poor-quality intelligence about precisely what was happening west of the Appalachian Mountains; and, of course, if Union forces threatened at several points at once, how should the Confederacy best deploy its slowly depleting forces: should a portion of Lee's army of Northern Virginia be sent west?

Secretary of War James Seddon thought so; he argued that holding Vicksburg was the Confederacy's principal strategic priority. He proposed sending some of Longstreet's Corps—probably including General Pickett's division—to the Mississippi. Senior Confederate generals, including, initially, General Longstreet, supported Seddon's plan. Lee, however, sharply resisted any portion of his army being detached. To Seddon, Lee argued that by the time Pickett's division reached Vicksburg, it would be too late—either Vicksburg would have fallen, or the tropical summer climate would have forced Grant to retire.[50] On May 11, Lee told Davis that from his reading of Northern newspapers (always the principal source of not-always-reliable information on the enemy's movements), it appeared that the Army of the Potomac was to be reinforced. As Lee correctly summarized, "the enemy in every department outnumbers us," and the imbalance of men was getting worse,[51] and Lee was right to assume the trend would continue. There were more than three military-age white men in the North for every one white Southerner. If the price of saving Vicksburg by diminishing the Army of Northern Virginia was to lose Richmond, would that, in the end, aid the Confederacy? Clearly, the answer was no.

But unlike Jefferson Davis's other commanders, Lee did not just bring him problems; he brought him solutions—or at least the hope of them. He argued that the best course of action was to take the war onto Northern soil. Some historians have criticized Lee for his parochialism—and it is probably true that deep down he was more concerned with Virginia, his home state, than with what happened in Mississippi. But Lee's Virginia-centric position was also strategically sound. If the size of his force diminished any further, Lee was surely right that he would have no choice but to retreat to the fortifications around Richmond, and the war of dash, hope, and optimism would be over. An offensive movement by the Army of Northern Virginia would also throw into disarray whatever offensive plans Lee imagined the Union had been developing for 1863. "If I can do nothing more," he mused to Jefferson Davis, an invasion of the North would "embarrass... [the Federals'] plan of campaign."[52] He said the same in his official report after the event: at minimum, his aim was to "disturb" the Federal Army's plan for a summer campaign.[53]

And then there was Lee's conviction that defeating the Army of the Potomac in Pennsylvania would boost the anti-war movement in the North, which, quite correctly, he saw as ultimately the only way of ending the war. On this issue, he was more clear-sighted than most other leading Confederates. "We should neglect no honorable means of dividing and weakening our enemies that they may feel some of the difficulties experienced by ourselves," he wrote. Venturing beyond the narrowly military realm, Lee urged Davis to take a pragmatic rather than a dogmatic approach to the possibility of peace negotiations. It would be prudent, he suggested, to allow the Northern "peace party" to believe—or "affect to believe"—that an offer of peace might be a route to reunion. "Should the belief that peace will bring back the Union become general, the war would no longer be supported, and that after all is what we are interested in bringing about.... When peace is proposed to us, it will be time enough to discuss its terms."[54] Perhaps success on Northern soil might even convince Britain or France to recognize Southern independence—a just-about-plausible deus ex machina in which Confederates invested huge hopes.

But quite apart from such high-level political strategy, there was a far more pressing reason for the invasion: the army was slowly starving. It had run out of cattle, fodder for the horses was scarce, and the men's rations were dwindling. Colonel Arthur Fremantle, a British military observer who wrote a perceptive account of his time with the Army of Northern Virginia, reported that the northern part of the state "is now completely cleaned out. It is almost uncultivated, and no animals are grazing where there used to be hundreds."[55] To the voracious demands of the army and the disruption and destruction of war could be added a drought in 1862 which had led to a poor harvest. The whole of Longstreet's Corps had been sent to southeastern Virginia to gather supplies; they even missed the battle of Chancellorsville because of it. An invasion would give some respite to Virginia farmers while enabling the army to gather cattle, horses, and grain for the winter ahead. In the end, Lee had good reason to fear that only by going north could he hope to gather the supplies he needed to keep his army together. Food shortages, rampant inflation, political discontent, and endless rumors of slave uprisings combined with the military situation generated mounting anxiety among Confederate leaders. When the arsenal in Richmond supplying the Army of Northern Virginia had to be closed for two months after an explosion, it seemed depressingly symbolic.

Even as he prepared to move, Lee feared the Army of the Potomac would launch an offensive first.[56] The only viable alternatives seemed to be to fall back to Richmond and settle for a siege that would eventually end in surrender (as was happening at Vicksburg) or gamble on an audacious assault. And so, audacious as it was, the Pennsylvania invasion was rooted in Southern weakness more than strength.

In the correspondence of Confederate leaders during May and June, there was a palpable sense that the war was approaching a decisive turning point. For the South, it was now or never. In Lee's words, "there is always a hazard in military movements, but we must decide between the positive loss of inactivity and the risks of action."[57] In a reported conversation after the war, Lee recognized the risks but, even in retrospect, believed he had no other choice: "He knew oftentimes that he was playing a very bold game, but it was the only possible one."[58] And if it went well, maybe there was, as Faulkner's character dreamed, a world to be won. According to one account, Lee was convinced that "the occupation of [Philadelphia in 1863] would have given us peace."[59]

Jefferson Davis probably sanctioned the decision to invade Pennsylvania at a meeting in Richmond on May 15, but it was Robert E. Lee's project from beginning to end, its fate ultimately his responsibility.[60] There has been no shortage of people who have criticized the premise of the whole operation. With the benefit of hindsight, one influential Northern journalist, William Swinton, described the Pennsylvania campaign as a "seductive but fatal adventure," misguided "in its inception, for it was an enterprise...without any well-determined military object."[61] This was obviously a partisan judgment, but there was some truth to it: while Lee seems to have had genuine hope that he may have the opportunity to strike a decisive blow if he moved onto Northern soil, he seems to have had no firm plans for how that might be done. In his official report, Lee simply stated that his movements were intended to draw the Army of the Potomac away from its position opposite Fredericksburg where "it could not be attacked except at disadvantage" and "if practicable to transfer the scene of hostilities beyond the Potomac."[62] There was no plan for a long-term occupation of Northern soil (though some over-excited Southern newspapers fantasized about occupying Baltimore or Philadelphia). Being in Pennsylvania for a few weeks or months was the main point; what to do once there was less obvious. But Lee must have known that the overwhelmingly likely consequence of the invasion was a major battle. He hoped, he wrote, for "a fair opportunity to strike a blow." As one of the great historians of the Gettysburg campaign put it, "Only a commander who had supreme confidence in himself and his army would dare be so opportunistic."[63]

After the war, and especially after Lee died in 1870, James Longstreet made the lordly claim that he had given his "assent" to the Gettysburg campaign only on the understanding that "we were not to deliver an offensive battle but to so maneuver that the enemy should be forced to attack us."[64] But hindsight can blind. The contemporary record suggests that Longstreet backed the invasion plan with no reservations.[65] If the Pennsylvania gambit did not, in the end, come off as planned, part of the reason was that once he crossed the Potomac, Lee was hampered by a lack of intelligence about the enemy's position. This was a significant explanation for why—as we shall see—the Confederate Army stumbled into battle at Gettysburg on ground that was, to put it mildly, disadvantageous. But the fact that the invasion did not end as Lee would have hoped is not in itself evidence that he was wrong to try.

2

The Confederate Invasion, June–July 1863

The army that Lee led into the North was larger than it had been for almost a year and—as it turned out—much larger than it would be again. After units on detached service in North Carolina and southeastern Virginia had been recalled, Lee had about sixty-seven thousand infantry and artillerymen and about twelve thousand four hundred cavalrymen under his command. The army was newly divided into three large corps—previously, it had been two even larger ones, with Stonewall Jackson commanding one and James Longstreet the other, but Lee considered thirty thousand fighting men to be too many for one commander to handle since "they are always beyond the range of his vision, & frequently beyond his reach."[1] Longstreet still commanded the First Corps. The other two were led by men who had previously headed up divisions in Jackson's Corps. Taking over the Second Corps was Richard S. Ewell, an industrious but perpetually fidgety eccentric who refused to eat anything other than wheat boiled in milk. On one occasion he asked a subordinate officer with genuine puzzlement, "What do you suppose President Davis made me a major-general for?"—a question that many others asked at the time, and indeed have done ever since.[2] The other newly promoted commander, in charge of the new Third Corps, was A. P. Hill, a slender and emotional man who put on a red shirt for battle and was notoriously irascible.[3] The weakness of Lee's corps commanders has been a major theme of Gettysburg literature, especially of the "Lost Cause" variety.

And while the misjudgments of Ewell, Hill, and Longstreet have often been much exaggerated, it is probably true that, without Stonewall, Lee lacked a lieutenant on whom he could completely rely. At the very least, the Army of Northern Virginia entered Pennsylvania that summer with an untested senior command.

Lee's plan was to invade Pennsylvania via the Shenandoah and Cumberland Valleys, a route that took his men through fertile fields with mountains on either side to shield his movement from the enemy. Once across the Potomac, Lee had no plans to maintain supply lines since his horses and men would take what they needed from the local farmers, but he did want to maintain a communications line back to Richmond, which was not easy to do in the absence of a well-placed railroad. Still, by late May, Lee had finalized his plan. The only concern that held him back was the possibility that Union forces would suddenly move on Richmond as soon as he marched north. But reconnaissance by Wade Hampton's cavalry along the Rappahannock convinced Lee by June 2 that Hooker planned no immediate aggressive movement. From Lee's perspective, so far at least, the Yankees were playing their usual role of always being two steps behind.

On June 3, the Army of Northern Virginia began withdrawing from its defenses at Fredericksburg. The plan was to assemble two-thirds of the army thirty miles away at Culpepper Court House, well past Hooker's right flank, leaving A. P. Hill's Corps at Fredericksburg for the time being.[4] "I recall the morning vividly," wrote the artilleryman Edward Porter Alexander.

"A beautiful bright June day, & about 11 A.M. a courier from Longstreet's headqrs. brought the order. Although it was only to march to Culpeper C. H. we knew that it meant another great battle with the enemy's army...I remember the hurried preparations, the parting with my wife & little daughter, & the looking back as long as even the tops of the locust trees & oaks about the house could be seen. And I can recall, too, the pride & confidence I felt in my splendid battalion, as it filed out of the fields into the road, with every chest & ammunition wagon filled, & every horse in fair order, & every detail fit for a campaign. It was just a month to the very hour almost that Pickett's charge at Gettysburg was repulsed."[5]

In those balmy summer days, as the army began to move, the confidence of Lee's men reached its apogee. At Culpepper on June 5, the dashing young cavalry commander, Jeb Stuart—a man who never knowingly passed over an opportunity for theatrics—organized a grand review of his horsemen for which invitations were issued "far and near." Thousands arrived by train to watch twelve thousand mounted men trot, then gallop, and then "charge at full speed past the reviewing stand, yelling just as they do in a real charge, and brandishing their sabers above their heads." The effect, recalled Stuart's aide-de-camp, W. W. Blackford, "was thrilling, even to us, while the ladies clasped their hands and sank into the arms, sometimes, of their escorts in a swoon, if the escorts were handy, but if not they did not." That night they held a ball. There was "firelight to dance by, and moonlight for the strolls."[6]

It was a quick descent from moonlight and magnolias to bloody battle. The following Tuesday, Federal cavalry commanded by General Buford crossed the Rappahannock undetected by rebel pickets just north of Culpepper at Brandy Station and launched a surprise attack on Stuart—a surprise being precisely what the nimble all-seeing rebel cavalry was supposed to prevent. In what was to become the largest solely cavalry engagement of the war, the Confederates held their ground and prevented Union forces from discovering the whereabouts of the bulk of the Army of Northern Virginia. Yet, for the first time—and just four days after his hubristic grand review—Stuart looked vulnerable. Among the wounded on the rebel side was one of Robert E. Lee's sons.[7] Even a Confederate newspaper report of the Battle of Brandy Station referred rather acidly to the Army of Northern Virginia's "puffed up cavalry" suffering the "consequences of negligence and bad management."[8] The US cavalry was better equipped than the rebels, with Sharps carbines—short, breech-loading rifles—as well as sabers and revolvers.[9] In retrospect, when they had lost the war, defeated Confederates found it all too easy to read into this cavalry engagement the sign of things to come.

As soon as reports reached Washington that Lee had left the protection of his entrenchments along the Rappahannock River, Lincoln saw an opportunity: to lure Lee's army into Pennsylvania, leaving Richmond exposed, then quickly advance on the Confederate capital, cut off Lee's return route, and destroy him.[10] One of the leading military historians of the Gettysburg campaign, Stephen W. Sears, argues that, although he was deeply distracted by a personal spat with General-in-Chief Henry Halleck, Hooker had developed a clear plan to do precisely that. This was exactly the Union response Lee feared and which he was gambling they would never have the nerve to undertake. And sure enough, so embittered were relationships among senior commanders in the Army of the Potomac following the disaster of Chancellorsville that Hooker's resolution (if such it was) was not shared by other senior officers in the Army of the Potomac. Marsena Patrick said of Hooker at this time: "He acts like a man without a plan and is entirely at a loss what to do, or how to match the enemy, or counteract his movements.... His role now is that of Micawber 'waiting for something to turn up,' and when something turns up he plays like a gambler."[11] In the long list of "what-ifs" about the Gettysburg campaign, it is just about plausible to include the possibility that, had Hooker shown capable leadership, he may have been able to call Lee's bluff and threaten Richmond in June 1863. As it was, the Union Army behaved as Lee had expected them to, rushing to catch up with the rebel leader who was again setting the agenda.

By mid-June, the Army of Northern Virginia was concentrated mainly in the Shenandoah Valley, while the Army of the Potomac was strung out along the Orange and Alexandria Railroad and beginning to push west toward the Bull Run Mountains. All this marching took place during a heat wave, and men in both armies suffered badly from heat stroke. Ewell's Corps was the first to cross the Potomac on June 15 after defeating Union forces holding Winchester and Martinsburg. Hill's and Longstreet's Corps followed on June 24 and 25.

Meanwhile, Jeb Stuart's cavalry set out on a dramatic ride around Hooker's east flank, burning bridges and creating havoc on the outskirts of Washington. But with the entire Army of the Potomac between him and the Army of Northern Virginia, Stuart lost contact with Lee, failing in his primary duty of intelligence gathering. As a result, Lee didn't know the Federal Army had crossed the Potomac in pursuit until two days after the event, and Stuart didn't arrive at Gettysburg until late on the second day of the battle.

In the post-war years, Lost Cause defenders of Lee made Stuart (who was killed in May 1864) a scapegoat for having failed to act as his chief's "eyes and ears." There is some reason to believe that Lee was irritated at the time: when Stuart eventually arrived at Gettysburg, Lee supposedly greeted him with a withering "Well, General, you are here at last."[12] But whatever the tactical consequences, Stuart had fun on the ride—capturing Union baggage trains, chasing Federal cavalry, burning the US army barracks at Carlisle, and boasting that if it weren't for his fatigued horses, he would have marched straight into Washington and taken "Abe and his cabinet prisoners." And the disruption he caused undoubtedly contributed to the North's fear that, at least in the eastern theater, the Confederates could do pretty much whatever they liked.

By June 24, the bulk of Lee's army was in Maryland and Pennsylvania (Map 2.1). As events panned out, the rebels had less than a week to plunder enemy country, but they made the most of it. The army fanned out, covering a ninety-mile arc from Chambersburg in Franklin County, through Adams County and up as far as Carlisle, targeting crops, livestock, and Black people as they went. As the army marched north, they sent their plunder south along a macadamized road which ran through the Cumberland Valley and south through the Shenandoah Valley to Staunton, Virginia. In Winchester, a local woman reported "large herds of cattle are passing through every day, sent back from Pennsylvania. Our army is to be subsisting entirely in the enemy's country."[13] Politics, as well as subsistence, helped determine whose property was targeted. When rebel forces began to set fire to the ironworks owned by the radical Republican politician Thaddeus Stevens, the works superintendent remonstrated that the people hardest hit would be the "hundred poor laborers" employed there. The rebel commanding officer, General Jubal Early, replied that Mr. Stevens was an "enemy of the South, in favor of confiscating their property and arming their negroes, and the property must be destroyed."[14] Stevens estimated that he lost about 75,000 dollars in seized property but was sanguine. "We must all expect to suffer by this wicked war," he wrote. "I have not felt a moment's trouble for my share of it. If, finally, the government shall be reestablished over our whole territory; and not a vestige of Slavery left, I shall deem it a cheap purchase."[15]

Looking back with the benefit of hindsight on the march into Pennsylvania, Confederate private John Dooley, son of a successful Irish immigrant in Richmond, later claimed that there pervaded "our ranks a solemn feeling, as if some unforeseen danger was ever dropping darksome shadows over the road we unshrinkingly tread."[16] But the contemporary accounts suggest the rebels were in high spirits. We are "inspired...with almost invincible ardor," wrote one.[17] "We passed through some of the prettiest country that I ever saw in my life," wrote a Confederate infantryman in a letter home. "They has [some] of the finest land in it in the world and some of the ugliest women that I ever saw."[18] Long marches in high summer were hard, especially for men who were, in some cases, barefoot and suffering from the endemic diarrhea that cursed Civil War armies. This was a mobile military city, defecating as it moved, without the time to dig latrines, and pursued by millions of flies. But even an army that could be smelt before it was seen or heard could have a buoyant sense of purpose.

Union officers conceded the superior morale of the enemy forces. "The spirit of his army was much better than that of ours," admitted Charles Francis Adams, Jr., a captain in the 1st Massachusetts Cavalry.[19] Adams' fellow Harvard alumnus Francis C. Barlow thought Confederate troops "more heroic, more modest and more in earnest

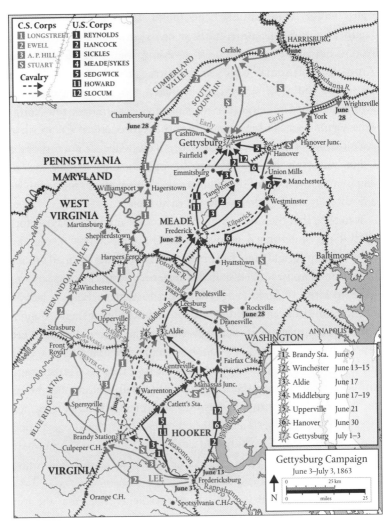

Map 2.1. Map of Lee's advance into Pennsylvania, June 3–July 3, 1863.

than we are. Their whole tone is much finer than ours. Except among those on our side who are fighting this war upon anti-slavery grounds, there is not much earnestness nor are there many noble feelings and sentiments involved."[20] This was exactly the view of post-war Lost

Cause writers who dismissed the Yankee army as low-grade hired hands, so it is disconcerting, at first sight, to see it in the contemporary record. But Barlow's exception is revealing: there were those in the Army of the Potomac who saw their struggle as being for a higher cause: the ending of slavery in a reunified nation. A danger for the army—and the Union cause more generally—was that too few Northerners would see this bigger picture or think the sacrifice was worth it. An outcome of the Battle of Gettysburg, a consequence not just of the Union victory in July but of Lincoln's speech in November, was to dampen the cynicism of the doubters and fortify the certainty of those already convinced of the nobility of their cause.

It may be that the over-confidence of Lee's army in the days before Gettysburg undermined its discipline. The temptations of plunder were too strong, and units were hard to keep together as small groups of soldiers marauded. Yet, as he led his army north, Lee appeared to have no sense of foreboding. According to General Isaac Ridgeway Trimble, one of Lee's subordinates, the commanding general thought a strategically meaningful victory was his for the taking. "My plan," Lee reportedly said on June 25, "is to throw an overwhelming force against the enemy's advance, as soon as I learn the road they take, crush them, and following up the sweep, beat them in detail, and in a few hours throw the whole Army into disorder and probably create a panic." According to Trimble, "General Lee then laid his spread fingers upon the map between Gettysburg and Emmitsburg and said, 'Somewhere hereabout, we shall fight a great battle, and if successful, will secure our independence and end the war.'"[21]

The flip side of this was that Union soldiers sensed that the war might be reaching a climax. The marches north to catch up with Lee's army on June 28 and 29 were brutal. Pounding for more than twenty-five miles a day down dusty roads, dehydrated men dropped from heat exhaustion by the wayside and were picked up by unsympathetic Provost Marshals on horseback. Yet the forced marches northward, exhausting as they were, raised spirits in the Army of the Potomac. Not only were the men in a free state among their own people for the first time—welcomed as saviors rather than reviled as marauders— but there was an exciting sense that Lee's gamble provided a genuine opportunity to end the war. When troops from the I Corps arrived in Emmitsburg, they were greeted with jubilation.[22] Charles Davis, a private from Massachusetts, remembered that "without regard to rank everybody on horseback was greeted with 'three cheers for the general!', which were given with a will." Women, he recalled, gathered in front of their homes with "pails of fresh water, milk, bread, cakes and pies, which they freely distributed among us." Some civilians may not have had an entirely positive impact on the troops' morale. Davis also remembered a farmer's wife near Emmitsburg who distributed bread and milk even while "sobbing and bemoaning the fate that awaited" us. "Oh boys, you don't know what's before you. I'm afraid many of ye'll be dead or mangled soon, for Lee's whole army is ahead of ye and there'll be terrible fighting."[23]

For the most part, until the collision at Gettysburg, the Confederates met little or no resistance. Pennsylvania Governor Andrew W. Curtin had issued proclamations calling for volunteers to repel the invaders, but the response was patchy, made worse by the reluctance of General Darius Crouch, who had been put in charge of organizing the Home Guards, to accept the service of African Americans. The apparent unwillingness of Pennsylvanians to pull their weight even in the face of invasion became a theme in the New York press, as did rumors of profiteering by civilians, selling whiskey, water, and bread to Union troops at exorbitant prices. Newspapers even claimed that locals were forcing wounded Union soldiers to pay for transportation.

The truth was that the Union Army at Gettysburg consisted of almost equal numbers of New Yorkers and Pennsylvanians. These two states accounted for more than half of all the men in the army. New York suffered the greatest number of casualties. The controversy over Pennsylvania's contribution had its roots a year earlier when Lincoln called for more volunteers with the threat that, if too few men came forward, he would have to use a draft. Pennsylvania struggled to fulfill its quota of men even though its Governor, Andrew

Curtin, was a Republican and a strong supporter of the war effort. But his state was deeply divided, and he proceeded cautiously, so much so that the War Department eventually had to send adjutant generals into the state to compel men into the army. Nineteenth-century Americans were unused to the idea that the state could compel military service. At the very least, they expected to be properly compensated through bounties for the deprivations families would suffer when the men were in uniform. In the Confederacy, a sense of an existential threat legitimized the creation of an astonishingly coercive central government which imposed conscription with few exemptions. In the South, men who did not fight faced a social stigma. By contrast, Northern communities retained a strong sense of being able to determine for themselves who should enlist and who should not. Pennsylvania had historically been a strongly Democratic state. In the many counties in Pennsylvania that Lincoln had not carried, there was strong resentment against prosperous Republican do-gooders who wanted working-class people to do their fighting. Conversely, middle-class Republicans were quick to see Democrats as disloyal. So, when New York reporters claimed to be astonished that Pennsylvanians were not taking to the streets to halt the rebel invasion, they were playing into a well-established stereotype. A cartoon in the New York illustrated newspaper *Harper's Weekly* (Figure 2.1) even depicted a Pennsylvanian profiteering by trying to charge a battle-weary Yankee soldier for a glass of river water.

Although Lee's invading army met little resistance, including from local militia, at least the Federal authorities had a reasonably good idea of where the invading force was and what it was doing, for their intelligence operation was greatly superior to that of the Confederacy.[24] Teams of spies behind enemy lines in the Shenandoah Valley tracked the movements of Lee's army as it advanced northward. And once Lee's army had crossed the Potomac, the Bureau of Military Intelligence spies were supplemented by literally hundreds of reports from local citizens. Lee allowed large numbers of refugees to pass through his lines, taking intelligence with them

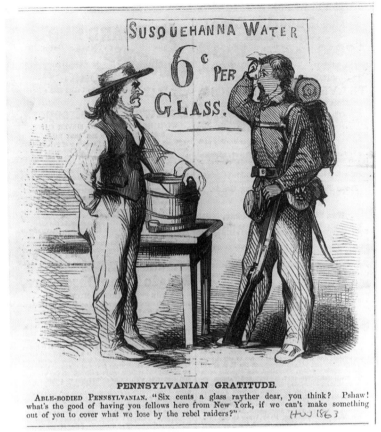

Figure 2.1. "Pennsylvanian Gratitude" Harper's Weekly, 1863. This ironically titled cartoon appearing in a New York illustrated paper during the invasion of Pennsylvania reveals the resentment of New Yorkers, or at least the middle-class readers of this illustrated paper, who perceived Pennsylvanians to be reluctant to make sacrifices even to defend their own soil.

about the position of his army. Lee appeared not to have the manpower to prevent it.

By the last week of June, the "enemy's campfires were in sight" of the town of Gettysburg, recalled one of its residents, Catherine Foster, an unmarried woman of 37 at the time of the battle. So precariously close to the area of operations of the Army of Northern Virginia, "our town," as Foster remembered it, had become "an isolated spot. None came in to bring us tidings, good or bad, and no one ventured out."[25] Rebel raiders had cut both the railroad and the telegraph lines.

Gettysburg's residents had been hunkering down for an invasion for weeks—businessmen had shipped goods to Carlisle or Philadelphia, banks had closed, and prudent farmers had moved livestock. Their first encounter with the invaders was on June 26 when a rebel cavalry detachment rode into the town demanding supplies. Tillie Pierce was at school near the Presbyterian seminary when someone shouted through the window that the rebels were coming, and her teacher, Mrs. Eyster, told the class, "Children, run home as quickly as you can!" As she fled home, Tillie saw dozens of Confederate cavalrymen at the central crossroads (known to locals as the "diamond"). "What a horrible sight!" Tillie recalled. "Clad almost in rags, covered with dust, riding wildly pell-mell down the hill toward our home! Shouting, yelling most unearthly, cursing, brandishing their revolvers and firing right and left."[26] The son of the landlord of the Globe Hotel downtown recognized a man riding with the rebel forces who had stayed in the hotel a few weeks previously in the guise of a traveling salesman and had asked questions about the farms and resources of the neighborhood; Confederates had been charting the lie of the land for some time. Also riding with this advance party of rebels and acting as a guide was Jim Purley, a Gettysburg native who had moved to Virginia ten years earlier.[27]

By June 27, Confederates ranged across three counties, but the center of operations—and General Lee's headquarters—were in the Cumberland Valley, as the northern end of the Shenandoah Valley was known. Here, sheltered by South Mountain from attacks from the East and with a natural escape route back south, was where most foraging and kidnapping took place. But, as Lee also knew, so long as he remained west of South Mountain his army would be a limited strategic threat. Therefore, the movement of a force commanded by Jubal Early to try to seize the mile-long bridge connecting Columbia and Wrightsville over the vast Susquehanna River was of potentially critical importance. Had Early's troops been able to capture and secure it, they would have put the state capital of Harrisburg under dire threat. In an engagement that deserves to rank as one of the most consequential of the invasion, Early's troops were held off on June 28 by a militia that included African American troops, probably the only time in the Pennsylvania campaign that rebel soldiers exchanged fire with uniformed Black men. "I regretted very much" this failure, Early wrote, since his plan had been to "cross my division over the Susquehanna, and cut the Pennsylvania Central Railroad, march upon Lancaster, lay that town under contribution, and then attack Harrisburg in the rear while it should be attacked in front by the rest of the Corps."[28]

By the evening of June 28, Lee had still heard nothing from Jeb Stuart and so assumed that the Army of the Potomac was in Virginia. On the one hand, this gave him a free hand in Pennsylvania. On the other, it raised the disturbing possibility that, rather than coming north to pursue him, the Federal Army might seize the opportunity to move on the lightly defended Richmond. To draw Hooker north, and not yet knowing of Early's failure to take the Columbia Bridge, Lee sent orders to his corps commanders that they should make an aggressive move toward Harrisburg. According to Charles Marshall, a dapper aide-de-camp to the Confederate commander, Lee assumed "there would be such alarm created by these movements that the Federal government would be obliged to withdraw its army from Virginia."[29] Yet no sooner had Marshall dispatched riders with the orders than Lee was informed that the Federal Army had already crossed the Potomac and was advancing toward them. The information came not from Jeb Stuart, who was still out of contact, but from a spy employed by Longstreet, an actor named Henry Thomas Harrison who, disguised as a Pennsylvanian farmer, had passed through rebel lines.

Lee immediately sent messengers to his corps and division commanders rescinding the previous orders and instructing them to concentrate at Cashtown, just east of South Mountain. This meant recalling Ewell's Corps, which was strung out across a thirty-mile arc toward Harrisburg, and Hill's, which was as far east as York. The order did not go down well with the troops since it appeared to signal that they were to advance no further.[30] But while this prompted disappointment, it was nevertheless a measure of the fundamental strategic success of Lee's Pennsylvania invasion up until this point. As one Confederate officer not unfairly summarized the situation, "Richmond has been relieved: scarcely a Federal soldier remains upon the soil of Virginia; and the burden of war has been transferred from that battle-worn State to the shoulders of the State of Pennsylvania."[31]

Lee understandably wanted to avoid a general engagement until his army was concentrated. "In the absence of the cavalry it was impossible to ascertain [the enemy's] intentions," Lee later complained, but until the enemy's plans became clear, it was wise to bring the disparate elements of his army together.[32] His worst fear was that the Army of the Potomac, which Harrison had reported to be moving northwest from Frederick, Maryland, might be intent on entering the Cumberland Valley to cut off the rebels' retreat, their supply of ammunition, and the supply chain down which plundered supplies were daily being sent south. Cashtown had the topographical features which made it "peculiarly favorable for a defensive battle," recalled Joseph B. Polley, a private in Hood's division. With his army in control of all the passes into the Cumberland Valley and with the mountains to his back, Polley argued that Lee could "safely count on drawing the enemy to his front and thus relieving his rear from danger."[33]

One of the fronts in the long-running post-war fight among former Confederates about what went wrong on the Gettysburg campaign turned on the alleged failings of Jeb Stuart. Lee's aide-de-camp, Charles Marshall, who was to become one of the post-war boosters of the Lost Cause myth, was among those who squarely blamed Stuart for everything that went wrong after Lee left the relative security of Chambersburg in the Cumberland Valley. Had he known exactly where the Army of the Potomac was heading, Marshall argued, Lee could have concentrated his army in Gettysburg by July 1. The movement to

Cashtown "was the result of a want of information which the cavalry alone could obtain for us."[34] "By his silence, [Stuart] caused Lee to move his army...not with the expectation or purpose of meeting the enemy but simply with the intention of preventing a movement which he supposed the enemy was making to obstruct his line of communication with Virginia and caused him to fight the Battle of Gettysburg without having his whole force present."[35]

Marshall's determination to blame Stuart while absolving the ever wise Lee smacks of special pleading, yet it is true that, had Lee had accurate intelligence about the northward movement of the Army of the Potomac—the kind of information that Stuart may have been able to provide—he could have concentrated his army at Gettysburg on July 1 or even a day earlier. As it was, divisions of Ewell's and Hill's Corps and the whole of Longstreet's Corps did not arrive until after the first day's fighting was complete. It is at least plausible that, as Marshall claimed, this was the "chief reason for not following up our success" on that first day.[36] Lee himself was not a man to cast about for scapegoats, but he felt badly let down by Stuart's lack of contact—officers recalled him displaying uncharacteristic "anxiety and impatience"—and in his post-battle reports referred repeatedly and pointedly to his lack of good intelligence on the whereabouts of the enemy.[37] Some eight miles to the southeast of Cashtown, Gettysburg was at the hub of eight roads radiating out in all directions of the compass. A glance at a map today makes it seem like a natural collision point for the two armies, each drawn toward the town as to the center of a web. Yet it was not self-evident in advance that the battle would take place there.

On June 28, as Lee's men ranged with impunity around Adams, Franklin, and Cumberland Counties, the commander of the Army of the Potomac was suddenly changed. Having concluded that Hooker was "more than just a failure" but would lose "the army and the capital," the Washington-based General-in-Chief Henry Halleck forced Hooker's indignant resignation after countermanding his order to evacuate Harpers Ferry.[38] Hooker was replaced by George G. Meade, a Philadelphian professional soldier who had provided solid leadership of the V Corps during the Battle of Chancellorsville. By the standards of his bombastic predecessor, Meade was undemonstrative and relatively unknown even within the army. Balding, with a rather ragged beard and mournful eyes, those who did know him found his appointment reassuring. Frank Haskell, aide-de-camp in the Union's II Corps, who had seen Meade at close quarters, thought him a "clear-headed, honest soldier... who would do his best always."[39]

Even so, the new commander's first orders did not go down well with his political bosses in Washington or his men. "The enemy are upon our soil," Meade wrote. "The whole country looks anxiously to this army to deliver it from the presence of the foe." This was pretty much what the newspapers were saying, but for Lincoln, the entire point of the war was that the whole country was "our soil" and he found utterly exasperating the implication that Meade saw his job as primarily defensive. For the troops under his command, however, it was Meade's final line that was provoking: "Corps commanders are authorized to order the instant death of any soldier who fails in his duty at this hour."[40] One Massachusetts private wrote, "The boys were pretty much of the opinion that the sting conveyed in the closing paragraph was undeserved and unnecessary.... Later on the boys thought it would be rather a good idea for the rank and file to issue a manifesto to the commander, expressing the hope that he would show more ability and judgment than his predecessors had shown when conducting a great battle and, above all, avoid issuing appeals or circulars reflecting the slightest doubt on the courage of the men."[41]

Meade was acutely aware that his army faced two potentially contradictory strategic imperatives—shielding Washington and defeating Lee's army. Yet the day after he took command, Meade appeared bullish. "I am going straight at them," he wrote to his wife, "and will settle this thing one way or the other."[42] Studying maps, Meade had begun to formulate more specific possibilities. His chief engineer, Gouverneur K. Warren, had identified an ideal location for a battle near Big Pipe Creek in Maryland in case the enemy assumed the offensive. If the aim was to defeat Lee once and for all, it was frustrating that Confederate forces were so scattered. Yet surely, Meade reasoned, Lee would be forced to concentrate his army once first contact was made. "I have pushed out the cavalry in all directions to feel for [the enemy]," Meade wrote to General John Reynolds, commanding the I Corps, at 11.30 a.m. on June 30. "And so soon as I can make up any positive opinion as to their position, I will move again."[43] As the eminent Civil War historian Bruce Catton once wrote, if Meade found a substantial enough piece of Lee's army and "prodded it vigorously, the separate parts would come together quickly enough."[44]

The "prodding"—fanning out to locate the enemy and perhaps draw him into battle—was the cavalry's job. The Union's First Cavalry Division, commanded by the experienced Brigadier General John Buford, was on the left flank (the westernmost side) of the advancing Union Army as it moved northward into Pennsylvania. Buford, wrote one of Meade's staff, had an expression that was "determined if not to say sinister. His ancient corduroys are tucked into a pair of ordinary cowhide boots, and his blue blouse is ornamented with holes; from one pocket thereof peeps a huge pipe, while the other is fat with a tobacco pouch. Notwithstanding this get-up he is a very soldierly looking man...of good-natured disposition, but not to be trifled with."[45]

After spending the previous day on a westward swing across the South Mountain, gathering intelligence about the enemy's movements, Buford led two of his three brigades northward into Gettysburg about midday on June 30. The I and XI Corps were expected to march northward from Emmitsburg the following day to be within range should there be contact with the enemy. Tillie Pierce and her friends sang "The Union Forever" to the cavalrymen as they rode down Washington Street, though she confessed that she only knew the words to the song's chorus and had to hum the verses. Townspeople, pleased to see Union men after their nasty brush with Ewell's rebels a few days earlier, plied them with drinking water, bread, and butter.

Buford quickly recognized that the low hills south of Gettysburg would provide the rebels with a strong defensive position. So, he determined to hold the town until Union reinforcements could arrive. That evening, bivouacking in the fields west of Seminary Ridge, Buford held a conference with his senior officers. The rebel army was concentrating, Buford told them, and he feared they would be attacked the following morning before the infantry arrived. One of his brigade commanders, Colonel Thomas Devin, thought Buford was too pessimistic—they could handle any frontal attack. "No, you won't," Buford replied. "They will attack you in the morning and come 'booming,' skirmishers three deep. You will have to fight like the devil to hold your own until supports arrive. The enemy must know the importance of this position, and will strain every nerve to secure it, and if we are able to hold it, we shall do well."[46]

At dusk that evening, June 30, a young woman named Lydia Clare climbed with her friends to the cupola of the Lutheran Theological Seminary, an elegant brick building on a ridge to the west of the town. Immediately in front were Buford's men, but on the horizon, they saw "as in panoramic view, the campfires of the enemy all along the blue mountainside, only eight miles distant."[47]

At about that time, eight miles away in Cashtown, Major General Henry Heth asked his corps commander, A. P. Hill, for permission to take his division into Gettysburg the following morning, July 1, to collect supplies. A whole division may have seemed rather excessive for a foraging expedition, but a "reconnaissance in force" seemed necessary because a portion of his division, the brigade commanded by a former diplomat and skilled linguist James J. Pettigrew, had ventured toward Gettysburg in search of supplies earlier that day but had to retreat when it sighted Union cavalry on Seminary Ridge. Lee's orders to avoid engaging the enemy until the army was concentrated justified caution. In addition, specific information that it was Buford's cavalry—and not merely a local volunteer force—that was occupying Gettysburg was passed to Pettigrew by a local Confederate sympathizer. According to the recollections of Lieutenant Louis Young of

Pettigrew's staff, Heth and Hill, the divisional and corps commanders, were skeptical that any portion of the Army of the Potomac was so close. "Blindness in part had come over our commanders," Young later claimed. "Slow to believe in the presence of an organized army of the enemy, [they] thought there must be a mistake in the report taken back by General Pettigrew." Consequently, when Heth's division, with General James A. Archer's brigade in the lead, marched down the Chambersburg Pike from Cashtown to Gettysburg early on the morning of July 1, they had little inkling that they were marching into battle. This was "a weakness on their part," Lieutenant Young considered with the benefit of hindsight, "which rendered them unprepared for what was to happen."[48]

As generations of historians have recorded, the Battle of Gettysburg was a "meeting engagement," meaning that neither side had planned to fight there at that time. Even so, Gettysburg was a natural point for the collision to happen. It had strategic importance thanks not only to its location at the hub of the region's road network but also because of the railroad to Harrisburg, which provided a supply route for the Union Army, and was why Confederate control of the town after the first day was potentially threatening. Furthermore, as the historian Troy D. Harman has pointed out, a battle on this scale could not have taken place without access to water to sustain a hundred and seventy-five thousand men and sixty thousand horses and mules. Gettysburg, positioned between two tributaries of the Monocacy River, Rock Creek to the east and Marsh Creek to the west, was therefore one of the few locations available for a conflict on this scale.[49]

*　*　*

The Chambersburg Pike ran in a straight line up and down a series of gentle ridges in a northwesterly direction out of the town. It was down this road that Heth's men came, beginning their march at first light, at around 5 a.m. on July 1. In the two hours that followed, as rebel foot soldiers plodded toward them, Buford's cavalry, bivouacking at the Gettysburg end of the road, were grooming their horses and preparing breakfast. But their pickets had been out all night. And at around 7.30 a.m., Company E of the 8th Illinois Cavalry, picketing near a bridge where the pike crossed over Marsh Creek, some three miles from the town, saw the column of rebel troops advancing. Lieutenant Marcellus Jones insisted on "the honor" of "opening this ball" by firing a shot at a Confederate officer on a gray horse.[50] A stone marker, erected in 1886 by the veterans of the 8th Illinois Cavalry, insists that this was the first shot of the battle, a claim that was—like almost everything about the battle—contested, in this case, most vigorously by veterans of the 9th New York Cavalry regiment who claimed that one of their own, Corporal Alpheus Hodges, had already fired at a mounted advance party of Confederates.

To the veterans and generations of battle enthusiasts, the question of who fired the first shot has mattered enormously, but the more significant point is simply that the advancing Confederates met resistance and a series of events were set in motion that triggered the war's biggest battle in a place and at a time that neither side had chosen. To General Buford, the most senior Union commander in the town on the morning of July 1, the stakes were high: whoever gained control of the high ground south of Gettysburg would have a huge tactical advantage in the full-scale engagement to come, and given the size of the advancing force, the enemy would get there first unless, as Buford laconically put it in his report, "arrangements were made for entertaining him until General Reynolds could reach the scene."[51]

As Heth's men approached Gettysburg, Reynolds, commander of the I Corps and a native Pennsylvanian, was about three miles away, riding north toward the town at the head of his leading infantry division. Buford's cavalrymen, around two thousand seven hundred and fifty of them, mounted the first line of resistance to the approaching Confederate troops. Heavily outnumbered, Buford aimed to "entertain" the rebels by delaying their advance until infantry reinforcements arrived—hopefully before the Confederates could occupy the high ground of Seminary Ridge. Dismounting and leaving one man in four to hold the horses, the cavalrymen fired their breech-loading carbines at Heth's men, reloading in a crouching position (instead of needing to stand as was necessary with muzzle-loading weapons). By half past ten in the morning, the vanguard of the I Corps of the Union Army, commanded by General John F. Reynolds, arrived. After conferring at the Lutheran Seminary, Reynolds concluded that this was as good a place as any for a battle and sent messengers scurrying back to the main body of the advancing I Corps, urging them to hurry. Reynolds could have allowed Buford to delay as much as possible and then taken control of the high ground south of the town. But he was a Pennsylvanian, and he was in a confrontational mood: it was necessary, he told one of his division commanders, "to attack the enemy at once to prevent them from plundering the whole state."[52]

Even at this stage, Confederate forces could have retreated to a defensible line. There was no strategic need for the rebels to occupy Gettysburg or engage in full-scale battle. Lee was still several miles away and had made clear that his commanders should avoid a general confrontation until his army was concentrated. But A. P. Hill, the rebel corps commander closest to the action at Gettysburg, scented a quick victory against what he imagined to be only a small Union force. And so the battle began.

3

The Battle, July 1–2

Wednesday, July 1, 1863, would be a clear, if costly, day of victory for Lee's army. In the morning, the action centered on fields and woods to the northwest of the town, close to where Buford's cavalry had first encountered rebel infantry. As troops from both armies arrived on the scene, what had begun as a routine skirmish became a full-scale and fast-moving battle. As troops arrived with cavalry messengers flying "over fences and fields like a shower of meteors," in the words of one observer, the residents of the Theological Seminary and farmers living on the ridge "came running down the hill faster than 'Double quick.'"[1] Instead of scattered groups of steadily retreating cavalrymen, by mid-morning Confederate troops faced several thousand infantrymen in close formation, blocking their path into Gettysburg (Map 3.1).

South of the Chambersburg road, the "Iron Brigade" from Wisconsin, sporting distinctive black wide-brimmed "Hardee" hats, counterattacked against startled Confederates who had expected to fight green local militia, not grizzled veterans. The rebels were pushed back down a gentle slope dotted with trees to a small stream. So sudden was the rebel reversal that Confederate General Archer was caught in the melee, overpowered by Private Patrick Maloney, an Irishman in the Iron Brigade, and taken prisoner—the first General in the Army of Northern Virginia captured by the enemy since Lee had taken command. Just behind Maloney as he wrestled Archer to the ground was another Irishman, Denis Burke Dailey, who took possession of the General's sword. Later that afternoon, when the Union Army's fortunes had taken a turn for the worse, Dailey found himself trapped in the basement of the house of Mary McAllister in the center of the town, where he offloaded the sword on his host, who hid it under a pile of kindling in the kitchen.[2]

The Union commander who bore more responsibility than any other for the decision to escalate the skirmish of the early morning, Major General John F. Reynolds, saw only a few minutes of this action. He was organizing the Iron Brigade line at some time between 10.15 and 11 a.m. when a bullet, perhaps from a rebel sharpshooter, struck him in the back of the neck, and he died almost instantly. The details of exactly where and when Reynolds was shot are one of the many endlessly debated Gettysburg unknowns. But his sudden death is not in dispute, nor is the romantic-novel-like fate of his fiancée Kate Hewitt who reacted to the news by joining the Daughters of Charity convent in Emmitsburg.[3] On Reynolds' death, the ranking division commander, Abner Doubleday, assumed command of the I Corps. Doubleday was a career soldier who had been second-in-command at Fort Sumter when the South Carolinians opened fire on it. He gained a curious post-war fame by claiming to have invented baseball, but the hours after his commander's sudden death were among the most testing of Doubleday's military career.

With Union troops having seized the upper hand to the south of the road, Doubleday's attention turned to the north. He sent the 6th Wisconsin, a regiment of the Iron Brigade, to attack the Confederate forces' right flank. This sudden assault forced Mississippi and North Carolina troops into a 15-foot-deep railroad cut that the Pennsylvania Railroad Company had left unfinished after the financial crisis of 1857. At first, this provided some cover for the rebels to fire at the advancing infantry. But despite losing half their men, the 6th Wisconsin, 95th New York, and 6th Brooklyn regiments somehow continued to advance, and when they reached the edge of the railroad cut and could fire down into it, the rebels' shelter became a slaughter pen. Hundreds of Confederates threw down their weapons and surrendered en masse.

Notwithstanding the bloodbath around the railroad cut, the bigger picture was that Federal troops were slowly pushed back to Seminary Ridge, the high ground to the west of the town from which, earlier that morning, cavalry commander Buford had first spotted the advancing rebels. As so often in this war, messages from commanders failed to reach the right men at the right time, exacerbating the confusion. The order to the 147th New York to pull back didn't get through on time because the regiment's Colonel was shot before he could inform his troops of the withdrawal. Caught in a trap, the 147th lost 207 of its 380 officers and men in just half an hour.[4] Meanwhile, the 76th New York and 56th Pennsylvania, exposed on the Union right flank, were decimated by onrushing Confederate troops. In under half an hour, 45 percent of the nearly one thousand two hundred Union soldiers north of the Chambersburg road were killed or wounded and out of action. By midday, Federal forces had secured their position on Seminary Ridge, but at a horrific cost.

All that morning, Union forces had been fighting to hold off Confederate troops coming at them from the northwest, and the line of battle was consequently oriented to face that direction. But, serendipitously for the rebels, Rodes' division of Ewell's Corps, marching west toward Cashtown in line with Lee's orders to concentrate there, got wind of the battle near Gettysburg and diverted toward the sound of gunfire.

By early afternoon, more Union forces had also arrived: the vanguard of the XI Corps marching from the south up the Taneytown and Emmitsburg roads reinforced Doubleday's beleaguered men. Under the command of Maine abolitionist Oliver O. Howard, many of the XI Corps' regiments were made up of first- or second-generation German immigrants. Some were veterans of the "First German Rifles," a regiment raised in 1861 by the Baden revolutionary leader Ludwig Blenker. The corps had then been led by another German revolutionary, Franz Sigel, until he resigned in a fit of pique just before the Battle of Chancellorsville. Two other "forty-eighters,"—veterans of the failed

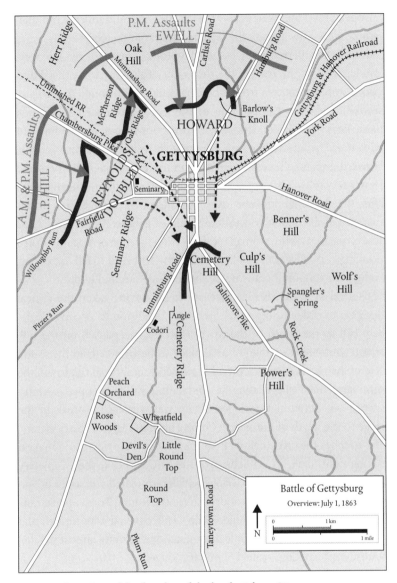

Map 3.1. Overview of the first day of the battle, July 1, 1863.

European revolutions of 1848—Carl Schurz and Alexander Schimmelfennig, were now among the leading officers in the corps.

Howard conferred with Doubleday, took command by seniority, and climbed to the roof of the three-story Fahnestock Brothers' dry-goods store downtown from where he could peer through the artillery smoke to identify the position of the forces from their regimental battle flags.[5] The Union troops were precariously holding the line, but with more troops arriving on the scene, fortunes could turn rapidly. Howard dispatched messengers to summon Dan Sickles' III Corps and Henry Slocum's XII Corps, though these troops did not arrive until after the day's fighting was over. All afternoon, tired Union troops marched at the double toward the sound of gunfire. As her family fled south, one Gettysburg woman recalled seeing the men of Slocum's Corps "looking... jaded and tired. Many had been compelled to fall out of line, and we came upon them lying by the roadside sick and hungry."[6]

General Howard also claimed credit for having taken the critical decision to order Adolph von Steinwehr's division to occupy Cemetery Hill to the south of the town. Howard had paused on the hill, which contained the town's burial place, as he arrived from the south. "Here," he recalled, "was a broad view which embraced the town, the seminary, the College and the undulating valley of open country spread out between the ridges. There was a beautiful break in the ridge to the north of me, where Culp's Hill abuts against the cemetery, and touches the creek below. It struck me that here one could make a strong right flank."[7] Carl Schurz of the XI Corps described Cemetery Hill as "the northern end of a ridge which terminated due south in two steep, rocky knolls partly wooded, called the Round Tops—half a mile distant on our right a hill called Culp's Hill, covered with timber; and opposite our left, about a mile distant, a ridge running almost parallel with Cemetery Ridge, called Seminary Ridge."[8]

But Cemetery Hill was only supposed to be a fallback position if the town could not be held; ideally, its defensive potential would not be needed. Howard's immediate task was to repulse the new threat from Rodes' division from the north and prevent the rebels from taking control of the town. He sent one of his divisions, temporarily commanded by Alexander Schimmelfennig, to occupy Oak Hill, a prominent rise today marked by the vast limestone face of the Peace Memorial erected with glowing optimism in 1933. But Rodes' rebel troops got to Oak Hill first, forcing Schimmelfennig to deploy his men haphazardly in the fields and woods below. Rodes sent three brigades to attack the right flank of the Union's I Corps, which had been fighting all morning, and the left flank of the newly deployed XI Corps. For an hour, the fight rolled across the fields and woods north of the town, with the I Corps troops just about withstanding the rebel assaults. A brigade of North Carolinians led by Brigadier General Alfred Iverson suffered devastating losses—more than eight hundred of the 1,350 men—in a poorly executed assault against veteran New Yorkers. Further to the west along the Chambersburg Pike, the "Bucktail Brigade" of Pennsylvanians held off a fierce attack by a different North Carolina brigade.

As these assaults were taking place, and with Meade still several miles away to the south, General Lee arrived at the scene. His first instinct was not to press the attack any further. After all, less than half of his army was present: there were still divisions of Hill and Ewell's Corps on the march from the east, while Longstreet's Corps was still several miles to the west coming up from Chambersburg. And Stuart's cavalry remained out of contact, as elusive as ever. By contrast, for all Lee knew, Meade's entire army could concentrate at Gettysburg at any point. Furthermore, Rodes' attacks appeared to be stalling. The Army of Northern Virginia had been in foraging not battle mode, and Lee was conscious that they were still awaiting the arrival of supply wagons carrying much-needed ammunition. A number of Longstreet's commands, including Law's Brigade of Hood's Division and Pickett's Division, had been detailed to protect and collect the supplies.[9] In short, there were many reasons to think that now was not the ideal time for a full-scale battle.

But then again, there was never a perfect time for a battle. And any hesitation on Lee's part was probably banished with the arrival of

Major General Jubal Early's division of Ewell's Corps, who appeared from the northeast. This was pure chance—Early's intended destination that day was Cashtown, not Gettysburg—but his men arrived just at the time and place where they could most make a difference. Suddenly Early could pile on the pressure on the exposed right flank of Howard's XI Corps. Lee had not envisioned a general engagement that day, but that afternoon, in the fields north of Gettysburg, surrounded by the smoke of artillery fire, he sensed another decisive victory.

As quickly as Confederate troops arrived, they joined the assault. Two fresh brigades in Heth's division re-opened the attack along the line of the Chambersburg Pike, which had failed to break through in the morning. One of these, General James J. Pettigrew's Brigade, enveloped the left flank of the much-depleted Iron Brigade and, in fierce fighting, pushed the Union troops back toward the town where they made a temporary stand at the Lutheran Theological Seminary. This was some of the most savage action of the entire war; the 26th North Carolina regiment lost around six hundred of its 839 men, while the 24th Michigan lost all but a hundred of its roughly five hundred soldiers engaged that day.[10] That evening, nineteen-year-old Private Tom Setser searched for his cousin Eli who had fallen in the fight. He told his family in Caldwell County, North Carolina, "I could all but walk over the field on dead and wounded." Eventually he found his cousin and childhood playmate bleeding profusely with a shattered thigh. He waited all night with him until Eli was carried away in a hospital wagon, later dying of his injuries. "Tom," Eli said, as the cousins said a final goodbye, "Tell my folks how it was."[11]

Union wounded were carried or stumbled back into the town where Gettysburg women had turned the First Presbyterian Church into a makeshift hospital. "We did all we could for the wounded men," wrote Mary McAllister. "Every pew was full; some sitting, some lying, some leaning on others. [The surgeons] cut off the legs and arms and threw them out of the windows."[12]

Meanwhile, Early's division began an assault from the northeast against the outnumbered Union XI Corps. One brigade, under

Brigadier General Schimmelfennig, was deployed on the left. Another, commanded by Brigadier General Francis C. Barlow, was on the right, but Barlow controversially advanced further north than Schimmelfennig's division, creating a salient in the Union line. His motives for doing so must have appeared sound at the time because he ordered his men to occupy a slight rise (today known as "Barlow's Knoll") that he feared could be used by the enemy as an artillery position. If so, it was doubly fruitless because Early subjected the XI Corps to a colossal artillery bombardment anyway and followed up with a frontal attack a mile wide and consisting of three brigades. Among the hapless Union defenders of the salient, exposed to attacks at their front and on their flanks, were the nine hundred men of the Brigade commanded by Colonel Leopold von Gilsa, a former officer in the Prussian army, who at Chancellorsville in May had succumbed to Stonewall Jackson's dramatic flanking attack and been pilloried in the press ever since. The fate of the German regiments that day further fueled anti-immigrant prejudice in the North.

While all this was happening, more Confederate troops arrived down the Chambersburg Pike from the northwest and were fed into the action, piling pressure on the remnants of the Union I Corps, who had thrown up improvised breastworks in front of the Theological Seminary building. The defenders were bolstered by twenty artillery guns closely spaced, which fired canister and shells into the closed ranks of oncoming North Carolinians from Alfred M. Scales' brigade in one of the deadliest, most concentrated artillery bombardments of the war. All but two field officers in Scales' brigade were killed or severely wounded, including Scales.

The angle of Early's assault threatened to cut off the Yankee's retreat route through the town. Outmaneuvered, Union troops began to retreat in various states of disorder. "Our men who were exhausted & wounded kept pouring into our cellar," recalled Annie Young, making it "so close from the *blood* and water on the muddy floor that we could hardly endure it."[13] Emma Gilbert, the wife of a Gettysburg coachmaker, recalled peering from the high window of her neighbor's cellar where she was hiding with seven of her children and seeing a dead body in the street just a few feet away. "When one of his own side came past, he would decently cover his face. Then would come one of the opposite side, would kick him and remove some article of his clothing until the poor man was almost nude." "The water in the gutters was tinged with blood."[14] At 6 p.m., when Sallie Myers and her family came up from their cellar, where they had been hiding with some wounded members of the XI Corps, they were confronted by "two men and two horses" lying dead in the town square.[15] Southern troops were as prejudiced about immigrant fighters for the Union as the New York press. One rebel private claimed, no doubt with massive exaggeration, that a "Dutch Colonel" (he meant a German speaker), commanding about two hundred and fifty men, came "up to me and cried out that he surrendered...I made him throw his sword on the ground and sent the whole party back to our rear guard, under the escort of only *one* Confederate soldier."[16]

It was nearly 5 p.m. when General Ewell, commander of the Second Corps, rode into the town square to take stock of the situation. Officers hustled Union prisoners to the rear while troops searched for water, food, and liquor. And for the next three days—until the final Confederate retreat on July 4—the town of Gettysburg was occupied by the rebel army. It was an exhausting experience for the townspeople; their accounts mix horror, indignation, and anxiety with the occasional dash of excitement at being at the epicenter of the storm. Annie Young recalled General Ewell and his staff invading her home and taking tea with her in a surreal replication of middle-class sociability. "They were all very polite & kind," she recalled. "I sat at the head of the table & gave them their coffee so I had a fine opportunity to see them all. With a *few* I was completely *captivated*."[17] That a woman could speak like this of dashing rebel soldiers a few years after the war speaks volumes about the post-war culture of reconciliation. But it is also possible that it is an insight into white women's slight sense of distance, of being onlookers. For privileged populations like respectable white women, the dangers of this conflict were usually very slight compared to the barbarity of other conflicts.

For the few remaining Black people in the town, the occupation potentially meant the end of their freedom. One local resident, Albertus McCreary recalled that "colored people living in the western part of town"—where there was a long-established Black neighborhood—were "gathered together by the Confederates and marched out of town." At least one escaped. A woman called Liz, identified as a washerwoman, was seen being marched away "crying and moaning." But she reappeared after the battle, and her white neighbors crowded around to find out how she had escaped. Liz told them she had slipped away just by the Lutheran Church without the guard noticing, climbed to the Belfry and had hidden there, unbeknownst to anyone throughout the battle, without anything to eat or drink.[18]

* * *

With the town lost, Union troops regrouped south of the town on Cemetery hill, the fallback position selected earlier that day. Although their retreat had been chaotic, they managed to retain almost all their artillery, which was rapidly moved into position. When General Howard reached the summit of the hill, he encountered General Winfield Scott Hancock, the commander of II Corps. The latter revealed that he had orders in his pocket from General Meade to take overall command of the battlefield, even though Howard outranked him. Despite what was a rather tense encounter (for it was impossible for Howard not to feel that Hancock's arrival reflected Meade's lack of confidence in him), the two men agreed that, by a mixture of accident and design, and despite the humiliating defeats of the day, they held, in Hancock's words, "the strongest position by nature upon which to fight a battle I ever saw."[19] Hancock's arrival, in any case, was reassuring to the men. As one Union soldier recalled, "His person was well-known, his presence inspired confidence, and it implied also the near-approach of his army-corps."[20]

When Meade finally arrived later that night and examined the terrain, he too was satisfied with the position in which his army had found itself. "We may fight it out here just as well as anywhere," he told his staff.[21] Meade was right to recognize the defensive potential of Culp's Hill and Cemetery Hill and the gentle ridge that ran from there to the south. It was not an impregnable position; the slopes were gentle and relatively uncluttered by obstacles to assaulting forces, and, except for a few stone walls, the defenders did not have any natural entrenchments. Yet visitors to the battlefield today can see for themselves that, from the top of the ridge, Meade's army had clear lines of sight.

Given this obvious advantage to the side occupying Cemetery and Culp's Hills, one of Gettysburg's most enduring controversies is whether Ewell should have pressed home his advantage on the evening of July 1 and pushed the retreating Union soldiers from the high ground. On his arrival in the town, Ewell had held a hurried conclave with his senior officers. Jubal Early argued that his division was in good enough shape to exploit the Union retreat. Yet, when Generals Ewell and Early ventured to the south of the town to survey the prospect of an attack, they could see prominently placed batteries of artillery facing down the slopes. Even so, they agreed that given the potential strategic gains of displacing the Union Army from so advantageous a spot, it was worth attempting, so long as Lee could provide some support from the right, presumably from A. P. Hill's Corps. When word was sent to Lee, however, the reply came back that no reserves were available. If the hill were to be taken, Ewell would have to do it alone.

After the war—when former Confederates feuded over who among them was to blame—there was a misty idea that Ewell had suffered a failure of nerve that cost the battle. Those keenest to blame Ewell claimed he had disobeyed Lee's orders by not advancing. But the order in question was opaque. It instructed Ewell to "carry the hill occupied by the enemy" if he "found it practicable." This kind of discretionary order was not unusual for Lee. As the influential Civil War historian

James McPherson pointed out, when Stonewall Jackson was alive, Lee could rely on him to interpret such an order in a fighting spirit. But Ewell was no Jackson, and, after the war, there was no shortage of Confederate veterans who claimed that they had been bursting to storm Cemetery Hill that night if only the order had come. William Calder, a North Carolina soldier, told his mother that not to advance on the hill was "the great mistake...which lost us all the advantage we had gained and caused the subsequent death of so many gallant men."[22] A Louisianan claimed he heard "many officers and men exclaim 'would that Jackson were here!'" when they discovered no attack was to be ordered that night.[23]

However, other witnesses with a good sense of the balance of forces thought Ewell's caution justified. For example, the Confederate artillery commander, Edward Porter Alexander, was sure that "any attack we could have that afternoon would have failed."[24] This may well be one of the many examples of Confederates arguing over their own decisions without giving enough credit to their enemies. Carl Schurz was surely right that even had Cemetery Hill been taken by the rebels that day, Meade would have "had time to change his dispositions" and pulled back to Pipe Creek, initially his favored defensive spot, where the battle would then have been fought.[25] Most military historians think Ewell's decision was the right one, but that has not stopped it from being one of those Gettysburg "what-ifs" that will not die.

Lee's unwillingness to offer immediate support to an attack on Cemetery Hill on the evening of July 1 may well indicate that he was still uncertain about whether this was the time and place for an all-out battle. He still did not know—in the absence of intelligence from Stuart's cavalry—quite how much of the Army of the Potomac lay in front of him. He did not know that Meade ordered five more Union Corps and the Artillery reserve to reinforce the shattered divisions on Cemetery Hill. But based on what he knew or felt, Lee went to bed that night, determined to continue the battle the following day. Union forces may have ended the day occupying advantageous high ground, yet they had been driven there in a ragged formation after their defense of Gettysburg collapsed in the face of Confederate pressure. The confident Army of Northern Virginia had every reason to think that having once again dominated the Army of the Potomac in a fast-moving battle, they could finish the job in the morning.

Lee's initial plan for July 2 was to attack by advancing his troops up the Emmitsburg Road toward the top of Cemetery Hill (Map 3.2). He hoped that by pressuring the Union lines from an oblique angle, they would collapse in on themselves. His first instinct was to shorten his lines by ordering Ewell to move his corps west from the town into position next to Hill's Corps on Seminary Ridge. But Ewell persuaded his commander that his men would be demoralized by withdrawing from positions they had fought so hard to take. He also claimed that he could easily take Culp's Hill, a wooded rise that overlooked Cemetery Hill, which Ewell falsely believed to be undefended.[26] Compared to the unresolved argument about whether Ewell should have attempted to assault Cemetery Hill that first evening, this dispute between Lee and Ewell is not one of the more famous of the battle's might-have-beens. Still, the battle would have looked very different had Lee concentrated all three corps of his army, facing the Union Army in a nearly straight line. By acceding to Ewell's insistence that he remain in place, curling around the Federal Army at their most easily defensible point on Cemetery Hill, Lee was accepting that his troops would have a more extended line than their enemy's. By not concentrating all his men on Seminary Ridge, Lee made communication between the right and left flanks of the Confederate line even harder than it would otherwise have been. Lee's revised plan was that the Confederates would attack at each end of the Union line instead of striking the center of Meade's army. To the north, Ewell's Corps would make a "demonstration" against the Union's right flank on Cemetery Hill, which could be converted into a full-scale assault if possible. Meanwhile, Longstreet's Corps would strike Meade's left flank at the south end of Cemetery Ridge, dealing the Yankees a fatal, perhaps even final, blow.

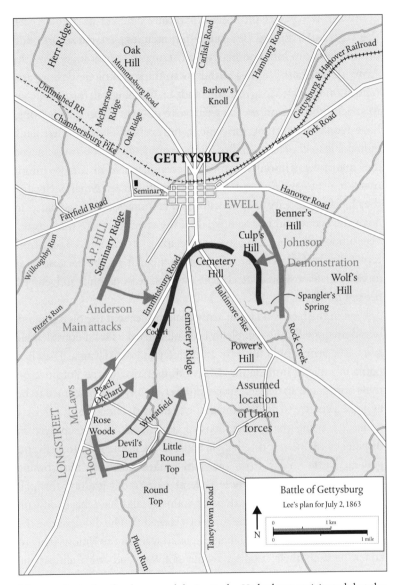

Map 3.2. Lee's plan for the second day's attacks. He had not anticipated that the Union line would be extended south to Little Round Top.

In vain, Longstreet proposed a radically different alternative: "All that we have to do is to file around [the enemies'] left and secure good ground between him and his capital." Longstreet was suggesting the Army of Northern Virginia withdraw to the south of Gettysburg and reposition for defense across the roads to Washington, forcing Meade to attack.[27] But the phrase "all we have to do" was rather glib. It would have required a turning movement, moving south with a left flank vulnerable to contact with the Union Army. Even if the army achieved this maneuver without too many losses, it would also have meant marching into unfamiliar terrain—and without Jeb Stuart's cavalry, they had less capacity to conduct proper reconnaissance in advance. In any case, Lee would not be moved. "If the enemy is there tomorrow," Lee supposedly told Longstreet, "we must attack him." Longstreet replied (or so he later claimed), "If he is there, it will be because he is anxious that we should attack him—a good reason, in my judgement, for not doing so."[28]

Even in the face of a Union army that had secured the high ground, withdrawing was unpalatable to Lee and carried its own considerable risks. The army could not stay indefinitely in Pennsylvania. They had come to inflict a humiliating defeat on the Army of the Potomac on their home soil, and after a successful day on July 1, now seemed to be as good a chance to do it as any that was likely to come along. Lee later conceded, using the passive construction he so often employed in dispatches to Richmond, that "it had not been intended to deliver a general battle so far from our base unless attacked, but coming unexpectedly upon the whole Federal Army, to withdraw through the mountains with our extensive trains would have been difficult and dangerous." At the same time, he claimed that he did not have the option of digging in on Seminary Ridge to wait for the Union Army to attack because their supplies would not last, and, with almost the entire Union Army in front of them, widespread foraging was not an option. "Encouraged by the successful issue of the engagement of the first day," Lee concluded, "and in view of the valuable results that would ensue from the defeat of the army of General Meade, it was thought advisable to renew the attack."[29]

Lee's post hoc rationalization is thin, as even some of his allies later conceded. Edward Porter Alexander, for example, was especially unimpressed by Lee's claim that a lack of supplies prevented the Army of Northern Virginia from, at the very least, simply entrenching their position on Seminary Ridge. This is his wonderfully dry summary: "When it is remembered that we stayed for three days longer on that very ground, two of them days of desperate battle, ending in the discouragement of a bloody repulse, & then successfully withdrew all our trains & most of the wounded through the mountains; and finding the Potomac too high to ford, protected them and foraged successfully for over a week in a very restricted territory along the river until we could build a bridge, it does not seem improbable that we could have faced Meade safely on the 2nd at Gettysburg without assaulting him in his wonderfully strong position."

So, Lee did not have to attack on July 2. He could have remained where he was, pursued Longstreet's plan of maneuvering between the Union Army and Washington, or he could have withdrawn with the "prestige of victory" back to Cashtown. He could have dared Longstreet to attack him first, which, given the political pressure on the Army of the Potomac, he surely, in the end, would have done. But, as numerous witnesses observed, Lee seemed to lack his usual composure that first evening in Gettysburg. According to Longstreet, Lee "seemed under a subdued excitement" which "occasionally took possession of him when the 'hunt was up.'"[30] Justus Scheibert, a Prussian military observer embedded with the Army of Northern Virginia, reported that "Lee was not at his ease, but was riding to and fro, frequently changing his position, making anxious enquiries here and there, and looking careworn." Lee's uncharacteristic "uneasiness during the days of the battle," Scheibert thought, "was contagious to the whole army."[31]

There is some evidence that Lee may not have been well. He may have been suffering from both an attack of diarrhea and the aftereffects of the heart attack he had suffered earlier in the year (he was to die of a heart condition five years after the war). As many historians have speculated, he may also have been struggling without Stonewall Jackson's élan and wise counsel. Nor was he used to commanders who disagreed flatly with him, as both Ewell and Longstreet had done. He had explicitly instructed General Heth to avoid a general engagement, yet here they were face to face with an unknown portion of Meade's army at a time and place not of Lee's choosing. Yet the successes of July 1 gave Lee that familiar scent of victory. According to the British military observer Arthur Fremantle, while Longstreet "spoke of the enemy's position as 'very formidable'" and warned (correctly) that they would "intrench themselves very strongly during the night," the general's staff were confident of success. "The universal feeling in the army," Fremantle reported, "was one of profound contempt for an enemy whom they have beaten so constantly, and under so many disadvantages."[32]

Lee may have been in an irritable frame of mind that evening, but he shared his junior officers' sense of invincibility, and all his instincts told him to keep the initiative. The extraordinary victory against improbable odds at Chancellorsville was fresh in his memory. In contrast, Longstreet, who had not been present at Chancellorsville, held up the Battle of Fredericksburg in December 1862 as the ideal victory. There, Confederates had destroyed wave after wave of Federal assaults from behind stone walls and entrenchments, "crippling and demoralizing" the Federal Army, as Longstreet later put it, "with trifling loss to our own troops."[33] For the rest of his life—he lived until 1904—Longstreet irritated fellow Confederates by claiming he had warned Lee that it was folly to attack Meade on Cemetery Ridge. He distanced himself from the outcome of the battle in its immediate aftermath, writing on July 24, 1863, that "the battle was not made as I would have made it" and claiming that had the army moved to cut off Meade from Washington, they could have "destroyed the Federal army, marched into Washington, and dictated our terms."[34]

Maybe. But back in the world of what happened, the Federal Army spent the night of July 1 further strengthening its position while Lee planned the next day's assaults. Soldiers on Cemetery Hill and along Cemetery Ridge piled logs, branches, and stones as makeshift defenses, while additional troops arrived to shore up the Union line. Troops in both armies slept fitfully that hot night of July 1, hearing the groans of the wounded, all anxiously awaiting what they expected to be a climactic battle the next day.

* * *

Shortly after first light, Meade rode along Union lines on Cemetery Ridge, surveying the ground. In a dispatch to Washington, he had promised to attack if he was not himself attacked, but that, surely, was a political sop to his anxious and instinctively bellicose political masters. All Meade's instincts must have told him that he would fight a defensive battle here, which indeed he did. Compared to other leaders in the Army of the Potomac—Winfield Scott Hancock, for example—Meade did not exude charisma. Watching the Commanding General that morning, Carl Schurz recalled that "there was nothing in his appearance or bearing—not a smile nor a sympathetic word addressed to those around him—that might have made the hearts of soldiers warm up to him, or that called forth a cheer." Yet he gave a convincing impression of competence. "This simple, cold, serious soldier with his business-like air did inspire confidence. The officers and men, as much as were permitted, crowded around and looked up to him with curious eyes, and then turned away, not enthusiastic, but clearly satisfied."[35]

All through the night and the morning of July 2, troops marched toward Gettysburg as fast as they could. The 20th Maine, a regiment in the Union's V Corps, was one of those marching through the darkness, reaching Gettysburg at 7 a.m. As the exhausted but adrenaline-pumped men from Maine tramped along dark roads, a rumor spread that the ghost of George Washington had been seen riding through the fields of Gettysburg. Their colonel, Joshua Lawrence Chamberlain, confessed that he almost believed the rumor himself.[36] By noon, both armies were practically all present on the battlefield. One of the Army of the Potomac's Corps (the VI, commanded by John Sedgwick) was still many miles away to the east, but otherwise, the whole Federal Army had gathered. If General Lee wanted to strike on July 2 in the belief that Meade's army had not yet concentrated, it was, unbeknownst to him, by then, already too late. On the Confederate side, General Pickett's division of Longstreet's Corps was still off to the west in Cashtown, one brigade of Hood's division still several hours' march away, and the elusive Stuart's cavalry had still not arrived, but otherwise, the Army of Northern Virginia was all present. The previously quiet fields were filled with tens of thousands of men, baggage trains, horses, artillery guns on carriages, and all the other detritus of large armies.

Visitors to the battlefield today can glean a sense of the sheer number of men involved in this fight by noting the official bronze markers placed by the US War Department in the early twentieth century when it owned the battlefield. Each denotes where the seventy Union and fifty-six Confederate brigades fought (unsurprisingly, the exact positioning has been the subject of controversy). Each of the twenty-two Union divisions and ten Confederate divisions also has an official marker, as do the locations of the artillery batteries on each side. As tourists to Gettysburg are told, Meade's army was arranged in a "fishhook" shape, with the point of the hook at Culp's Hill, curving around Cemetery Hill, the "shank" of the hook running down Cemetery Ridge, and—this Lee had not anticipated—with Little Round Top resembling the "eye" at the southern end. Union Signal Corps observers had a clear view of Confederate lines from the Union's extreme left flank on Little Round Top, making a surprise attack extremely difficult.

All through the humid morning of July 2, Union troops watched for an attack that didn't come. Lee made mistakes at Gettysburg—perhaps the most fundamental being to choose to fight on July 2 at all—but if an attack was to happen, he had been right to want it to come as soon as possible, before the Union defenders had time to strengthen their line. "We anxiously hoped that his attack would not come too early for our comfort," recalled Carl Schurz.[37] To his critics, the delay was another strike against Longstreet. Maybe Longstreet should not have insisted on waiting until Law's brigade of Hood's division arrived (he didn't want to fight "with one boot off," he said), though the challenge of balancing a desire to move quickly against the understandable desire to wait for more men was a familiar one for commanders. Longstreet probably had little choice, however, but to march his corps on a circuitous route for more than twenty miles to evade the watching Union signal officers on Little Round Top. If he had not done so, his assault would have lost any element of surprise. But the consequence was that they were tired and dehydrated by 4 p.m. when the troops were finally in position to attack. Relations among the Confederate leaders deteriorated throughout the day. Longstreet, still unconvinced by the whole plan, felt that Lee was undermining his command by trying to micromanage the attack, while General Lafayette McLaws, who Lee had designated to lead the first wave of the attack, was getting increasingly irritated with Longstreet, who he described as "a man of small capacity, very obstinate, not at all chivalrous, exceedingly conceited and totally selfish."[38] Time was dragging on, and things were not going well for the Confederates.

A further complication to Lee's plans for July 2 was that the Union's "fishhook" position had been bent out of shape at its southern end (Map 3.3). This had not been Meade's intention. In the morning, the troops were arrayed in a straight line along Cemetery Ridge, but by the afternoon, the section of the Union line commanded by General Daniel E. Sickles had bulged forward by about a mile to form a salient.

Sickles, who was to play a prominent role in the post-war contest over the memory and meaning of the battle, was, to put it delicately, a colorful character. The only one of the seven Union corps commanders not to have been to West Point, Sickles had been a Tammany Hall Democratic congressman from New York before the war. In 1857, the extravagantly mustachioed Sickles was the defendant in a sensational murder trial. He was acquitted after shooting his wife's lover in broad daylight in Lafayette Square in front of the White House. His defense attorney, a fellow Democratic politician, convinced the jury—no doubt made up of men who thought shooting an unfaithful wife's lover was entirely justifiable—that his client had been temporarily insane when he committed the crime. And in a twist that would be implausible if this were fiction, the attorney who made legal history this way was now the Secretary of War in Lincoln's cabinet, Edwin B. Stanton. Sickles, needless to say, owed his position to political connection rather than military qualification. To be fair, he was one of a handful of the few "political generals" to show genuine military talent. But July 2 at Gettysburg was to be his last day in command.

On that morning at Gettysburg, Sickles had been deeply unimpressed by the position he'd been ordered to defend, which was the southernmost third of Cemetery Ridge where it sloped downward toward the base of Little Round Top. If you go to Gettysburg today and stand where Sickles was sent and look west, it is not hard to see why he was unhappy. At this point, the "ridge" is no longer a ridge at all but is at a lower elevation than the farmland just to the west, where now, as in 1863, there is a peach orchard. Three months earlier, at Chancellorsville, Sickles had been ordered to give up some high ground which was then used to deadly effect by Confederate artillery. He didn't want to be burned twice. And so, at 2 p.m., the general ordered his men to advance to take the higher ground. In doing so, he doubled the length of his defensive line, which meant that, even by committing all his reserves, Sickles did not have enough men to defend the line adequately and still connect to Winfield Scott Hancock's Corps on his right and the "anchor" of Little Round Top to his left. The man who had gotten away with murder had created gaps in the Union line.

From further up Cemetery Ridge, General John Gibbon, divisional commander in Hancock's II Corps, was bewildered by the sight of Union troops advancing down the Emmitsburg Road toward the distant peach orchard. "We could not conceive what it meant, as we had heard of no order for an advance and did not understand the meaning of making this break in the line."[39] When Meade was told of Sickles' unauthorized advance, he was apoplectic. Riding over to inspect the new forward line for himself, he made quite clear to Sickles why he thought it was dangerous, as well as insubordinate. He pointed out that Sickles' new position was "neutral ground" in the sense that the artillery guns of both armies commanded it from Cemetery Ridge and Seminary Ridge respectively. Therefore "the very reason you cannot hold it applies to them." Sickles asked if he should pull his men back to their original line. "I wish to God you could," replied Meade, "but the enemy won't let you!"[40]

The rancorous Meade–Sickles feud over whether the creation of this salient saved or nearly doomed the Union cause consumed extraordinary amounts of time and energy after the war, but it is ultimately unresolvable. To the end of his days—and he lived to the age of 94— Sickles insisted that in occupying the peach orchard, he had saved the Union cause at Gettysburg. Many, if by no means all, military historians have begged to differ, as, most emphatically, did General Meade. The truth is that Sickles' freelance strategizing disrupted both Meade's careful defensive plan *and* Lee's offensive. From Meade's point of view, aside from Sickles' manifest insubordination, his maneuver had created new vulnerabilities in the Union's defense. His advance swapped a short, straight defensive line for a salient which could be attacked from three sides. Meade called up the Union Army's Fifth Corps, newly under the command of George Sykes and in reserve two miles to the east, to reinforce Sickles. Meanwhile, the artillery chief Henry Hunt ordered up five batteries to support the precariously exposed New York battery commanded by James Smith at the end of the Union line.

Potentially the most serious consequence of Sickles' move was that it opened up a vulnerability on the Union's left flank. When he ordered the ten thousand men of the Third Corps forward, Sickles put no troops on Little Round Top, even though that was where Meade had explicitly told him to anchor the left flank (anchor, that is, in the sense that if the end of the line were in so defensible a position, it would be difficult for the enemy to outflank them and attack Union troops in the rear). Had the Confederates seized this opportunity and moved artillery onto Little Round Top, they would have dominated the Union Army's position on Cemetery Ridge, the alternative history scenario imagined by Ward Moore in 1953.

This terrifying vulnerability came to Meade's attention because he sent chief engineer Gouverneur Warren there to assess the strength of the force Sickles had posted. Warren was staggered to discover that not only were there no more than a few signalmen on the top of the hill but that Confederate troops were advancing. Immediately Warren sent for troops to be diverted to the position that Meade had always intended for them to hold. Fortunately for the Army of the Potomac's future, Warren's messenger encountered Colonel Strong Vincent, commanding the Fifth Corps' lead brigade as it hurried up from the rear. Without double-checking with his superiors, Vincent—although a lawyer, not a trained soldier—immediately recognized the urgency of the request. He immediately galloped to Little Round Top, accompanied by his orderly carrying the white triangular brigade flag with a navy border and a red Maltese cross. The brigade followed, tracking up a farm road and finding a path up the hill.

If Sickles going rogue had thrown Meade's defensive plans into disarray, forcing the Army of the Potomac to scramble to adapt, it was also challenging for Longstreet. Rather than being able to push up the Emmitsburg Road to attack the Union line on Cemetery Ridge from an oblique angle, the Confederates were confronted by Union troops closer to their right than they had expected.

For a couple of hours, with Little Round Top undefended contrary to Meade's intentions, the end of the Union line lay at the ten-acre area known—even before the slaughter there on July 2—as "Devil's Den." Nestled near a small creek right at the base of Little Round Top, Devil's Den, among all the mythologized and ghost-ridden places on the Gettysburg battlefield, is the one with the most intrinsically sinister appearance. It is an unusual geological formation of huge protruding igneous rocks. According to local folklore, an evil serpent skulked between the boulders. From Devil's Den, the Union line ran north along a ridge on the western side of a creek before turning northwestward from the wheatfield to the peach orchard and bending northeast along the Emmitsburg road to form the dangerously exposed salient.

In the face of Sickles' Corps' unexpected placement, one of Longstreet's divisional commanders, John Bell Hood, argued for a change of plan and requested that, rather than advance up Emmitsburg Road into the thick of Sickles men, he be allowed to move around the Federal left flank—around Little Round Top—and attack them in the rear. Even though this was not so dissimilar an idea from the one that Longstreet had proposed to Lee the night before, he refused Hood's request on the grounds that it would be too big a deviation from Lee's orders.

Hood's attack nevertheless was compelled to deviate from the plan to march up Emmitsburg Road. The terrain and the position of the Union line made it impossible to follow the original line of attack. And then, only a few minutes after launching the attack, Hood was severely injured by a shell that burst right above his head, "withering" his left arm. He was evacuated from the battlefield leaving his brigade without central direction. Amid the confusion created by shell fire, a landscape filled with natural obstacles, and a fallen commander, Evander M. Law's Alabamans and Jerome Bonaparte Robertson's Texans and Arkansans were forced to adapt their attack plans continually. The 44th and 48th Alabama regiments of Law's brigade and the 1st Texas and 3rd Arkansas of Robertson's brigade advanced through woods and smashed into the Union defenders around Devil's Den while other regiments made toward Little Round Top.

In Devil's Den, men battled hand to hand, never certain where their enemies were amid the bewildering array of rocks. In less than half an hour, the 20th Indiana lost more than half its men, including its colonel and lieutenant colonel. General Law recalled that in this corner of the battlefield, "the ground was rough and difficult, broken by rocks and boulders, which rendered an orderly advance impossible." Time

GREAT BATTLES

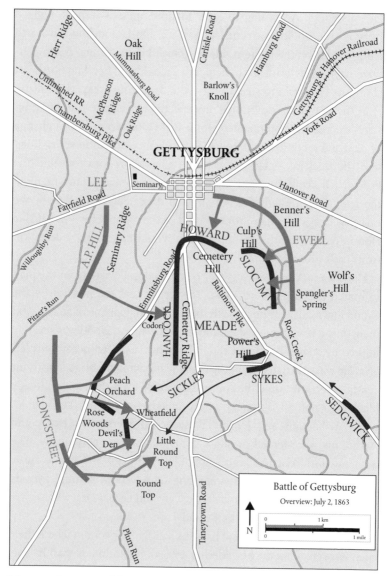

Map 3.3. Overview of the second day of the battle. Note the salient around the Peach Orchard created by General Sickles' unauthorized forward movement.

THE STRUGGLE FOR DEVIL'S DEN.

Figure 3.1. A sketch of the fighting in Devil's Den, reproduced on p. 347 of the 1887 book *Battles and Leaders of the Civil War, being for the most part contributions by Union and Confederate officers, based upon 'the Century War Series,'* vol. 3.

after time, Union defenders were on one side of a massive boulder and rebels on the other. In some cases, recalled Law, "My men, with reckless daring, mounted to the top of the large rocks in order to get a better view and deliver their fire with greater effect. One of these, Sergeant Barbee of the Texas brigade, having reached a rock a little in advance of the line, stood erect on the top of it, loading and firing as coolly as if unconscious of the danger while the air around him was fairly swarming with bullets. He soon fell, helpless from several wounds, but he held his rock, lying upon the top of it until the litter-bearers carried him off."[41]

As the Confederate attackers gained more and more ground, Colonel Van Horne Ellis of the 124th New York, a regiment that had already lost 40 percent of its men at Chancellorsville, led a spectacular counterattack, charging into Devil's Den and hurling themselves recklessly at the 1st Texas. Ellis was shot and killed only a minute into the attack, as was his major. Scarcely a hundred men from the regiment staggered back to their original line. A little later, the 40th New York lost more than a third of its men in a brutal struggle with Georgian and Alabaman troops in a rocky area on the edge of Plum Run creek that the soldiers would christen "the Slaughter Pen." "We could hear the charges of canister passing over us with the noise of partridges in flight," wrote one Confederate private of the fight in Devil's Den. He continued: "Immediately to [my] right, Taylor Darwin, orderly sergeant of Company I, suddenly stopped, quivered, and sank to the earth dead, a ball having passed through his brain. There was Rube Franks, of the same company, just returned from his home in Alabama, his new uniform bright with color, the envy of all his comrades, his gladsome face beaming as if his sweetheart's kiss had materialized on his lips, calling to his comrades, 'Come on, boys; come on! The 5th Texas will get there before the 4th [Alabama]! Come on, boys, come on!' he shortly afterwards met the fatal shot."[42] Against tough competition, the late afternoon of July 2, between around 4 p.m. and 6 p.m., at this southern end of the Union line, can lay claim to being the nastiest period of fighting in the battle.

As fast as the Confederates piled into the fight, more Union reserves would appear, yet the rebels pushed the Union soldiers back through attack and counterattack. Eventually, just as Union artillery commander Henry Hunt had feared, the enemy seized three of the four Parrott rifles of Smith's New York battery stationed above Devil's Den. Rebel troops claimed possession of Devil's Den and the ridge behind it in what General Law remembered as being "less than an hour from the time we advanced our attack."[43]

Meanwhile, just a quarter of a mile up the slopes from Devil's Den, Colonel Strong Vincent had hurriedly posted his 1,350 men to defend the partially wooded, boulder-strewn hill. The 20th Maine, commanded by Colonel Joshua Lawrence Chamberlain, was on the extreme left flank. The 83rd Pennsylvania, the 44th New York, and the 16th Michigan curved around the hilltop to join up with the rest of the Union line on Cemetery Ridge. As the men in Vincent's brigade recognized, the stakes were incredibly high; the consequence of failing to hold the hill may well be the collapse of the entire Union line. "I place you here!" Vincent told Chamberlain. "This is the left of the Union line. You understand. You are to hold this ground at all costs!" Retreat was not an option.[44]

The thirty-four-year-old Chamberlain was raised by deeply religious parents to think of slavery as wrong. Still, his views became more radical when, as an undergraduate at Bowdoin, he listened with a small group of friends to Harriet Beecher Stowe reading drafts of her novel *Uncle Tom's Cabin.* Chamberlain later succeeded Harriet's husband, Calvin Stowe, as the holder of the Chair in Rhetoric in the college. Chamberlain's forebears were citizen soldiers who had served in the American Revolution. In 1862, the professor left Bowdoin, recruited a regiment and became its lieutenant colonel. "This war, so costly of blood and treasure, will not cease," Chamberlain told the Governor of Maine, "until the men of the North are willing to leave good positions" as he was doing. Blending an unyielding sense of duty to God and country that so exemplified the public culture of the mid-nineteenth-century United States, Chamberlain pledged to set a personal example by sacrificing his "dearest personal interests, to rescue our Country from desolation, and defend our National existence against treachery at home and jealousy abroad."[45] The hour or more in which the 20th Maine desperately defended Little Round Top on July 2, 1863, was the pivotal moment in Chamberlain's long life. For many others, that evening was their last.

Peering through the trees down the hill through young oak and pine trees, the men of the 20th Maine waited in silence for the assault they knew was coming. Some cracked jokes to defuse the tension; others fidgeted with their cartridge boxes or muskets. Chamberlain walked "up and down the line," recalled one of his men, offering "a last word of encouragement or caution." After only a few minutes' wait, Confederate artillery fire suddenly stopped and was replaced by the sound of musket fire as Alabamans and Texans advanced as best they could up the slopes, firing from behind trees and boulders. Confederates had taken similar positions by storm in the past, but on this day, they failed. A long march in broiling sunshine had left them dehydrated. Without water, they could not clean off the residue of black powder on their rifle barrels, making it harder and harder for them to reload. Furthermore, the three lead rebel regiments attacking Little Round Top, the 4th and 5th Texas and 4th Alabama, were not under unified command but essentially fought as separate entities; their effectiveness was further blunted when the two Texas colonels were wounded early in the assault. These troops were followed by two more Alabama regiments under the command of Colonel William C. Oates, on the furthest right of the Confederate line, whose orders were to find the extreme left of the Union line and try to turn it. It was Oates' men who pushed Chamberlain's Maine regiment hardest.

From above, Union cannon, hurriedly placed on the summit of Little Round Top, blasted shot and shell into the valley below but could not directly help Vincent's brigade as the men struggled desperately to hold off the attackers. Ably supported by some experienced junior officers, Chamberlain managed to get his men to extend their line while under fire and "refuse" it—in other words, bend it back into a horseshoe shape. Believing they had outflanked the Union defenders, Oates' men unexpectedly ran into severe fire from behind rocks. Oates recalled that his assault was met by the "most destructive fire I ever saw," and his line "wavered like a man trying to walk against a strong wind."[46] All around, Confederate and Union soldiers thudded to the ground as minié balls tore into their flesh and bone. "Squads of the enemy broke through our line in several places, and the fight was literally hand to hand," wrote Chamberlain. "The edge of the fight rolled backward and forward like a wave. The dead and wounded were now in our front and then in our rear."[47] All around were "shouts of defiance, rally, and desperation; and underneath murmured entreaty and stifled moans; gasping prayer, snatched of Sabbath song; whispers of loved names; everywhere men torn and broken, staggering, creeping, quivering on the earth, and dead faces with strangely fixed eyes staring stark into the sky. Things which cannot be told—nor dreamed."[48]

The fight at Little Round Top is the most storied episode in this most storied of battles. Many of the accounts tell of moments of heroic chivalry of the kind that Victorian readers loved. One example is Chamberlain's description of the last moments of Private George Washington Buck, who had been demoted before the battle by a cartoonish bully of a quartermaster, Alden Litchfield ("a large, rough, overbearing man, one who disgraced his uniform every day by his brutal treatment of the men").[49] Bleeding profusely from a shoulder wound, Buck knew he was dying. As his colonel knelt to offer comfort, the private whispered, "Tell my mother I did not die a coward." To this Chamberlain responded, "You die a sergeant, I promote you for faithful service and noble courage on the field of Gettysburg!"[50] Another example, from among the attacking Alabamans, was Captain James Ellison, a particular favorite of Colonel Oates. At one point, Oates saw Ellison out in front of his men gesturing with his hand to his ear, signaling to the colonel that he had not heard a command. When Oates yelled an order to renew the attack, he heard Ellison cry, "Forward, my men, forward!" before, the very next instant, the young captain was killed by a bullet to the head. "He fell on his back," Oates wrote, "threw up his arms, clenched his hands, gave one quiver and was dead. I thought him one of the finest specimens of manhood I ever beheld."[51] A third example of an oft-told tale of heroism on Little Round Top concerned the 20th Maine color sergeant. As had been the case in battles for hundreds of years, Civil War armies relied on a regimental flag to guide soldiers through the smoke of battle. The enemy would target the color guard in the same way that they would target officers, to disorient a regiment, and it was the ultimate humiliation for a regiment for the enemy to capture the flag. And so, in the Battle of Little Round Top, much was later made of the heroism of Sergeant Andrew Tozier, who held up the regimental colors while badly wounded. "In the center [of the 20th Maine line], wreathed in battle smoke, stood the Color-Sergeant," recalled Chamberlain, "his color-staff planted in the ground at his side, the upper part clasped in his elbow, so holding the flag upright, with musket and cartridges seized from the fallen comrade at his side he was defending his sacred trust in the manner of the songs of chivalry."[52] From tales such as this—and there were many more at Gettysburg—Americans on both sides emerged from the war with a burnished ideal of heroic sacrifice.

With about a third of the regiment dead or severely wounded, Chamberlain saw yet another wave of attackers coming at his men up from the valley. "It did not seem possible to withstand another shock like this coming on," Chamberlain recounted. With their ammunition nearly out, and no reserves in sight, "only a desperate chance was left to us." Chamberlain ordered a bayonet charge, holding his right in place while the left swung around down the hill. With a flair for the dramatic, Chamberlain later recounted the moment in breathless prose. "Five minutes more of such a defensive, and the last roll-call would sound for us. Desperate as the chances were, there was nothing for it but to take the offensive. I stepped to the colors. The men turned toward me. One word was enough,—BAYONET! It caught like fire, and swept along the ranks."[53] It is impossible to know whether most of the Maine men could hear their colonel or think about him much under the pressure of battle. Maybe their counterattack was spontaneous. But whoever deserves the credit, it was a success. A private in Chamberlain's regiment recalled the stunning effect of the charge on the rebels. "Thinking we had been reinforced [they] threw down their arms and [cried] out 'don't fire! We surrender'." As the 20th Maine drove attackers across the front of the next Union regiment in line, the 83rd Pennsylvania and the 44th New York, more than two hundred rebels were captured (unsurprisingly, the exact numbers are unclear), which itself is an indicator of the low morale of the attacking force. The cost in casualties, however, was pitifully high. By nightfall, the official count showed that of the 358 men of the 20th Maine engaged in battle, twenty-nine had been killed outright and ninety-one wounded, many of them fatally. The enemy had reportedly captured five.[54]

Today, the monument to the 20th Maine is the most visited site in the Gettysburg National Military Park. The story of the 20th Maine's heroic defense of Little Round Top has captured the public's imagination since Chamberlain was made a central character in Michael Shaara's Pulitzer Prize-winning novel *The Killer Angels*, published in 1974. In the 1993 film based on the book, Jeff Daniels starred as Chamberlain, conveying clear-eyed courage combined with an endearing scholarly sensitivity. The 20th Maine's bayonet charge was extraordinary, but other regiments in Vincent's brigade—and on different parts of the battlefield—suffered higher casualties than the 20th Maine. Colonel Vincent himself was mortally wounded, as was the general of the brigade sent in as reinforcements and the commander of the Union artillery battery on the hill.

But against the odds, Chamberlain lived. He survived the battle, went on to be awarded the Congressional Medal of Honor, rose to the rank of brigadier general and was chosen by General Grant to accept the surrender of the Army of Northern Virginia at Appomattox. Even so, Michael Shaara could not have made him a central character in his novel had Chamberlain not shaped his image through speeches and writings over many decades. With integrity but not a little dramatic flair, Chamberlain conjured a mystique around his—and his regiment's—wartime service (a reputation he pressed into use in four successful campaigns for Maine governor). One of his most quoted passages comes from a speech he gave on the battlefield in 1889 at a ceremony to dedicate a monument to the soldiers of Maine who fought and died there: "In great deeds, something abides. On great fields, something stays. Forms change and pass; bodies disappear, but spirits linger to consecrate the ground for the vision-place of souls. And reverent men and women from afar, and generations that know us not and that we know not of, heart-drawn to see where and by whom great things were suffered and done for them."[55] If you spent a couple of hours on Little Round Top on a busy summer day, you will hear this speech read aloud by a schoolteacher or tour guide. If it is read well, it is as sobering to hear as any war literature ever written.

Despite the Chamberlain cult, the reality is that the defense of Little Round Top did not rely on the 20th Maine alone but also on the other regiments in Vincent Strong's brigade. Furthermore, even if Oates' Alabamans had captured the Maine men's position, they probably could not have held it for long, isolated as they were. Just as occurred elsewhere on the field that day, any breach in the Union line could more than likely have been plugged by reserves. A critical element in the Union defense of Little Round Top was the arrival of the 140th New York, commanded by Patrick H. O'Rorke, a young West Point-trained officer, who quickly recognized the vulnerability of the 16th Michigan's position on the opposite flank from Chamberlain's men, and led his men toward the onrushing rebels. O'Rorke was killed almost immediately by a bullet through his neck, but his men then overpowered the attacking Texans and Alabamans, securing the hill's right flank.

The southern anchor of the Union line at Little Round Top held firm, but further up Cemetery Ridge, there were moments of danger; in several places, the rebels pierced Union defenses. By about 7 p.m., the terrain occupied by Sickles' Corps in their unauthorized advance had been lost, and Meade—constantly surveying the whole battlefield as best he could—had to move men from the Union right to reinforce and plug gaps along the ridge.

Throughout the late afternoon, the armies had pushed back and forth over what became known as "the Wheatfield" and the Peach Orchard, the elevated ground that had first attracted Sickles' attention and formed the apex of his salient. The fight included what Confederate artillery commander Porter Alexander later recalled as one of the fiercest artillery contests of the war. The Confederate batteries on Seminary Ridge were only about 500 meters from the Federal troops, a range which made their firing devastatingly effective. Longstreet committed all his forces to drive the Federal Army back from the salient. One of those injured in the melee was Sickles himself, whose right leg was struck by a cannonball as he and staff were evacuating their corps headquarters in the face of Barksdale's assault. As he was carried to the rear on a stretcher, Sickles asked an aide to light a cigar and stick it in his mouth at a jaunty angle in a display of insouciance. His leg had to be amputated just above the knee. Sickles sent the severed bone to the newly established Army Medical Museum and took friends to visit it, but July 2 was his last day of active service. This outcome was far from universally mourned within the Army of the Potomac. One Second Corps officer drily remarked, "The loss of his leg is a great gain to us, whatever it may be to him."[56] With Sickles out of action, Meade put Second Corps commander General Winfield Scott Hancock in overall charge of the Federal left wing, which restored order to the rattled Union defenders but was too late to hold Sickles' position.

The Mississippians turned the tide against Sickles' defenders. They smashed through the Third Corps defenders in the Peach Orchard before turning northeast and pushing Andrew Humphreys' division, which was struggling to hold a line along the Emmitsburg road, into full retreat. Among the last to enter the assault was the Mississippi brigade of General William Barksdale, who rode at the head of his troops with his hat off and his long white hair flowing. For a while, it looked as if Barksdale's men might be able to push through a gap onto Cemetery Ridge and threaten the whole Federal position until a powerful counterattack by a brigade led by Colonel George L. Willard. Barksdale was mortally wounded, one of the nine generals to die in the battle. Colonel Willard was also killed when a shell fragment smashed his skull.

Sickles' repositioning and the confused fighting around the Peach Orchard had disrupted the order of the original plan, but the basic idea remained. The Confederate assault was designed to come in waves rolling one after the other toward Union lines at an oblique angle, a tactic that Civil War generals, revealing once more the influence of French military theory, referred to as an *en echelon* attack. One such "wave" to the left of Barksdale's—a brigade of Alabamans from Richard Anderson's division of A. P. Hill's Corps, led by Cadmus Wilcox—crashed into the Union line at a weak point, destroying the remnants of Sickles' Third Corps and threatening to surge up through a gap in the Union line. According to several sources, General Hancock, having failed to rally stragglers from Sickles' Corps, recognized that Wilcox's onrushing men were only minutes away from seizing a Union battery on Cemetery Ridge, which could be turned on the rest of the Union line with devastating consequences. He turned to the only troops in good order nearby, the two hundred and sixty disciplined veterans of the 1st Minnesota Volunteers and ordered them to charge. Outnumbered four to one, "every man realized in an instant what that order meant," recalled one survivor. "Death or wounds to us all—the sacrifice of the regiment to gain a few minutes time and save the position and probably the battlefield, and every man saw and accepted the necessity for that sacrifice."[57]

The place of Chamberlain's Maine men is secure in popular memory, but the 1st Minnesota Volunteers have at least as strong a claim to have saved the Union on July 2. The Minnesotans advanced double-quick into the oncoming fire of lead, not pausing even as man after man fell. When they were close to the first rebel line, they charged with leveled bayonets, only firing once they reached what shelter could be found in the dry bed of Plum Run. Their charge held up the Alabamans for ten to fifteen minutes, enough time for Hancock to find reinforcements to protect the batteries on the ridge, but at a huge cost. Forty Minnesotans were killed outright or suffered mortal wounds. A further one hundred and seventy were severely wounded, a total casualty rate of 82 percent, one of the highest of any unit in a single action in the whole war.

The high-water mark of the Confederate assault on July 2 was reached by a brigade of Georgians led by Ambrose "Rans" Wright, a reluctant secessionist who had become a tough and savvy fighter. Wright's men advanced up Cemetery Ridge, capturing artillery batteries as they went but were left stranded without support and were forced to retreat. In just three hours in, their successive assaults along the Union line from Little Round Top northward by Longstreet and A. P. Hill's Corps had resulted in around six thousand Confederate casualties while approximately nine thousand Union men were killed, missing or wounded.[58]

Yet, just as Gettysburg was not where the commander of either army had planned a full-scale engagement, this part of the battlefield was where either commander intended to fight on July 2. Sickles had created a salient that was ultimately indefensible on ground that Meade had not wanted him to occupy. In doing so, however, he had at least prevented the Confederates from pursuing their original plan to push directly up the Emmitsburg Road, rolling up the Federals' left flank. That line of attack was unlikely to have succeeded anyway since it relied on the faulty intelligence that the Union Army had neglected to occupy Little Round Top properly. Had Sickles not gone rogue, Little Round Top would have been effectively defended all day; it was because he stretched his line so thinly that it was ever exposed at all.

Aside from Sickles, the Union command on July 2 cooperated well, benefiting in comparison to the Confederates from shorter lines of communication. While Lee remained static, observing the assault on the center of the Union line as best he could from his headquarters on Seminary Ride, Meade was in constant motion. So too was the energetic Winfield Scott Hancock, who, more than once after he took over command of the Union left, spotted a vulnerability in the defensive line just in time and found reinforcements. By 7 p.m., about an hour before sunset, the Confederate attacks on the Union left and center were about worn out; amid lingering smoke, wounded men lay in the fields groaning and gasping for water. But the last act of the day's battle was still to get underway.

Lee's original plan had envisioned an assault at both ends of the Union line. While Longstreet's Corps assailed the enemy's left flank, Ewell's orders were to mount a "demonstration" (a show of force) against the other end of the Union line on Culp's Hill and Cemetery Hill, which he should convert into an actual assault if possible. Ewell duly began an artillery bombardment at around 4 p.m. as Longstreet's men began their attack to the south. Charles Wainwright, a Union artillery officer positioned on Cemetery Hill, described the impact of a single shot from a Parrott rifle, the muzzle-loading cast-iron cannon used by both sides. Wainwright was just 10 yards from where a twenty-pound ball struck the center of a line of infantry lying behind a stone wall in the hope of protection. "Taking the line lengthways, it literally ploughed up the two or three yards of men, killing and wounding a dozen or more." The twenty-pound Parrott rifles were immensely heavy, requiring two teams of six horses to move them, so the armies more frequently used lighter ten-pound cannons. But the twenty-pounder was devastating in its impact even when, as in the instance Wainwright described that evening on Cemetery hill, the shell failed to explode. Wainwright recalled another which did burst, just under an artillery battery, the canister killing one man outright, "blowing another to pieces so that he died within half an hour, and wounded the other three" men.[59]

At around 7 p.m., Ewell finally ordered an infantry attack on Culp's Hill. By then, the Union defenses on Culp's Hill were dangerously overstretched. Five brigades from the hill had been diverted to reinforce the Union line elsewhere, leaving only one behind—about one thousand four hundred men commanded by the sixty-two-year-old George S. Greene, the oldest general on the battlefield who, as an assistant professor, had once taught Robert E. Lee at West Point. Greene's men, like the 20th Maine at the other end of the Union line, were stretched into a single battle line with no reserve, but at least they had the advantage of the breastworks they had been assembling all day from rocks and felled trees. Struggling up the wooded hill in the gathering dark, the attackers had the advantage of numbers, but all along the east side of the hill, they failed to overcome the Union's entrenchments.

But the Union entrenchments, strong as they may be against a frontal assault, were useless if the enemy managed to move around the side of them. Two Virginia regiments (the 23rd and 10th) did just that on the evening of July 2, outflanking the 137th New York, which was holding down the extreme right of the Union line in much the same way as, two miles to the south and two hours earlier, the 20th Maine had been holding down the extreme left. Colonel David Ireland, commanding the 137th New York, is far less famous than his counterpart Joshua Chamberlain. Although he survived Gettysburg, he died of dysentery in 1864 during the Atlanta campaign; for Ireland, there was to be no long post-war life to burnish the memory of his triumphs. Yet his regiment experienced a strikingly similar ordeal to the Maine men, made even worse by gathering darkness. "We were being fired on heavily from three sides," wrote Ireland in his report, "from the front of the works, from the right, and from a stone wall in our rear. Here we lost severely in killed and wounded." Company A was most exposed on the regiment's furthest right, fighting in the dark without breastworks to protect them and losing almost half of their men. With ammunition running low, a portion of the regiment bayonet-charged the oncoming rebels to give time for the rest of the regiment to regroup. At one point, the 71st Pennsylvania regiment from the Second Corps arrived to reinforce the New Yorkers only to quickly retreat, their colonel saying he "would not have his men murdered."[60] Like Chamberlain, Ireland ordered his regiment to rotate at a right angle—or "refuse the line"—a dangerous but essential maneuver in the face of an enemy firing at their unprotected right flank. The regiment reformed in a fortuitously positioned traverse trench dug earlier that day in a remarkably orderly fashion. The New Yorkers held on at great cost. The regimental monument erected on Culp's Hill in 1888 records forty killed, eighty-seven wounded, and ten "missing."

The rebels' twilight attack extended to Cemetery Hill, where General Jubal Early ordered two Confederate brigades to assault General Oliver O. Howard's Eleventh Corps. As had happened further down the Union line earlier in the day, the story on Cemetery Hill was of ferocious rebel attacks, occasionally puncturing the Union line but ultimately failing to hold an advanced position or exploit their gains. The German regiments in the Eleventh Corps once more earned the scorn of some of the rest of the army, Charles Wainwright, the Union artillerist, claiming that "not a single regiment of the Eleventh Corps exposed to attack stood fire, running away almost to a man" in the face of Harry T. Hays' brigade, who reveled in the nickname "Louisiana Tigers."[61] But overall, the Union lines held firm, and with self-conscious evenhandedness, Wainwright noted that an artillery battery manned by Germans fought tenaciously hand to hand to prevent their guns from falling into rebel hands.

The second day of battle drew to a close with the armies in virtually the same positions as they had been at dawn. Yet for Lee, the partial, temporary successes of the assaults appear to have validated his instinct that a great victory was within his army's grasp. "The result of this day's operations," he wrote with characteristic use of the passive voice that sought to drape his own highly contentious views with the veneer of self-evident truth, "induced the belief that with proper concert of action...we should ultimately succeed, and it was accordingly determined to continue the attack." In short, "the general plan was unchanged," he wrote. The third and final day of the battle would test Lee's faith in his army and his own judgment to destruction.

4

High Tide and Retreat, July 3 and Afterward

On July 1, rebel forces had soundly beaten the Union Army, but had ended the day on less advantageous ground. On July 2, having tasted victory on Northern soil, the rebels resisted the temptation to make a tactical withdrawal, and attacked. Yet, despite horrific losses on both sides, the position of the two armies were not fundamentally changed. And with each failed assault, the stakes rose for the Confederates, who were running very low on ammunition, were encumbered by miles of pillaged horses, cows, hogs, and corn—not to mention four thousand prisoners of war—and were forty-five miles along rutted tracks from Virginia. Throwing caution to the wind, on July 3, Lee ordered another attack. It was to be the last on Northern soil.

As the historian Stephen Sears has pointed out, there was a striking contrast between Meade's detailed knowledge of the condition of his own and his enemy's forces and Lee's relative ignorance. Agents for the United States Bureau of Military Intelligence had accurately informed Meade that Pickett's division had arrived to reinforce Lee. In contrast, Lee's ad hoc spy network, or his army's less than systematic interrogation of captured Union soldiers, provided no similar source of information about the strength of the Army of the Potomac. When he formulated his attack plans on the evening of July 2, the Confederate commander had not even received direct reports from Ewell or Longstreet. Stationing himself in his field headquarters throughout July 2, Lee's firsthand knowledge of the day's fighting was limited to what he could see through his binoculars. Perhaps this helps to explain Lee's decision to fight on. But perhaps—tired and unsettled as he was—he would have done so anyway, determined not to lose a chance to bring the war to a climax.

For General James Longstreet, however, the failure to break the Union defenses validated his doubts of the morning. The little ground the Confederates had gained (around Culp's Hill on their left and the Peach Orchard on the right) were of no real value and had come at far too high a price for an army in enemy territory in danger of being cut off from retreat. Although he was intensely proud of how well his men had fought that day ("the best three hours' fighting ever done by any troops on any battle-field"), Longstreet remained convinced that the assaults had been misguided and should certainly not be repeated the next day.

Normally, Longstreet and Lee would confer on the evening after a battle, but their relationship was so strained that neither seems to have tried to do so on July 2. Early the next morning, however, the two met, and Longstreet, by his own account, pressed for an alternative strategy. Of all the Gettysburg "what-ifs," this Lee–Longstreet encounter is the one that seems most consequential. There was a genuine decision to be made here; there was no reason why the Army of Northern Virginia needed to resume its assault on that enemy in that position that day. If Longstreet had prevailed, there would have been no Pickett's Charge that day.

Looking eastward, the two men could clearly make out the defensive line of the Union Army less than a mile away across the shallow valley between the two low rises of Seminary and Cemetery Ridges. They could have strolled across the fields to those guns in less than half an hour. In between were cornfields and grazing land bordered with snaking split-rail fences, some of which had been torn down. That morning, still shrouded in mist, lay the fallen from the shattering violence of the previous day: most dead, some barely alive. But by his own account, Longstreet wasn't looking east; he was looking south.

So storied is this encounter that it is easy to imagine how it might have gone. Just imagine: the blue-gray dawn light; General Lee appearing out of the mist on his majestic white horse; Longstreet, a tin cup of coffee in his hand, his eyes squinting at the Union positions, his mind running through the tactical possibilities. "My scouts have been out all night, sir," Longstreet says. "I believe we've found a way through those hills...if our turning movement is successful, we can sidestep the Yankees' left flank and push up towards his center." Surely, he argues, they could outflank the Army of the Potomac by marching to the south around the Union right wing, regain the initiative, find a defensible position, and compel Meade to attack. But as Longstreet makes his case, Lee shakes his head almost imperceptibly, then points toward a copse of trees on Cemetery Ridge at roughly the center of the Union lines. "The enemy is there, sir. We must strike him where he is." And Lee tells Longstreet that Meade would have responded to yesterday's assaults by strengthening his flanks, leaving the center weak. Pickett's division of Virginians had just arrived at the battlefield: they could lead a frontal assault that would succeed where yesterday's had failed. As Lee says this, he glances over his shoulder to where can be heard the occasional burst of laughter from Pickett's men, hidden in the trees of Seminary Ridge. They have been marching most of the night but are battle-ready. And as Lee knows all too well, Pickett the cavalier, his hair worn long and his beard groomed to the point of dandyishness, was eager for his slice of glory. Now, Longstreet is astonished. "General, I have been a soldier all my life; I have been with soldiers engaged in fights by couples, by squads, companies, regiments, divisions, and armies, and should know as well as anyone what soldiers can do. It is my opinion that no fifteen thousand men ever arrayed for battle can take that position. We have an alternative line of attack here, General. I am not proposing retreat, but that we maneuver to get between the enemy and Washington. Sir, I know my men and what they can do— and sir, yesterday, they did the best three hours' fighting done by any troops on any battlefield, and still, they failed. Surely, sir, we cannot risk the whole army on another frontal assault as you propose?" Lee

GREAT BATTLES

narrows his gray eyes and gazes at Longstreet. For a long moment, neither speaks. The fate of the battle hung in the balance for a long moment in the cool dawn air.

Perhaps the meeting happened like that, or perhaps not. The main source for my imaginative reconstruction is Longstreet's account. And Longstreet's agenda was to distance himself from the disaster that followed. What we know for certain, though, is that at the end of the discussion between the two generals, Lee was unmoved. The plan for an attack on the center of the Union position would go ahead. When Federal troops launched a dawn attempt to retake the trenches at the foot of Culp's Hill, Lee reasoned that if Meade was still concentrating his efforts on defending his flanks, his center would be weakened. And so, while Lee committed troops to the struggle on Culp's Hill and ordered Jeb Stuart's cavalry division to attack the Union Army in the rear and disrupt their supply lines to the east, these actions were sideshows. The main effort was to be a massive assault directed at Cemetery Ridge, precisely the course of action that Longstreet feared would lead to disaster—and precisely what General Meade had anticipated Lee would do.

There are historians who argue that Lee never intended the July 3 assault to veer toward the famous "copse" of trees but intended the objective to be another—and more prominent—group of trees known as Ziegler's Grove on Cemetery Hill.[1] Since Lee never commented at any length on what happened, and the orders he gave that day were, in key respects, characteristically vague, it is impossible to be certain how exactly he hoped an assault would work. But whether the intention was to attack at an oblique angle or in a direct line, Lee's presumption was that, with a big enough blow in the center, Meade's army could be broken in two.

As had happened the day before, Lee communicated his overall plan but allowed his subordinates to work out the details. This meant that, notwithstanding his doubts, Longstreet was left in command of the main assault. As for the other two Confederate corps commanders, Dick Ewell was in charge of the continuing struggle for Culp's

Hill, while A. P. Hill was unwell (probably with at attack of gonorrhea, which had afflicted him periodically ever since he contracted it while at West Point). Hill played no active role that day. Lee made clear that Pickett's freshly arrived Virginia division (containing brigades led by James L. Kemper, Lewis A. Armistead, and Richard B. Garnett) should take the lead along with a division of North Carolina troops led by John J. Pettigrew. They were supported by two North Carolina brigades from A. P. Hill's Corps under the command of Isaac R. Trimble. That made two and a half divisions altogether, a total of around twelve thousand men.[2] Two more brigades from Anderson's division of Hill's Corps led by Generals Cadmus Wilcox and David Lang were positioned to support Pickett's right flank. As on the previous day, getting all these troops into position took longer than Lee had hoped, delaying the attack by several hours, and in later years some Confederate veterans added this tardiness to the charge sheet against Longstreet.

Although it took hours before the main assault was ready, fighting started at first light on Culp's Hill on the extreme left of the Confederate line. Union artillery pounded positions they had lost the previous evening, but before the Federal Army could follow up with an infantry assault, the rebels counterattacked. The fight around Culp's Hill continued for six hours, making it the longest continual engagement in the battle. Three main attacks by rebel soldiers, the final one at around 10 a.m., tried and failed to storm well-entrenched Union positions. Federal troops attacked as well, with their final assault around noon killing or wounding nearly half of the 2nd Massachusetts regiment that led the attack.

According to Gettysburg legend, one of the Confederates killed in the attack on Culp's Hill that day was Wesley Culp, whose Uncle Henry owned the land. Wesley was one of the Gettysburg boys who had migrated to Shepherdstown Virginia to work in a carriage works and had enlisted in the 2nd Virginia Infantry. The story that he died as a member of an army invading his hometown is true, though he probably died on nearby Wolf Hill rather than on his family's property. Today, Gettysburg Ghost Tour guides speculate that his spirit still walks on the Culp Farm, where—allegedly, but not very plausibly—his body was buried by female relations after they recovered it from the battlefield. Wherever he fell, Culp's sacrifice was in vain. Almost a third of the men in Edward Johnson's Confederate division who were engaged around Culp's Hill fell on July 3.

Lee's hope was that the attacks on Culp's Hill would draw away Union defenders from the center of their line on Cemetery Hill. But if that was the intention, it utterly failed due to timing. The twenty-two thousand Confederate and Union soldiers battling for Culp's Hill were exhausted by noon and the fighting petered out. Yet by that stage, the main assault on the Federal center had still not begun.

In mid-morning, as the fighting continued around Culp's Hill on the Federal right, the Army of the Potomac's artillery commander, Henry J. Hunt, rode along the Union line, inspecting his gun placements. From the top of Cemetery Hill, looking westward toward the rebel lines, he saw what he grimly called "a magnificent display." "Our whole front for two miles was covered by batteries already in line or going into position." The ridges were "planted thick with cannon" and "never before had such a sight been witnessed on this continent, and rarely, if ever abroad." While Hunt had some incentive to talk up the artillery force against which his own would shortly be tested, there is, no doubt, much truth to his observation. For Union soldiers on Cemetery Ridge, the sight of so many Confederate cannons moving into position could only mean that they were about to face an onslaught of iron projectiles which some of them would not survive. As Hunt correctly predicted, what this impressive artillery buildup portended was "an assault on our center, to be preceded by a cannonade in order to crush our batteries and shake our infantry."[3]

Around 1 p.m., these Confederate cannons duly commenced what may have been the largest artillery bombardment of the war. Over a hundred and fifty Parrott and Rodman rifled guns, as well as older Napoleon smoothbores, blasted shells in the direction of the Union line (they "belched forth their death" as one rebel soldier put it), while Union artillery responded in kind.[4] The roar and crash of exploding shells was terrifying. Crouching or lying impotently by their guns, their field of vision shrouded by smoke, and knowing that there was no effective way of protecting themselves from whizzing shrapnel or a direct blast, the men remembered the bombardment with horror and awe. "I lost fifty of my men lying down," reported Union General Alexander Webb. A Confederate soldier recalled that a major in his regiment was "conversing with a friend during the shelling, both having their faces close to the ground, and his friend making some remark the Major asked him what he said; and after waiting a little while for an answer found on looking up that his friend was dead—dead by his side, and he did not hear the blow that killed him."[5]

Presumably, Lee hoped the artillery bombardment would fatally weaken Union defenses and tip the advantage to the offensive force, a tactic recently deployed with mixed success in the Crimean War and the Franco-Austrian War. Half a century later, the British Army put a similar, and similarly misplaced, faith in the power of artillery to "soften" their enemy's defenses on the first day of the Battle of the Somme. Back in the earliest days of Lee's command of the Army of Northern Virginia, on July 1, 1862, at the Battle of Malvern Hill, a series of confusing orders and miscommunications had hampered the effectiveness of the Confederate artillery bombardment, contributing to the failure of a series of infantry assaults against an elevated Union position. A year later, the problem and the outcome were eerily similar.

A good proportion of Confederate shells overshot their targets, landing relatively harmlessly on the far side of Cemetery Ridge rather than amid the huddled infantrymen. Faulty ignition fuses contributed to the problem, as did smoke that soon made the targets invisible, but as at Malvern Hill, a lack of coordination among the various battery commanders compounded the problem. The firing could have been concentrated in one spot; instead, it was scattered all over the Union line. The man formally in charge of Confederate artillery, William Nelson Pendleton, known to the men as "Old Mother Pendleton," was largely absent and utterly out of his depth, so much so that one sage historian concluded, "Lee bears responsibility for allowing a man so stupendously incompetent as Pendleton to rule the artillery."[6] Lee bears responsibility, too, for (once again) the vagueness of his orders, which gave Edward Porter Alexander—the de facto artillery commander—too little time and too little detailed understanding of what he was being expected to accomplish. Having failed to substantially dent the Union defense, Alexander had too little ammunition remaining to use his batteries for the other purpose which Lee may have had in mind: advancing behind the troops to give them cover. In any event, the author of one of the most exhaustive accounts of the third day's fighting concludes that the Confederate artillery bombardment failed to achieve any significant reduction of Union artillery power, and that, furthermore, "the Confederate infantry lost as many men [in the exchange of artillery fire] as the Union infantry, and probably more."[7]

Mistrust and misunderstanding between artillery and infantry commanders hampered both armies throughout the war, and the consequences were especially visible on July 3. On the rebel side, there was no effective coordination: even had they been on target, Confederate shells were aimed at too broad a field, and no one seemed to have thought in advance about exactly how best to advance the infantry behind the artillery fire. But on the Union side as well, recriminations over the use of artillery became a running sore in the post-war commentary on the battle. Union artillery chief Henry Hunt complained that General Winfield Scott Hancock had countermanded his instructions to his batteries to conserve their fire during the Confederate bombardment. Had Hancock not interfered, "I do not believe Pickett's division would have reached our line," Hunt later wrote. "We lost not only the fire of one-third of our guns but the resulting cross-fire which would have doubled its value."[8]

General Hancock, a man whom one historian has described as an "infantry chauvinist," had indeed overridden Hunt's plan by demanding that—for the sake of the morale of his men—Union batteries should return fire with fire.[9] But even if the full potential of the artillery was unrealized, it was devastating enough for the oncoming Confederates. As the rebel ranks came within range, the Union artillery opened fire. Smoothbore Napoleons slammed solid shot, sometimes knocking over whole files of men like tenpin bowls, while rifled pieces fired shells that either exploded on impact or overhead, raining shrapnel. Union gunners had rarely had so perfect an opportunity for enfilading fire across the length of the Confederate ranks. "I could sight down the entire length of their line," recalled one Union battery commander almost gleefully. "I watched my fire stop and break one column, all the men turning back in mass seeking cover in the woods."[10]

The assault known as "Pickett's Charge" was not undertaken by Pickett's division alone, and nor was it really a "charge" if, by that term, one imagines men advancing at a run. Instead, sometime after 2 p.m. (or perhaps as late as 3 p.m.—reports, as always, differ), ranks of men advanced slowly across the uneven fields toward the Union guns, pausing to clamber over fences, the lines disappearing and reappearing from the sight of the Union defenders when they went into slight dips in the land. The two wings of the attack—Pickett's division on the Confederate right and Pettigrew's on the left—moved at different paces, and the commanders struggled to close the gap between them. Yet the scale of the attack impressed itself on all who saw it. To Frank Haskell it was "an overwhelming resistless tide of an ocean of armed men sweeping upon us."[11] To Christopher Mead, a corporal in a New Jersey regiment, the enemy "made a splendid appearance with their colors flying in the breeze."[12] In the many dozens of accounts by Union soldiers describing what they faced, the word "magnificent" frequently appears. "On they came," recounted Mead, "driving our skirmishing line before them like so many frightened sheep, although they fought well until they saw there was no chance."[13] Many men that humid afternoon brooded on the outcome of the attack. Not just the day's fight, but the global struggle seemed—even at the time—to hang in the balance. Writing in his diary in the late morning of July 3, before the artillery bombardment began, a

Pennsylvania private wrote that if the South successfully launched an attack that day, it would be "all up with the USA."[14]

Viewing the advancing ranks of rebels from Cemetery Hill, Carl Schurz could not help but be impressed. "The alignment was perfect. The battle flags fluttered gaily over the bayonets glittering in the sunlight." But the "grand holiday parade on a festive ground" soon turned dark. "No sooner had the attacking column appeared on the open than our batteries, which had in the meantime been re-formed and well supplied with ammunition, opened upon them from the front and from the right and left, with a terrific fire. Through our field-glasses we could distinctly see the gaps torn in their ranks, and the ground dotted with dark spots—their dead and wounded. Now and then a cheer went up from our lines when our men observed some of our shells striking right among the advancing enemy and scattering death and destruction around. But the brave rebels promptly filled the gaps from behind or by closing up on their colors, and unshaken and unhesitatingly they continued their onward march."[15]

Although this is usually described as a frontal assault, a lack of foresight in the troops' jumping-off positions meant that Pickett's division had to execute a turning movement only 500 meters from Union guns in order to close ranks with Pettigrew's on their left, exposing them to withering fire. Yet what is truly extraordinary about the record of that hour of exceptional violence is how many rebel soldiers continued to advance through blistering shrapnel, obeying orders not to stop and fire even as their comrades fell one by one beside them. They struggled across rising ground toward the "copse" of trees at the Union center, and toward a stone wall from behind which Union soldiers, crammed together and passing loaded rifles to the best shots among them, blasted a steady volley of musket fire.

Most men in Pettigrew's division could struggle no further than the Emmitsburg Road, which ran at an oblique angle across the line of the Confederate attack. General Isaac Trimble saw Pettigrew's men "sink into the earth under the tempest of fire poured into them." The slightly sunken road gave some measure of protection to the rebel troops, and the roadside fence provided a good cover from which to fire back at the defenders, but there was no way forward. Within the range of musket fire as well as cannon, the straggled groups of Pettigrew's men who pushed toward the ridge from the Emmitsburg Road faced a destructive rain of fire as intense as anything experienced on the battlefield. A Delaware soldier recalled that "grape, canister, Minnie, buck and ball were simultaneously poured in one incessant stream into the advancing column of the enemy."[16] Isaac Trimble was one of many officers to fall that day, his leg shattered by a bullet. When an aide asked the general if he should rally the men, Trimble replied, "It's all over! Let the men go back."[17] About half an hour after they had emerged from the woods on Seminary Ridge, the traumatized survivors of Trimble's division began picking their way back to where they had started.

Meanwhile, on the right wing of the attacking force, the vanguard of Pickett's division was within touching distance of a minor salient in the Federal defenses. "The Angle"—or the "Bloody Angle" as it subsequently became known—was a right-angle formed by the stone wall and enclosing the "copse" of trees that had been a visual marker for the advancing rebels. Now in ragged groups rather than the parade ground lines with which they had begun, Garnett's brigade spotted a gap in the Union line where Pennsylvanian troops had fallen back. At that small point in the line, and for a few brief minutes, around two thousand Confederates came face to face with only a few hundred defending Federal troops. General Richard Garnett urged his men forward but was killed instantly by a bullet in the side of his head. According to some accounts, Garnett's terrified, wounded horse galloped wildly back to the rear, an emblem of Confederate fortunes.[18] But even as Garnett fell, General Lewis Armistead's brigade was close behind. Sticking his felt hat on the tip of his sword and raising it in the air for his men to see, Armistead led his men across the stone wall. Shrieking with rebel yells which were often indistinguishable from the screams of animals in pain, this was the Confederate high tide.

Fighting hand to hand with fists and bayonets, the rebels captured a Union battery before being overwhelmed. A Northern journalist tried to describe the desperation of the struggle: "Men fire into each other's faces, not five feet apart. There are bayonet thrusts, saber-strokes, pistol-shots; cool, deliberate movements on the part of some,—hot, passionate, desperate efforts with others; hand-to-hand contests; reck-lessness of life; tenacity of purpose; fiery determination; oaths, yells, curses, hurrahs, shoutings; men going down on their hands and knees, spinning round like tops, throwing out their arms, gulping up blood, falling—legless, armless, headless."[19]

To break through at the Angle, even if only for a few minutes, was a remarkable fighting achievement for Garnett and Armistead's men. Astonishingly, they even managed to capture fourteen men of the 69th Pennsylvania and took them back behind Confederate lines. They were among the more than five thousand Union POWs taken back with the rebel army as they retreated into Virginia, ending up in the notorious Libby Prison in Richmond.

The best estimates of total Confederate losses that afternoon are around six and a half thousand men. One of the most authoritative estimates is that 1,123 rebel soldiers were killed on the battlefield and more than four thousand wounded.[20] All three brigade commanders in Pickett's division were casualties. Garnett was shot dead, James L. Kemper seriously wounded, and Armistead shot in the chest just as he breached the stone wall, dying behind Union lines two days later. All told, Pickett's and Pettigrew's divisions suffered casualty rates of more than 50 percent. The defenders, naturally, lost fewer men both in numerical and certainly in proportional terms. The Army of the Potomac suffered around one thousand five hundred casualties on Cemetery Ridge that day.

Notwithstanding the subsequent Southern romance of this moment as a possible tipping point, and the puncturing for a short time of the Union defenses at the Angle, the defenders were never in serious danger of breaking. General Alexander Webb, the brigade commander responsible for defending the Union line at this point in

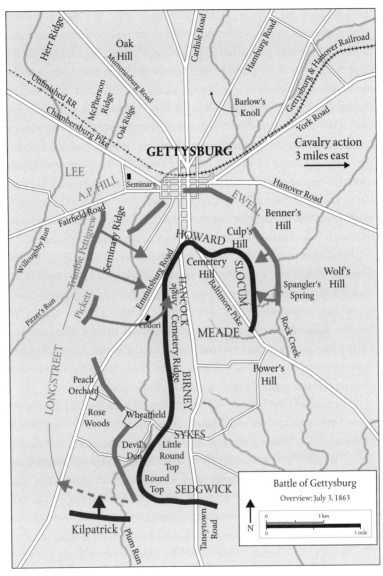

Map 4.1. Overview of the fighting on July 3, 1863. The fighting around Culp's Hill on the Union right began at dawn and lasted all morning. Longstreet's assault, known as "Pickett's Charge," began at around 1 p.m. after an artillery bombardment. After the repulse of Pickett's Charge, the two armies remained in essentially the same positions as they had at the start of the day. By nightfall, Longstreet had withdrawn his forces from the Peach Orchard and Devil's Den and Ewell had evacuated the town, concentrating Confederate forces on Cemetery Ridge, from where they would begin their retreat to Virginia.

the line, hurriedly sent in reinforcements to plug the gap, and there were more where they came from. But there was no equivalent force of attackers able to pile in behind Armistead's men. Lee had intended a large reserve force, of perhaps as many as eleven thousand men, to be in readiness to exploit any breach in the Union lines achieved by Pickett's division—and the failure of the "supports" was to become one of the bitterest post-battle disputes among Confederate survivors. Longstreet, who might have sent in further troops had he thought there was a chance of success, did not do so. To his post-war detractors, this was the final evidence of Longstreet's sullen refusal to enact Lee's plan. A private in Pickett's division who was shot in the legs just yards from the Union line but survived to tell the tale was convinced that with "but a little well-timed support . . . Gettysburg was ours."[21]

There were troops that could have been sent in support. Rodes' division was ready to move on the left flank and two brigades of Richard H. Anderson's division on the right. But Lee had given Longstreet the responsibility of determining whether the chances of success made it worth throwing in additional troops. Longstreet—unsurprisingly given his reservations about the entire operation—did not come to that conclusion. Rodes received a note telling him to stay where he was because "the attack had already failed."[22]

As groups of Confederate soldiers struggled back toward their lines, some Union troops pursued them, capturing some and killing others in skirmishes. "It was a time of indescribable enthusiasm and excitement," recalled a New Yorker. "Hats and caps and shouts filled the air. Sallies to the front were made, and battle-flags and trophies of our victory were gathered and brought in."[23] But Federal troops did not venture further than the Emmitsburg Road.

By the time the Confederate artillery opened their bombardment, Jeb Stuart's six thousand cavalry had ridden on a long flanking maneuver to the east of the town. Their aim was to get to the rear of the Federal Army and disrupt their lines of communication. If the main assault was successful, Stuart's cavalry would be able to cut off the retreating Union Army. Among the Union cavalry that raced to intercept Stuart was George Armstrong Custer, who had been made a general at the age of just 23. Custer's brigade lost 257 men that afternoon in a head-on charge. But in the end, the cavalry battle was a sideshow. When Stuart realized that there was no infantry breakthrough to exploit, he withdrew. There was cavalry action south of the main area of fighting as well later that afternoon. It was an ill-judged effort, led by Union cavalry commander Judson Kilpatrick, to launch frontal assaults on the Confederate right close to Devil's Den and the Round Tops. It is a heavy irony that the last action of the battle should have been a futile Union attack leading to a humiliating and costly retreat.

Even to men who had grown used to death, the scale of the slaughter, especially on July 2 and 3, was shocking. A volunteer surgeon with the United States Christian Commission was moved to scribble some verses about the maimed and dying men on the battlefield: "Blood-wet before the altar stairs / of Freedom—and Secession! / all one in pain and gaping wounds / all one in war's possession!"[24] The official record states that over the three days of fighting 3,155 officers and men of the Army of the Potomac had been killed in action, and 14,531 had been wounded (many dying later of their injuries or associated disease). A total of 5,369 Union soldiers were captured, mostly on July 1. Confederate losses were not recorded so precisely at the time, but the best estimates suggest four thousand killed, twelve thousand wounded, and six thousand taken prisoner. An even balance sheet, except that this represented a greater proportional loss for the Army of Northern Virginia (30 percent) compared to 21 percent of the Army of the Potomac's numbers. And the Confederacy was far less capable of replacing the men it had lost than was the Union.

Was a different outcome possible on July 3? Veterans and scholars have debated the subject for a hundred and fifty years without coming to any agreement. While the defending forces clearly had an advantage given the range and accuracy of their firepower, there were examples of successful offensive actions against well-entrenched opposition. At Missionary Ridge in Tennessee in November 1863, Union forces successfully stormed a rebel fortification atop a more imposing slope than at Gettysburg. Meade's forces were able to shelter behind stone walls in places, but elsewhere there were no natural defenses, and, while on Culp's Hill the defenders had constructed effective entrenchments, there were none along the mile-long defensive line on Cemetery Ridge. If you walk the route of Armistead's attacking force today, you will notice that, although there is a gentle slope upward toward the "High Water Mark," there are also undulations in the ground that give cover and would occasionally have hidden the advancing ranks from view. In other circumstances, with a different balance of forces, perhaps the attack might have worked. Cemetery Ridge is hardly a natural fortress.

In 2015, mathematical modeling by two scholars published in *Social Science Quarterly* suggests that had Lee committed up to three more brigades the attack could have successfully taken Union positions.[25] This backs up the conclusion of Professor Edwin B. Coddington, author of one of the most comprehensive and considered studies of the Gettysburg campaign, published in 1963, who argued that the Union position was "difficult but not impossible to take."[26] But even if Coddington and the mathematical modelers are right, breaking the Union lines was a necessary but not sufficient condition for a Confederate victory. If more men had been committed to the assault, it would have exposed the remainder of the army to a counterattack. Lee was hardly risk-averse as a commander but adding more men to the initial assault would have been a truly high-stakes gamble. Much would thereafter have depended on how well Meade rallied his forces—and he had more better-armed men than Lee, and capable corps commanders, even without the wounded Winfield Scott Hancock. In this realm of might-have-beens, the cavalry battle may have become critical, for if the Army of the Potomac was cut off from its supply lines, even temporarily, or surrounded on three sides, they would have been in serious danger. Meade had many fallback options, whereas Lee had few. Strategically, Lee's army was in a far more vulnerable position, operating miles from its home base in hostile country and with its stocks of armaments almost totally depleted. Yet in war, as in politics, perceptions can make reality. Had Lee's army held Cemetery Ridge by nightfall on July 3, it would have profoundly altered the public perception of the battle, even if their success was temporary, the losses were just as great, and the army's fundamental strategic position remained unaltered.

So, different outcomes were possible on July 3. But any alternative ending would have depended, far more than most observers have accepted, not just on decisions made by Lee and his generals but on what their opponents did. It is easy to discount the achievements of the Federal forces, especially on the third day when they had the advantage of fighting on the defense. But the fact is that the Army of the Potomac overperformed expectations on July 2 and 3. They had the advantage of interior lines and good defensive ground. They were better supplied than the rebels. And yet they were also more cohesive and tenacious, and better led, than many—notably Robert E. Lee—had anticipated.

*   *   *

So dominant is Pickett's Charge in the story of Gettysburg that it can come as a shock to discover men who had only a vague idea of what had taken place that evening. On the Union extreme left, removed from the direct Confederate assault, Private Wilbur Fisk recalled his comrades trying to piece together what had happened from the scraps they had heard. "The officers continually represented things as favorable. They always do." But the accounts of stragglers variously reported rebel breakthroughs or total rebel collapses. "The night closed the struggle and we lay down tolerably sure the battle had not gone against us."[27]

On Seminary Ridge, Lee and other officers made efforts to rally the devastated remnants of the army. To the eyes of the British military observer Arthur Fremantle, Lee remained "perfectly sublime," addressing words of encouragement to each soldier he met. "This has been a sad day for us, Colonel," Lee said, "but we can't always expect to gain victories." Other post-war reports describe Lee as having been far less composed that afternoon, some even claiming he apologized to his men. Such hand-wringing seems unlikely from the generally tight-lipped Lee. But he did not try to shift the blame onto others, however frustrated he must have been by the execution of his plan.

Confederate commanders had little time to count the cost of the catastrophic assault, for they feared an immediate counterattack and needed to prepare for it. There was a Union Army corps (the 5th) in reserve which had not been deployed that evening, and others still in good fighting form. Meade later claimed that he had intended the left of the Union line to make just such an attack but, considering "the condition of the forces" and the time it would take, he determined that it had gotten too late.[28] This was not surprising. The Army of the Potomac was in a defensive mindset, Meade was a brand-new

Figure 4.1. Sketch by Edwin Forbes, a staff artist for *Frank Leslie's Illustrated*, of Union soldiers relaxing after the battle, entitled "Behind the breastworks on the right, July 4, 1863." Forbes' pencil sketches were turned into engravings for publication or into oil paintings and lithographs. On July 4, the Confederates expected an attack from the Union army which never came.

commander who had yet to forge the army into a cohesive force or fully gain the trust of his corps commanders. Yet the fact remains that Lee's army would have been highly vulnerable had the Army of the Potomac been willing or able to advance. And there was no shortage of senior Army of the Potomac officers who were later to claim that this was Meade's greatest error. Carl Schurz argued that, had Meade counterattacked in the three hours of daylight after the repulse of Pickett's Charge, he could have achieved a "real victory over Lee's army, a victory which might have stopped this mainstay of the Confederacy of most of its power of mischief." Instead, Lee "was given ample time to rally and reform his shattered host, and, contracting his lines, establish himself in his strong defensive position on Seminary Ridge. There he stood—a whole day longer, like a wounded lion— wounded but still defiant."[29]

Schurz was writing with the benefit of hindsight, but that does not make his argument invalid. There would have been a risk for Meade in attacking on July 3, and no certainty of success. But, as events were to show, there was also risk in doing nothing. The opportunity to hit Lee's army when it was in a shattered and disorganized condition did not come again for a long time.

* * *

The seeds of Gettysburg's epochal status were sown on Independence Day, July 4, 1863, as war reporters filed their stories. In those first drafts of history were most of the ingredients of the later myths, claims and recriminations that were to dominate the battle's afterlife. For Northerners, two interconnected themes dominated. The first was to lay a claim to Gettysburg as greater than any of the great battles of the past. It was a victory "greater than that of Marathon...greater than the decisive battle of Blenheim...greater than any battle fought by the forces of the French republic at the time of the Revolution; greater than any fought in the civil wars of England; greater than Waterloo, which only lasted a single day, and fixed the fate of Europe."[30] This was an engagement on a physical scale that eclipsed those other storied encounters and was thus fitting to the world-historical presumptions of the relatively young American republic. The second theme anticipated the central idea of Lincoln's interpretation of Gettysburg: that the battle marked a rebirth, or re-consecration of the nation. The *New York Times* correspondent was stirred to sub-Byronic praise for the "envied" dead who at Gettysburg had "baptized with your blood the second birth of Freedom in America."[31] The *Boston Journal*'s reporter saw "a country redeemed, saved, baptized, consecrated anew to the coming ages."[32]

Journalists' immediate certainty that this had been the "greatest" and the "decisive" battle of the war cannot be explained by the numbers of men engaged or the duration of the battle—though both factors were certainly at play. Nor did the length of the battle or the numbers of slain men make it in itself a marker of a "second birth of freedom." Instead, it was two other factors that made this *the* decisive confrontation of the war. First, the location, on "Northern" soil, which had raised the stakes so terrifyingly high. And, second, as the New York lawyer George Templeton Strong put it, the breaking of the "charm of Robert Lee's invincibility." There was a genuine psychological challenge for Northerners who had convinced themselves their armies were facing an opponent with dark powers. The sense of freedom from that pall was no doubt part of why so many writers responded to the battle with imagery of an "overcast sky" clearing into "unclouded starlight."[33]

* * *

Perhaps it should have been a warning to the Northerners who used those meteorological metaphors that, on July 4, the heat wave ended and the rain came pouring down. Lee consolidated his forces, ordering Longstreet to withdraw from the area around Devil's Den and the Peach Orchard which had been won at such cost on the second day. He also told Ewell, after two days of trying and failing to puncture the Union defenses on Cemetery Hill and Culp's Hill, to evacuate the town and move up to Seminary Ridge. Perhaps if Lee had concentrated his forces on Seminary Ridge in this way on the evening of the first day, the outcome of the battle would have been different. By the morning of United States Independence Day, Lee had at last concentrated his army, but only in preparation for retreat.

The task of safely retreating across the Potomac River was in some ways more formidable than any the Army of Northern Virginia had faced. It took ten days for Lee's army to make its escape, and a further two weeks after that for the two armies to be back where they had started, facing each other either side of the Rappahannock River. That Lee managed to get almost all his surviving army and most of his supply train safely back into Virginia was an immense feat. As so often before, however, Lee's achievement was also a reflection on his opponents, for the aftermath of the battle was not Meade's finest hour.

The first stage of the escape was to get the army back over South Mountain into the Cumberland Valley. Throughout the battle, Lee had protected two passes, one along the Chambersburg Road (present-day Route 30), the other, the Monterey Pass, further south. Both routes were used in the retreat. The northernmost route was longer but was an easier climb, so Lee sent a supply train that way under the protection of cavalry commander John Imboden. The rest of the army moved on the southwesterly route, beginning their trek after nightfall on July 4. The army was traveling with, in total, six thousand wagons—so many that Imboden's supply train stretched for seventeen miles. Among the marching troops were ambulance wagons carrying eight thousand five hundred sick and injured soldiers.[34]

Imboden's supply train was harassed by local militia and hampered by roads that were churned up by the torrential rain that had begun falling. The main body of the army fought several engagements with Union cavalry but avoided a major infantry confrontation. The Army of the Potomac's pursuit was cautious. Still nervous about the danger of Lee getting between his army and Washington, Meade wanted as much intelligence as possible about the enemy's movements before committing troops, but the delays this created cost him vital time. The VI Corps commanded by General John Sedgwick pursued the retreating Confederates as far as the top of Monterey Pass. There were skirmishes between Sedgwick's men and Ewell's Corps, which brought up the rear of the Confederate forces, but no full assault.

Screened by Stuart's cavalry, the Army of Northern Virginia reached the Potomac on July 11 and constructed impressive defensive earthworks. Heavy rains had swollen the river so that it was no longer possible to ford, as it had been when the rebels marched north a few weeks earlier. Under huge pressure Confederate engineers began rapidly constructing pontoon bridges. Meade made plans to attack, but delayed for a day, issuing orders for an advance to begin on July 14. But by that morning, the Army of Northern Virginia had slipped away. "We had them in our grasp," said Lincoln. "We had only to stretch forth our hands and they were ours. And nothing I could say or do could make the army move."[35] If Gettysburg is remembered as the place where the South could have won the war but didn't, it is no less the place where the North could have won the war but didn't.

How could so golden an opportunity as to destroy Lee's army have been missed? "There is bad faith somewhere," Lincoln fumed to Secretary of War Edwin Stanton. When General-in-chief Henry Halleck informed him of the President's "great dissatisfaction" Meade immediately offered to resign, indignant that his on-the-ground assessment of what was practically feasible for his exhausted and ravaged army was being second-guessed by deskbound men in Washington. Lincoln refused the resignation but sat down to write a long explanation of his frustrations. "You had at least twenty thousand veteran troops directly with you, and as many more raw ones within supporting distance, all in addition to those who fought with you at Gettysburg; while it is not possible that [Lee] had received a single recruit; and yet you stood and let the flood run down, bridges be built, and the enemy move away at his leisure, without attacking ... He was within your easy grasp, and to have closed upon him would, in connection with our other late successes, have ended the war. As it is, the war will be prolonged indefinitely.... Your golden opportunity is gone, and I am distressed immensely." It was a powerful critique and, in the largest sense, true. As Lincoln pointed out, "If you could not safely attack Lee last Monday [when he was still in Pennsylvania, trapped north of the flooded Potomac], how can you possibly do so South of the river, when you can take with you very few more than two thirds of the force you then had in hand?"[36] Yet Lincoln did not send the letter; he filed it away, evidently judging that to send it having rejected Meade's resignation would be counterproductive. And indeed, Meade remained formally in command of the Army of the Potomac until the end of the war, even though Lincoln appointed Grant to a new command outranking him.

Not everyone had Lincoln's restraint. The commander of the Army of the Potomac had powerful enemies who sought to convince the public that the general's timidity and ineptness had led to missed opportunities and wasted lives. The North may have won the battle, but there were many who were determined to litigate its course and meaning, even while the war was still in progress. Among the general's most dogged and ungenerous foes was the radical Republican majority on the Joint Congressional Committee on the Conduct of the War, which was set up following the Union's defeat at the first Battle of Bull Run in 1861 with a wide, roving brief to probe "the disasters that have attended the public arms." To the committee's leading members— Senator Ben Wade and Representatives Zachariah Chandler and George Washington Julian—Meade's major failing was that he was not General Hooker. Notwithstanding his earlier Democratic and antiabolitionist views, "Fighting Joe" had appeared to be exactly what the committee wanted from a commander of the Army of the Potomac: charismatic, brash, avowedly aggressive, and more than willing to change his political views if it was expedient to do so. Even the disaster of Chancellorsville didn't dent his support. Lincoln's decision to remove him on the eve of Gettysburg was therefore deeply unpopular, and Meade's grumpy stolidity and political naivety made him, in the committee's eyes, a very poor substitute.

In February 1864, the joint committee opened hearings on the Battle of Gettysburg with General Dan Sickles as their star witness. Resentful that he hadn't been restored to his old corps command when he returned from sick leave, and stung by the official report of the battle which criticized his forward position on July 2 while defending Meade's decision-making throughout, Sickles gave the committee the indictment they wanted. Meade, he alleged—with no supporting evidence—had wanted to avoid fighting at Gettysburg in the first place. Little wonder, then, that he had failed to pursue Lee's army effectively after the battle. Sickles' testimony established the remarkably durable myth that Meade had intended to retreat to a defensive line at Pipe Creek and that he had been induced to make a fight at Gettysburg only because of the decisions of his subordinate commanders. The implication was that Meade's alleged hesitancy was not merely a measure of his personality but of his politics. General Doubleday gave Sickles some helpful backup, testifying that since Meade had been in command "no man who is...anti-slavery...can expect decent treatment." Secretary of War Stanton warned Meade that the committee "had gotten up this halloobaloo" [sic] in order to try and reinstate Hooker, but that there "was no chance of it succeeding."[37] The committee's recommendation that Meade be dismissed was duly ignored by Lincoln, but it contributed to the radical narrative that fervent anti-slavery politics led to "vigorous" military tactics and vice versa.

Sickles' slanderous charges against Meade were gleefully amplified by the press. Sickles himself was probably the author of an anonymous article in the *New York Herald* condemning Meade for his recalcitrance and lauding "that sagacious officer, General Sickles." All this was accompanied by a brazen defense by Sickles of his unauthorized decision to move his corps to what turned out to be an indefensible position. "I took up that line," Sickles told the congressional committee, "because it enabled me to hold commanding ground, which, if the enemy had been allowed to take—as they would have taken it if I had not occupied it in force—would have rendered our position on the left untenable." The trouble with this argument was that the enemy took Sickles' advanced position anyway, after heavy fighting, and because of the salient it had created, had an easier target than they otherwise would have had. The *New York Herald* published a rebuttal to its earlier pro-Sickles piece arguing that "instead of saving the army [as he claimed], General Sickles nearly ruined it by a sad error—an unaccountable one." No matter: there was no way that Sickles would ever admit to the most obvious explanation for his actions on July 2, which was that he had made a mistake which had cost the army dearly. For him, this internecine Battle of Gettysburg would never end. He was still fighting it when he died in 1914.

* * *

One way of looking at the outcome was that Lee's army had retreated from the field in good order and without conceding any ground. On that measure the battle was a draw. And then, by successfully retreating into Virginia, he had created the basis for an unlikely victory narrative. If the British could turn Dunkirk into a source of pride in World War II, there was far more hopeful material to work with in the Gettysburg campaign.

The response in the South to news of Lee's return to Virginia was mixed. As news and rumors filtered through, there were initial hopes that the battle had gone well.[38] When the scale of the casualties became clear, and as stories were told of the futility of the frontal assault on July 3, critics of the Davis administration attacked both the invasion itself, and the conduct of the climactic battle. Charleston's *Mercury* called the invasion "foolish and disastrous."[39] A more balanced and probably fairly typical view was expressed by the *Richmond Examiner*, which regretted that Lee had "made one failure" but called on its readers to "thank Heaven that we have so great and good a General; a man who has the good sense to know how to save his army, even after such an unsuccessful campaign."[40] The dominant emotion in newspapers and private diaries was, first, shock at the evidence of a setback, followed by a determination to understand and accept the judgment of God and continue the struggle. "Alas that such valor should be unavailing!" wrote a North Carolina editor. "The heart bleeds and the tear unbidden starts from the eye, when we think of the noble and gallant thousands of our countrymen who went down in that fiery vortex."[41]

Much of this commentary in the South in the immediate aftermath of the retreat suggests a recognition on the part of Southern writers that the invasion of Pennsylvania had been a gamble, albeit a necessary one given the pressures the Confederacy faced. But neither the armchair commentators nor, more importantly, Robert E. Lee had resolved how to balance the two main goals of the invasion. On the one hand, it was a gigantic foraging expedition; on the other, an opportunity to score a knockout blow that might win the war. The first aim could best be achieved if the army remained in the mountains, plundered the countryside for as much as it would yield, while keeping open a rapid route back into Virginia and avoiding a full-scale battle. The second aim could only be accomplished in a grand climactic engagement. It required a level of risk and audacity that Lee possessed, perhaps in over-abundance, but his commanders mostly did not.

The basis of Lee's whole approach to military command was aggression. When this worked, it was devastating and brilliant; when it didn't, as on the second and third days at Gettysburg, it made him look impetuous. But even when it was successful, the aggressiveness of the Army of Northern Virginia came at a very high price. "Don't you see your system feeds upon itself?" Colonel Fremantle claimed to have said to Lee. "You cannot fill the places of these men. Your troops do wonders, but every time at a cost you cannot afford." Very likely Lee understood this completely but thought there was no alternative. A defensive strategy, minimizing the loss of his own troops, might have bought time, but the Confederacy would still have faced the same overwhelming imbalance of men and resources. Lee was correct in his perception that the only path to victory was to destroy the Northern people's willingness to fight. If the most effective way to do that was to destroy Union armies with élan, even at the cost of the lives of men who he could not replace, so be it. But the logic of this approach also meant that with each bloody encounter, the stakes were raised ever higher. Lee's decisions to continue the battle on July 2 and 3 should not therefore be ascribed solely to bloody-mindedness or a misreading of the situation in front of him (though both of those were factors). Instead, it was born of a conviction that this was his army's only chance of a knockout blow.

Taken as a whole, the Gettysburg campaign demonstrated both Lee's weaknesses and his strengths. His fixation on the need for a decisive victory over the Army of the Potomac led to the sacrifice of the lives of thousands of men in assaults on July 2 and 3 that were unlikely to succeed. Earlier, it had led him to reject the redeployments of Longstreet's Corps to the West, which might have avoided or mitigated critical losses of the Mississippi River (including Vicksburg and then Port Hudson, Louisiana) or middle and southeastern Tennessee (including Chattanooga). And his management of his forces in the assaults of July 2 and 3 lacked the control and good communication with divisional commanders that would have given it a greater chance of success. Yet he retained the confidence of his men. They, after all, knew better than any civilian critic how necessary were the supplies plundered in Pennsylvania. The historian who has made the most careful study of Lee's retreat estimates that the army returned to Virginia with twenty thousand horses and mules, thirty thousand cows, twenty-five thousand sheep, "thousands" of hogs, thousands of tons of grain and hay, thousands of barrels of flour, and hundreds of wagonloads of saddles, boots, spare cartwheels, coal, oil, paper, and cloth. The plunder provided fodder for the army's horses and (almost unheard of) fresh meat for the men.[42] That fall, the Army of Northern Virginia lived better than it had since 1861. Eventually, the food and fodder ran out, but without it, who knows if the army would have held together for as long as it did.

In the end, then, whether the Pennsylvania invasion was a success for Lee depends on what one sees as its main purpose. Judged as a gigantic foraging operation, it was a success that bought the Confederacy precious time. But judged by Lee's other goal—to inflict a knockout blow on Northern soil—it was a desperate failure.

5

Aftermath, 1863–1865

When the soldiers departed, civilians surveyed the damage: the town's shattered windows and bullet-marked walls and roofs, the ransacked stores and churned-up streets. Local boys found that lead bullets, which could be gathered in handfuls in some parts of the battlefield, were an easy source of income since lead was in high demand in the wartime North. The few African Americans who had remained—either because they were too infirm to flee or because their white employers pressured them to stay—emerged from hiding places and tried to piece together their lives. Soldiers were "buried in wide, yawning trenches," recorded one observer.[1] The bodies "were only slightly covered with earth," recalled another visitor, "and you could feel the body by pressing the earth with your foot. One man's left hand...stuck out of the grave looking like an old parched well worn buck-skin glove."[2] Hogs uncovered some of those shallow graves. The remains of three thousand horses and mules also lay rotting on the battlefield, bloated and picked over by crows, until they were buried or burned. The stench was so great, reported one local resident that we can "neither eat, drink nor sleep."[3] The smell of decomposing bodies persisted as late as October.[4]

The fields on which the battle had been fought were churned up; crops, fences, and barns were destroyed. Returning farmers had no chance of a harvest that year. Seeing an opportunity, a local lawyer, David McConaughy, created the Gettysburg Battlefield Memorial Association (GMBA) in August 1863 and offered stock to raise funds to buy up battlefield land. The association's aim, McConaughy explained, was to ensure that Gettysburg would be "the shrine of loyalty and patriotism, whither in all times will come the sons of America and the pilgrims of all lands, to view with wonder and veneration the sacred scenes of heroic struggles, in which were involved the life of the nation and the perpetuity of liberty."[5] Gettysburg, said McConaughy, was now "sacred ground."[6]

In the weeks after the battle, curious or grieving visitors began to inscribe across the battlefield a path from one key site to the next that one historian has compared to the Stations of the Cross.[7] Picking their way through the improvised wooden crosses that marked shallow burial places, visitors trooped to Seminary Ridge, to Little Round Top, and back up to Cemetery Hill. The early pilgrims, who came to see where a loved one had fallen, were accompanied by the sensation-seekers who wanted to see for themselves the ground where the famous battle had been fought. Visitors typically returned home with a relic scavenged from the battlefield. Ambrose Emory, a clerk from Baltimore who visited the battlefield in August, went home with a bayonet, a brass epaulette, a 12-inch solid shot, and a Bible inscribed "R. W. Davies, Virginia."[8] But if their pickings were not spectacular enough, there was always the option of purchasing something more impressive from a relic vendor. They "attach considerable humbug" to their offerings, reported a journalist, claiming every bullet sold was "the agency by which some prominent Union or Confederate officer was sent to eternity."[9] Gettysburg merchandise, which went on sale as early as July 1863, included sheet music, battlefield guidebooks, engravings, and stereographs that went on sale in the months after the battle. The historian Jim Weeks highlights an advertisement from December 1863 in which two enterprising photographers pushed "a full set of our Photographic Views of the Battle-field of Gettysburg" as a "splendid gift" for Christmas.[10] Bullets and shrapnel from Gettysburg were sold to raise money for wounded soldiers at a grand fair in Philadelphia in 1864.

Throughout the summer of 1863, field hospitals remained around the town, treating soldiers too ill to be moved. But if the first priority

GREAT BATTLES

was to care for injured soldiers, a close second was to take care of the bodies. For months after the battle, notices were placed in the local press by relatives appealing for information about the location of missing sons and fathers. But soldiers wore no dog tags in this war, and identifying remains was often impossible. There were celebrated successes, however. The body of thirty-two-year-old Amos Humiston of the 154th New York was identified after the press publicized a photograph of his wife and children found clutched in his hand.[11]

Even as the cleanup operation was underway, plans were being laid to memorialize the dead. The large-circulation New York City papers took a great interest in the battlefield over that summer, no doubt because it was so much more accessible to visitors than those in the South, but also because of the desire to make it the war's turning point—or "*The Battle* of this Second War of Independence," as a local newspaper put it.[12] The fields and woodland where the battle raged, declared the *New York Herald* in July, were now "one of the nation's altars." And therefore, there was "doubtful propriety" in removing "the remains of soldiers who lost their lives in the glorious battle." Far better, the newspaper's correspondent suggested, "to expend the same sum which a removal will cost in a proper general monument, upon which all the names of the dead heroes, from Major General Reynolds down to the humblest private, should be inscribed."[13] Efforts to memorialize General Reynolds were, in fact, already underway. He was by far the highest-profile casualty of the battle on the Union side. His dramatic death—shot while organizing the town's defense against Heth's advancing troops on July 1—made him one of the war's most celebrated hero-martyrs. Officers of the 1st Corps of the Army of the Potomac raised funds from officers and men and enlisted public subscriptions for a bronze statue, which was the first to be erected on the battlefield.[14]

There was already a cemetery in the heart of the battlefield. The Evergreen Cemetery on Cemetery Hill had been dedicated only nine years before the battle, so there were not yet many graves. But it was the natural focus for the project to inter the Union dead close to where they had fallen. Another Gettysburg lawyer, David Wills, persuaded Pennsylvania Governor Andrew Curtin to back a plan for the state to fund the purchase of land to create a national cemetery. By the end of August, Wills had purchased 17 acres of land from David McConaughy, who had snapped up the Cemetery Hill site for his Gettysburg Battlefield Memorial Association (GBMA). Provost Marshals assisted by local men including Basil Biggs, a local African American farmer, undertook the work of meticulously separating the Union from the Confederate dead, disinterring them from their battlefield graves and reburying them in the new cemetery.[15] Samuel Weaver, who oversaw the exhumations, claimed, "I firmly believe that there has not been a single mistake made in the removal of the soldiers to the Cemetery by taking the body of a rebel for a Union soldier." However the process of identification usually rested on educated guesses based on fragments of clothing or the location of the body.[16] The corpses of Confederate soldiers remained where they were, buried in unmarked graves across the battlefield.[17]

For the Union dead, Wills hired the landscape architect William Saunders to design a cemetery of "simple grandeur."[18] The aim was to create a space for contemplation at a place that had been made sacred not only by the burial of the dead but by the Army of the Potomac's successful defense of Cemetery Hill on July 2 and 3. The Soldier's National Cemetery, as it was known, was adjacent to the town's Evergreen Cemetery. The three and a half thousand Union dead were laid in semi-circular ranks.[19]

On November 19, 1863, although only half the bodies had been buried, the new national cemetery was dedicated. Special trains brought thousands of out-of-town visitors, overwhelming the hotels and boarding houses. The national press descended, with reporters fascinated to visit the fields routinely referred to as sacred ground. Locals who knew all about the battle, or claimed to, offered tours or regaled the visitors with firsthand descriptions of the battles' "horror and glory."[20] Even in November, this was still a landscape strewn by

Figure 5.1. Photograph by James F. Gibson for Brady's Studio of bloated corpses lying on the battlefield several days after the battle. The first task facing the residents of the town was burying the dead.

"soiled fragments of uniforms, in which heroes had fought and died, remnants of haversacks and cartridge-boxes," and skeletons of horses.[21] Amid this carnage the cemetery promised tranquility. The father of one who was buried there later reflected that "the spectacle of so large a field crowded with the graves of the slain brings home to the heart an overpowering sense of the horror and wickedness of war."[22] The aim of the cemetery's dedication ceremony was to offer some higher meaning to counter the overwhelming sense of loss.

* * *

The world now remembers that Lincoln came to Gettysburg and gave the speech that defined the war, but his presence there was almost an afterthought, and what he quite accurately called his "short, short, short" speech (it was only 272 words) was completed at the last minute. The President was invited by David Wills, the thirty-four-year-old Gettysburg lawyer who had led the local effort to memorialize the battle.[23] A radical Republican in a predominantly Democratic town, Wills had the ear of Republican Pennsylvania Governor Andrew W. Curtin. And it was almost certainly the governor, fresh from victory in a tense re-election battle against an anti-war opponent, who suggested that Lincoln be invited. Even so, the President's role was to be strictly limited. Wills' letter of invitation was sent on November 2, just over two weeks before the date of the ceremony. Lincoln was not asked to give a speech as such, but formally to "set apart these grounds to their Sacred use by a few appropriate remarks."[24] Understanding that his role in the drama was no more than a supporting act, Lincoln accepted the invitation—even though there was much pressing business in Washington. He was eager to see the battlefield and knew that whatever he said there would have intensified meaning.[25]

Lincoln's party arrived by rail on November 18, the evening before the ceremony, and spent the night at David Wills' house in the center of the town. The roads that led to Gettysburg, like the spokes of a cartwheel, were filled, reported one newspaper, with "citizens from every quarter thronging into the village in every kind of vehicle—old Pennsylvania wagons, spring wagons, carts, family carriages, buggies, and more fashionable modern vehicles, all crowded with citizens."[26] There was a festive air in the town that evening, and there must have been some residents of the traditionally Democratic-voting town who shuddered at the open displays of abolitionism. The crowds sang "John Brown's Body" and shouted for the President, who appeared briefly and spoke a few words.[27]

Early next morning, Lincoln toured the battlefield on horseback. He made a particular point of visiting the spot where General Reynolds had died, and when he returned to the Wills' house for breakfast, it was evident to his companions that the President was very affected by having seen for himself the ground on which the battle raged.

In mid-morning a rather ragged procession formed with an honor guard of the Invalid Corps and a Marine band to accompany the speakers and distinguished guests from the town up to the cemetery.

They passed houses draped in mourning or flying the Stars and Stripes along the short route. At 6 feet 4 inches and wearing a 7-inch stovepipe hat, Lincoln towered above everyone—"the tallest and the grandest rider in the procession," as one observer recalled.[28]

The pressmen scurried into place, and the crowds jostled for position to get the best view of the speakers on the rickety platform. But once the ceremony began, the solemnity of the occasion impressed everyone present except for a reporter for a Democratic Party-supporting paper who ostentatiously smoked and smirked until his fellow pressmen sat on him. Even the President's studiedly cynical young secretary John Hay found himself gradually caught up in the rites of nation-building that unfolded.

The first act was a prayer by a well-known Methodist pastor, Thomas Stockton, whose cadaverous face and sonorous voice struck observers as perfectly fitting for the occasion. In a long prayer, he framed the events of July 1–3 on what he called this "Field of Deliverance" as an apocalyptic struggle between slavery and freedom. The rebel army, Reverend Stockton declaimed, sought to encircle "the chain of Slavery around the form of Freedom, binding life and death together forever." Yet "from the coasts beneath the Eastern star, from the shores of Northern lakes and rivers, from the flowers of Western prairies, and from the homes of the Midway and the Border" came the Union Army, which was led by "Thy hand to these hills" where they "took their stand upon the rocks." Union soldiers, Stockton intoned, "came here to die for us, and for mankind."[29] Stockton spoke of the blood of Union soldiers having brought national redemption; he said little of what the future might bring. But as the crowd joined him in saying the words of the Lord's Prayer, many were moved to tears.

After two hymns, the main event was a two-hour-long oration by Edward Everett. A former Governor of Massachusetts, Senator, Minister to the Court of St James, and Secretary of State, Everett was one of those veterans of public life whose age and moderation made him a "statesman" rather than a politician. A life-long Whig until that party collapsed, no one in public life in the mid-nineteenth century was more associated with the veneration of the Union and its founders. He had been the driving force behind the purchase as a national shrine of George Washington's home, Mount Vernon—now in a state that was in arms to break up Washington's republic. But when war broke out, Everett, like many others who had hoped to appease the Southern malcontents, was now an unbending supporter of Lincoln's war policy.[30]

In his address, Everett narrated the Gettysburg campaign in some detail, dramatizing the stakes by imagining the consequences of an alternative outcome: Washington could have fallen, the national government forced to flee.[31] Everett tackled head-on the question of why a nation created in a rebellion against the British Empire should now be so intolerant of a rebellion against itself. The answer was that while rebellion against Charles I or George III was just, that did not make rebellion itself just. The leaders of the rebellion had been fully included in the councils of the nation, unlike the leaders of the rebellious colonies in the 1770s. But more than that, this rebellion was motivated not by love of liberty but by wickedness and self-interest. Unlike the Cromwellians of 1640, the Whigs of 1688, or the colonists of 1776, the rebels were not rebelling against arbitrary power but against a free government in which they themselves had participated. And they were doing so to create an oligarchy based on "the corner-stone of slavery."[32] If there was a parallel in English history for the utter illegitimacy of a rebellion it was, for Everett, the Jacobite rising of 1745 which sought to overthrow the "liberty" won in the Glorious Revolution and to replace it with autocracy. For someone like Everett, who, as he confessed in his speech, had trodden for "perhaps too long" in the path of "hopeless compromise," the barbarism of the Southern rebellion was especially shocking because it betrayed all his fondest hopes. Worst of all was the refusal of the rebels to "give quarter" to Black troops and Lee's army "selling into slavery free colored men from the North who fell into their hands."[33]

Like the Reverend Stockton, Everett honored the fallen and castigated the rebels but said little about the future. That job was left to Lincoln. This, in full, is what Lincoln said:

Four score and seven years ago our fathers brought forth, on this continent, a new nation, conceived in Liberty, and dedicated to the proposition that all men are created equal.

Now we are engaged in a great civil war, testing whether that nation, or any nation so conceived and so dedicated, can long endure. We are met on a great battle-field of that war. We have come to dedicate a portion of that field, as a final resting place for those who here gave their lives that that nation might live. It is altogether fitting and proper that we should do this.

But, in a larger sense, we can not dedicate—we can not consecrate—we can not hallow—this ground. The brave men, living and dead, who struggled here, have consecrated it, far above our poor power to add or detract. The world will little note, nor long remember what we say here, but it can never forget what they did here. It is for us the living, rather, to be dedicated here to the unfinished work which they who fought here have thus far so nobly advanced. It is rather for us to be here dedicated to the great task remaining before us—that from these honored dead we take increased devotion to that cause for which they here gave the last full measure of devotion—that we here highly resolve that these dead shall not have died in vain—that this nation, under God, shall have a new birth of freedom—and that government of the people, by the people, for the people, shall not perish from the earth.[34]

The Gettysburg Address looms so large in American memory that there is a whole sub-genre of literature devoted solely to working out when and how Lincoln wrote it. There are folksy stories of Lincoln writing the speech on the train on his way to Gettysburg, or composing it in a single sitting after a spiritual experience. Much ink has been spilt over such apparently trivial details as whether he spoke the words "under God"—a sub-clause included in some extant drafts of the speech but not in others. The painstaking textual analysis and documentary reconstruction of the historian Martin P. Johnson has cut through some of these myths. We can now be reasonably confident that Lincoln wrote the first part of the speech in Washington but reworked the ending after he had visited the battlefield on the morning of his speech. Seeing where his "gallant and brave friend, Gen. Reynolds" was killed seems to have given Lincoln an even more intense sense of place. Before he rose to deliver his speech, the President underlined one single word: "The world will little note, nor long remember what we say here; while it can never forget what they did here."[35] That emphasized "did" was the pivot point of the speech: the moment when he moved from acknowledging the past and present to the active commitment now required of the living in the coming months.

But whatever the mechanics and timing of the writing process, we know that this was Lincoln's most succinct attempt to draw meaning from what, even then, appeared to be the war's defining battle. The two-minute speech drew on Lincoln's long-held and oft-expressed understanding of the Providential nature of the American Union, but also on his new understanding of the challenges the nation faced at that moment. It was a speech for the ages—transcendent in its vision of the United States as a work in progress—but also a partisan manifesto setting out the terms on which he wanted the war to end.

The speech followed a simple tripartite format: moving from the past to the present and then the future. His opening ("Four score and seven years ago"), an echo of the 90th Psalm in the King James Version of the Bible, rooted the moment of creation of the United States not in military victory over the British or the 1783 Treaty of Paris which recognized American sovereignty, nor even in the ratification of the Constitution, but in the Declaration of Independence of 1776. Unlike other nations, the United States was not a product of war or international diplomacy; still less was it a primordial entity. It was "conceived in liberty"; created for a purpose. If that was so, then the nation must strive for those ideals or die. This is the core idea of American exceptionalism: imagining the nation as an ideological project with Providential meaning for all mankind. But Lincoln's sleight of hand was to invoke the Declaration's ringing phrase "all men are created equal," not as Jefferson had described it, as a "self-evident truth," but as a "proposition" to which the nation was "dedicated." This was very different: if a "self-evident truth" was beyond contestation, a "proposition" was a claim to be proved or disproved through experiment and experience. The scholar Gary Wills argued that Lincoln's "alchemy" at Gettysburg was seamlessly to merge the Declaration of Independence's commitment to equality with the preservation of the

Constitution and the Union even though nowhere in the Constitution is there any formal commitment to equality (or to liberty or the right to vote or anything else).[36] Lincoln was certainly not the first to do this, but it is true that this speech, far more than any other text, crystallizes the idea that the institutional structure of the nation (the Constitution) is inseparable from the underpinning idea.

This "dedication" to equality and its "conception" "in" liberty made the United States a universal nation, but it was also, like other nations, rooted in territory. It had been brought forth not anywhere but somewhere: "on this continent."[37] This was a reminder of one of Lincoln's familiar themes, which was the "impossibility" of secession. "Physically speaking we cannot separate," he said in his inaugural address in 1861.[38] In 1862, he explained that a nation "may be said to consist of its territory, its people, and its laws," but it was the land, "the national homestead," which gave it permanence: "One generation passeth away, and another cometh, but the earth abideth forever."[39] Even if separation occurred, Lincoln thought, it would be temporary, however much blood the separation might have cost. The land would endure. Many Northerners—as well as secessionists in the South— thought differently. For example, the writer Nathaniel Hawthorne, a Democrat who was deeply conflicted about the legitimacy of the war, emphasized the unknowability of "the vast extent of our country— too vast by far to be taken into one small human heart."[40] But Lincoln thought the ultimate impossibility of separation was a self-evident truth: one way or another, in the end, reunion would be forced. The outstanding question, though, was the character and meaning of that Union, for even if the outward form remained, if it no longer retained its dedication to equality, in a very real sense, it would have died.

This opening sentence led Lincoln to the present: to the "great civil war" that, in an echo of the Christian idea of a trial of faith, was "testing" whether not only the United States but "any nation so conceived and so dedicated could long endure." Both the struggle and the sacrifice had a dignity and a purpose of universal and transcendent significance. The underlying assumptions of American nationalism were here laid bare in all their hyperbole and hubris, fusing the Enlightenment's claim to have divined universal truths with the exceptionalist claim that America was the "redeemer" nation. If the rebels triumphed, the "proposition" on which the nation was founded would be falsified. And that would mean that no nation ever again could aspire, as America had, to equality and liberty. "We are met," Lincoln said, "on a great battlefield of that war," and, coming to the emotional pivot-point of his speech, he declared that while "the world will little note nor long remember what we say here, it can never forget what they *did* here."[41] Given Lincoln's reportedly slow and deliberate delivery, one can imagine the dramatic impact of that word "did" and what it conveyed and the pause that would have followed after a smattering of applause from the crowd. From "continent" to "nation" to "battlefield" to "here," Lincoln moved from the wide horizons to the soil beneath his feet, ground which had been "consecrated" by brave men living and dead.

One might have expected that in his "few, appropriate remarks," the President would have contemplated the sacrifice of those who had given their lives so that the nation might live. But Lincoln did much more: he did not just dedicate the cemetery but demanded renewed dedication among the living to the "great task" remaining. To ensure that the dead shall not have "died in vain," the living must increase their devotion to the cause for which, Lincoln said, the dead of Gettysburg had given their "last full measure of devotion." That task was, of course, to defeat the rebellion. Was there an irony in the fate of a government of, for, and by the people lying in the hands of the army? If so, it was not one that Lincoln would have recognized. Instead, he saw the task of a free people as being to preserve—by force since force had been used against them—the only government in the world dedicated to the equality of man. The "great task" of the living was, then, to preserve the Union in order to ensure that popular government did not "perish from the earth."

For Lincoln, as for most nineteenth-century Americans, human history consisted of a Manichean global struggle between autocracy and democracy, a struggle in which the beacon of freedom was now being held aloft by the United States, the "last, best hope of earth" as Lincoln called it and in which the rebellion was on the side of autocracy. For Lincoln, human enslavement was the ultimate antithesis of democracy. "As I would not be a slave, so I would not be a master," he had written before the war. "This expresses my idea of democracy."[42] It was therefore axiomatic—a "self-evident truth" one might say—that if the rebels won, democracy would lose; the experiment of founding a republic based on the ideals of equality and liberty would fail; and therefore "government of the people, for the people, by the people" would "perish from the earth." The stakes in the war's pivotal battle could not be higher, not just for Americans but for all believers in freedom everywhere.

But even that was not all. For in addition to preserving government of, for, and by the people, the cause for which the dead had fallen also encompassed a "new birth of freedom" for the nation. What did this mean? The obvious interpretation, given our contemporary sensibility, is that Lincoln was referring to the ending of slavery. And indeed, by the time he came to Gettysburg, Lincoln was utterly committed to abolition. The Emancipation Proclamation transformed the politics of emancipation—by committing the Federal government, for the first time, to free at least some enslaved people—but it offered no solid basis for ensuring that freedom would be permanent. The Proclamation existed in the tenuous and temporary realm of "military necessity," so there was no reason to think it would have any legal standing after the war. But Lincoln had made clear in public his desire that "all men everywhere" should be free and that the promise of freedom having been made "must be kept."[43] A consistent thread in Lincoln's thought since at least the summer of 1862 was that slavery was not only wrong but the taproot of the rebellion. Therefore, it must be removed by any means necessary if the nation were ever again to know peace and security.

Black troops did not fight at Gettysburg, but they were clearly in Lincoln's mind by November. In the days before giving his address at the National Cemetery, Lincoln had been working on his Annual Message to Congress. In it, he reflected on the year since the Emancipation Proclamation had come into effect and the Union began to employ Black troops. It was a policy, he acknowledged, that "gave to the future a new aspect, about which hope, and fear, and doubt, contended in uncertain conflict." African Americans had fought with valor in battles further south, around the same time as Gettysburg, notably at Fort Wagner in South Carolina on July 18, 1863, proving themselves, in Lincoln's words, "as good soldiers as any."[44]

Enlisting Black men in the Union Army had political as well as military consequences. Just weeks after the Battle of Gettysburg, in response to shocking episodes in which Confederates killed African American Union troops after they had surrendered, Lincoln issued a formal commitment to the nation's responsibility for the equal protection of all its citizens "of whatever class, color, or condition."[45] This was the first time the United States had committed to such a proposition. Later, after Lincoln's assassination, it was enshrined in the language of the Fourteenth Amendment. Lincoln's Annual Message also included a plan for post-war reconstruction, which—although it has since been derided for its moderation—committed the administration to the hitherto radical proposition that there would be no reunion with slaveholders.

Given all this, it seems reasonable to assume that the "new birth of freedom" Lincoln referred to meant freedom for enslaved people. But there was a broader and deeper meaning, too. Ending slavery would cleanse the Union of a terrible contradiction—the existence of unfreedom in a land of freedom. It was a contradiction that Lincoln, along with most white Americans, had long tolerated in order to perpetuate the higher good of national preservation. But secession changed everything. Once, preserving the Union had required slavery to be tolerated; now, it required its destruction.

That perspective was highly partisan. By November 1863, Northern Democrats had come to see Lincoln's administration, and the Republican Party as a whole, as a profound threat to liberty. They simply could not understand, or did not accept, Lincoln's certainty that ending slavery was possible or necessary, and they genuinely feared that war measures like conscription and the suspension of habeas corpus were harbingers of the end of the republic. Supporters of the Lincoln administration treated Democrats as if all were actively disloyal. In a bitterly divided North, there was no occasion—not even the consecration of a soldiers' cemetery—that could transcend partisanship. Still, as the party in government waging a war for the nation, the Republican Party wrapped themselves in the language of patriotism, even abandoning the name "Republican" in order to build pro-war coalitions under the banner of the Union Party. Since the town of Gettysburg had historically voted for the Democrats, and since there were many locals present, it seems likely that there were plenty of Democrats in the crowd that day. But the only prominent Democrat present was Horatio Seymour of New York, who was "not smiled upon by that earnest company," recalled a young journalist for the *Philadelphia Press*. There was a "Puritan spirit abroad, and you can imagine the feeling with which a company of Roundheads would have welcomed a prince of the Cavaliers."[46]

Listeners recalled Lincoln speaking with "an archaic voice in an ascending key," in "high clarion tones, which the people of Illinois had so often heard."[47] Some remembered him unfolding a piece of paper from which he read his remarks, a contrast to Everett, who had committed his far longer address to memory. No one expected the President to be so brief. John Russell Young, the reporter for the *Philadelphia Press*, was distracted by the amusing sight of a photographer carefully arranging his equipment to take a shot of Lincoln speaking and just getting it into position when the President sat down: "There was a general ripple of laughter at his dismay."[48]

It is easy to discount as high Victorian hyperbole the reports of grown men with tears flowing as they were swayed by the emotions of the opening prayer, Everett's soaring oration, and Lincoln's earnest, powerful address. Yet this was a culture in which tears flowed, especially in the commemoration of war dead. "There was not a dry eye in the vast assemblage," recalled one battle veteran in 1866 who had been in Lincoln's audience three years earlier, "and from the loud sobs that interrupted the President during some parts of his address, it was at times impossible to hear what he had to say."[49] If this seems over-wrought to the point of parody, the fact that it was uttered and (presumably) received without any hint of irony suggests how quickly the myth of the Gettysburg Address took hold. As a quasi-spiritual moment of national rebirth, it was altogether fitting and proper that the speech should have affected people in this way. There is a variant of the Gettysburg Address myth according to which the speech was regarded with indifference by those who heard it, its genius only later recognized by newspaper readers. But even this story (which in any case does not seem to accord with the evidence) merely adds to the miracle of the Address by portraying a crowd who, like Mary Magda-lene mistaking the risen Lord for a gardener, failed initially to recog-nize it for what it was.

* * *

Because the war ended with the total defeat of the Confederate rebel-lion, the Gettysburg Address can be read, in retrospect, as a meditation on the meaning of Union victory. But at the time it was delivered, no one could be confident of the war's outcome. That was true despite the psychological boost to the North of Lee's defeat, as well as the simultaneous fall of Vicksburg. The path to Confederate victory re-mained what it had always been: undermining the North's will to keep on fighting. But in the fall of 1863, it was the Confederacy that faced a crisis of confidence. In elections for the Second Confederate Congress, anti-administration candidates gained seats. In North Carolina, which, proportionally, had suffered more casualties in the Gettysburg cam-paign than any other Confederate state, more than a hundred public meetings were held calling for the State to make a separate peace with the United States.[50] Desertion from the army increased sharply, although so did a revival movement that swept through the Army of Northern Virginia after its retreat from Pennsylvania.

In late 1863 and early 1864, the Army of the Potomac remained largely quiet, replenishing its ranks and preparing for the spring when the roads would be clear of mud and snow and, once more, they would try to push for Richmond. But any respite this gave to the battered Army of Northern Virginia was balanced by the continual progress made by Union armies in the West. Confederate General Braxton Bragg was forced to evacuate Chattanooga, Tennessee, a major rail hub. Confederates successfully counterattacked at the Battle of Chickamauga on September 19–20, 1863, leaving them in control of high ground—a far better position on Missionary Ridge and Lookout Mountain than the Union Army had held at Gettysburg. This gave a blast of hope to anxious white Southerners. It seemed that a dramatic knockout blow against the Union Army on their home soil, such as Lee had attempted at Gettysburg, was no longer on the cards. Yet surely, wrote John B. Jones, a clerk in Richmond, "the government of the United States must now see the impossibility of subjugating the Southern people, spread over such a vast extent of territory."[51] General Ulysses S. Grant, however, was certainly not thinking like that. Appointed by Lincoln commander of all Union armies west of the Appalachians, Grant made an immediate impact. On November 24–25, Federal forces in Tennessee achieved what Lee had failed to do and drove the enemy from seemingly impregnable positions through a frontal assault. Unlike Longstreet's attackers at Gettysburg on July 3, the Union forces at Missionary Ridge were able to keep out of the firing range of the defenders as they climbed the 400-foot ridge, taking cover in gullies and behind rocks.

The victory at Gettysburg mattered because of what it prevented—a politically disastrous defeat on Northern soil. But its significance was amplified by the series of victories in the West that followed. They meant that, by the end of 1863, large swathes of Tennessee, Arkansas, Louisiana, and Mississippi were in Union hands, as well as strategically important enclaves in Virginia and the Carolinas. In the historically impoverished Appalachian regions of Virginia, North Carolina, and Tennessee, there had been few enslaved people, and secession had widely been seen as a project run by aristocratic slaveholders, and anti-war feeling soared. Bands of deserters disappeared into the mountains.

Perhaps even more tellingly, after the summer of 1863, there was no more talk of foreign intervention to aid the South. That had always been the Confederacy's deus ex machina, the external force that they hoped would sweep in and prevent their destruction. British foreign secretary Lord John Russell had been itching to offer mediation, notwithstanding his embarrassment at failing to prevent a Liverpool-built ship from sailing in 1862 and becoming the *Alabama*, the Confederacy's most lucrative blockade runner. As late as October 1862, the Chancellor of the Exchequer and future Prime Minister William Gladstone had made a speech in Newcastle-upon-Tyne in which he had strongly indicated that he regarded the Confederacy as already having achieved the status of nationhood. Gladstone knew about Lincoln's preliminary Emancipation Proclamation when he gave that speech—it had been printed in *The Times* the previous day—but he regarded it as incendiary and desperate. It did not change his view, shared by many liberal-minded, anti-slavery people in Britain, that the war had a "thoroughly purposeless character, since it has long been (I think) clear enough that Secession is virtually an established fact, & that Jeff Davis & his comrades have made a nation."[52] Gladstone's apparently pro-Confederate speech—described by a leading Gladstone biographer as "premeditated and popular"—was especially notable since it was given on Tyneside, a hotbed of radicalism; it was far from just *The Times* editorial writers and Conservative MPs who favored British intervention.[53] A year later, however, there was no more talk of Britain coming to the aid of the South. The Emancipation Proclamation had turned out to matter, after all. The war was inextricably now bound up with the fate of slavery. British Liberals were often still romantically attached to the Southern cause—national self-determination was, after all, the defining cause of the age, and it was British admirers who paid for a statue of Stonewall Jackson in Richmond—but Britain was far too invested in the idea of itself as an anti-slavery power to stand in the way of a Union victory that would bring a "new birth of freedom."

An obvious rejoinder to the claim that the turning point of the war was in July 1863 was that it took until April 1865 for Lee to surrender and for the Confederacy finally to collapse. Part of the answer to this lies in the remarkable resilience of Southern white society. With the benefit of hindsight, we know that there would never again be a rebel invasion of the North. But in an increasingly asymmetrical war, with marginalized segments of the white Southern population in open rebellion against the war effort, the Confederacy's resilience is a remarkable phenomenon. Of course, Southern newspapers minimized the scale of the defeats, and the privations of the home front—the malnutrition caused by a lack of food, the impoverishment of working families without a male breadwinner—were almost so familiar that they became a source of pride. The capacity to keep going is nowhere more evident than within the Army of Northern Virginia itself, which became, after Gettysburg, more than ever Lee's army. The historian J. Tracy Power has shown that "Lee's Miserables" (as they wittily described themselves) had remarkable faith in their commander even as late as February 1865, by which time the army, on meager rations, was entrenched outside Petersburg, Virginia, outnumbered more than two to one, with their options running out.

Another part of the explanation for why the Confederacy lasted so long is the time it took for the North to bring to bear its superiority in manpower and resources. Gradually the Northern economy was becoming more efficient at war production. The railroads were being used more astutely to supply the army, and the draft—or the threat of it—was drawing men into the ranks in sufficient numbers to replace those who were being lost through death, injury, or the end of their terms of service.

Maximizing the Union's inherent advantages also required learning strategic lessons. One lesson was the need for coordinated advances on all fronts simultaneously to prevent the Confederacy from transferring troops from one battlefront to another. Another was the importance of targeting the South's capacity to wage war as well as just the armies themselves. Union forces had done this from the start, but by the end of 1863, they were doing so in a more purposeful way. Just as Lee had aimed to break the Northern will to fight with a victory in Pennsylvania, Union commanders increasingly recognized the need to subjugate white Southerners, to force them to recognize the futility of their war for independence. We are "not only fighting hostile armies," wrote General William T. Sherman, "but a hostile people, and must make old and young, rich and poor, feel the hard hand of war."[54] Key to the attrition of the Confederacy's economic capacity—and hence of its ability to wage war—were raids, including from Union-held enclaves in the South. Union naval dominance allowed them to establish beachheads all along the Confederacy's coastline, among the best-known being Fortress Monroe in Virginia and the Sea Islands in South Carolina, where African Americans ran as well as labored in the cotton plantations where they had formerly been enslaved. Raids became more important strategically by 1864. Sherman's "march to the sea" after the fall of Atlanta in September 1864 was effectively a raid on a spectacular scale designed to awe the white South into submission but also to destroy their capacity to fight with forensic determination.

In the final analysis, bringing to bear the North's advantages in men and material also required a new psychology of command. It meant being willing to bleed Union armies in the knowledge that they could be replenished, whereas the Confederate armies could not. As President Lincoln recognized, the Confederacy could not be defeated simply by occupying territory. Their armies had to be destroyed. Meade, with his utterly ill-judged celebration of rebel armies being driven from "our soil," was just the latest in a long line of Union generals who failed to grasp this point. But Grant and Sherman grasped it, and they were now the men in charge. In March 1864, Lincoln appointed Grant—the victor at Vicksburg—general-in-chief of all the Union armies, replacing the beady, scholarly Henry Halleck.

Even after Grant came East and took charge of the Army of the Potomac—outranking but not replacing Meade—it took more than a year to force a Confederate surrender. In the first three years of the war, the typical routine was for the armies to come out of their winter camps in the spring, fight a battle lasting no more than a day or two, and then retreat to lick their wounds before the next encounter. In fact, this was how warfare had always been conducted and was why the life of a soldier for hundreds of years had been mainly shaped by the tedium of camp life punctured by short, terrifying experiences of combat. This assumption about how wars were conducted no doubt influenced Meade's willingness to stay put on July 4. But in May and June 1864, General Grant ripped up that script, pushing the Army of the Potomac to fight day after day, pushing Lee's ever-shrinking army back toward Richmond. After a particularly horrific encounter at the Wilderness, close to the site of the Army of Northern Virginia's great victory at Chancellorsville, Grant ordered his army to continue to march south the next day, not re-cross the Rappahannock as Hooker had done a year earlier. Even though they had suffered terribly, battle-hardened Union troops cheered when they realized that they were not retreating. "We marched free. The men began to sing," recalled one.[55] But unlike at Gettysburg, the Union Army was now mainly on the offensive and consequently was losing men at a previously unimaginable rate. In six weeks in May and June, fifty-five thousand Union soldiers were killed or wounded in action. And still, Lee managed somehow always to escape, avoiding the all-out confrontation that Grant now sought and Lee, unlike the previous year, wanted to avoid.

While Grant was bleeding the Army of the Potomac and failing to inflict the final blow on Lee, Sherman was in a stalemate of his own. Having taken command of the Union armies in Tennessee, he had pushed into Georgia, but the key railroad hub of Atlanta was holding out. If the massive loss of life Northerners were suffering had led quickly to victory, that would have been one thing, but instead, by August 1864, the rebellion appeared as stubbornly alive as ever. Even radical anti-slavery Republicans like the mercurial editor of the *New*

York Tribune, Horace Greeley, called for peace negotiations with the Confederacy. The Democratic Party nominated for president former General George McClellan on a platform pledging to overturn the emancipation policy and calling for an immediate armistice. In his headquarters in Virginia, studying the Northern newspapers that were routinely smuggled through the lines, Lee must have hoped that finally, the anti-war movement in the Union would succeed.

But the tide of war turned. Atlanta fell on the night of September 1, the evacuating Confederate troops burning everything of military value as they left. Sherman set off on his march to "make Georgia howl" and the Democrats looked foolish for staking their electoral strategy on the "failure to restore the Union by the experiment of war." In November, Lincoln was re-elected by a comfortable, if not overwhelming, margin, helped by a solid majority among enlisted soldiers. The 1864 presidential election truly had been the last chance for a Confederate victory. Lincoln's re-election also ensured that emancipation would not be reversed. In January 1865, Congress passed, by the required two-thirds majority, the Thirteenth Amendment to the Constitution, abolishing slavery. When the Amendment was ratified by the states, it was no longer legal for any state to protect the idea that one human being could own, buy, and sell another. Even with this measure, the meaning of freedom for former slaves was contested with violence and in law. But without it, there would have been no secure legal basis even to resist re-enslavement. It was a new birth of freedom, of a kind.

In the spring of 1865, the final endgame was played out. Lee's army made a tactical retreat from their entrenchments outside Petersburg, abandoning Richmond and setting it in flames before the Confederate government loaded its treasury and its archives into railroad cars and fled west. At long last, the Confederate capital, which Northern newspapers had confidently expected to fall nearly four years previously, was in Union hands. On April 4, 1865, President Lincoln visited the ruined city, protected by a detachment of Black cavalry. Formerly enslaved people thronged the street cheering him.

On April 9, Lee accepted that the Army of Northern Virginia could fight no longer. An army which had known astonishing triumphs and had, no less impressively, survived for nearly two years after being so severely wounded at Gettysburg was now starving, ragged, and grossly outnumbered by the Army of the Potomac. In the parlor of a private home in the village of Appomattox Court House, Lee, in dress uniform, signed the terms of surrender. Grant later wrote that he felt "sad and depressed" at that moment, at the downfall of a "foe who had fought so long and so valiantly, and had suffered so much for a cause, though that cause was, I believe, one of the worst for which a people ever fought."[56] Robert E. Lee by now almost personified the Confederate nation, so much so that his surrender was regarded by nearly everyone as the effective end of the rebellion, even though the fugitive President Jefferson Davis had not officially given up the fight. The surrender would be a "turning point in history greater than the Revolutionary war was," predicted the *New York Herald*. And within that grand story of the advance of human freedom, Gettysburg retained its golden place.

6

Coming to Terms with Victory and Defeat, c.1865–1880

After the battle, a remarkable discovery was made in Gettysburg. A spring to the west of the town near Willoughby Run was found to have medicinal properties comparable to those of Vichy in France. By a remarkable coincidence the spring was discovered by a local businessman who was able to profit from the discovery by opening a new hotel. Visitors could soak up the memory and meaning of the great battle while also soaking up the mineral-enriched water. The waters, it was reported, could cure heart disease, gout, kidney trouble, and urinary infections, and even "improve the physique of both sexes."[1] The spring reinforced the association of the battlefield experience with the natural world, intensifying the piquant juxtaposition of mechanically enhanced human destruction with the "purity" of the landscape. Where once bodies had been maimed and destroyed, the landscape itself was now a healer. That healing was much needed because the aftershocks of the war continued to reverberate. For at least a decade after Appomattox, the central anxiety in American politics remained whether, and on what terms, political stability and national cohesion could be achieved.

Somehow, Americans needed to come to terms with the brutality and the death toll, and the Gettysburg spring offered a powerful metaphorical counterweight to violence that had taken place in those fields. From the earliest post-war days, the memorialization of the battle revealed a deep ambivalence about fighting and killing.

Amid all the celebration of military prowess, there was a persistent avoidance of the unglamorous reality of the violence of war in general and of this battle in particular. On the one hand, the extraordinary loss of life was integral to the battle's meaning. As Lincoln had said, the dead had "consecrated" those Pennsylvania fields: even as they sipped the healing waters of the spring, those early visitors could not help but contemplate the dead. The death toll was acknowledged in formal terms in the serried ranks of the headstones of the National Cemetery, and in sentimental terms in songs and poetry. Yet, on the other hand, the transformation of respectable Victorian men into killers was uncomfortable. Who really wanted to stare with unblinking eyes at the brutal reality of combat, the bloody gaping wounds, the guttural, animal fear of the men? Veterans processed their wartime experience in many ways, often by enduing with disciplined and righteous purpose the violence they had perpetrated and witnessed. But even among those who had fought, it was never entirely clear what place, if any, the savagery of combat had in the creation of a collective memory of the battle. This ambivalence was captured in the differing responses to one of the most remarkable pieces of art generated in the immediate post-war years, Peter F. Rothermel's epic 16-foot by 32-foot painting of Pickett's Charge.

A well-connected Philadelphia artist, Rothermel was commissioned for the generous sum of $25,000 to produce an artwork conveying "the larger meaning of the battle" of Gettysburg by a state legislative committee. Governor Andrew Curtin, an eager supporter of the plan, wanted a "historically true" painting to hang in the State Capitol which would commemorate for all time the turning point which, in Curtin's words, had sent the rebellion staggering backward into its grave, while valorizing the "tens of thousands of our gallant [Pennsylvania] soldiers" and "heroic commanders" who made it happen. Rothermel set about his task with great earnestness, interviewing battle survivors even while confessing that "there was much contradiction and confusion in the various reports of officers, eye-witnesses and writers in the interest of their special friends."[2] After two years of work, Rothermel produced a painting that depicted the fight at the Bloody Angle, at the climax of Pickett's Charge, when the assaulting troops began to fall back.

The painting does not shy away from the human pain of the fight. Looking west along the top of Cemetery Ridge toward the Round Tops from a spot just on the Union side of the stone wall, Rothermel created a hellish scene, the summer sky obscured by smoke, corpses visible underfoot, and white-faced men bleeding to death or struggling with bayonet and musket to kill before they are killed. At the dead center of the image is an everyman figure described by the artist as a "stalwart Federal soldier...beating back the enemy with the butt of his musket" and in the foreground is a gun propped against the stone wall on the Union side, inviting the viewer to pick it up and join the fight.[3] As one reviewer explained, Rothermel "bring[s] forward, almost to the feet of the spectator, multitudes of the bodies, bloody and wounded,

Figure 6.1. Peter F. Rothermel, *The Battle of Gettysburg: Pickett's Charge* (1870). Pennsylvania Historical and Museum Commission. The Union defenders are on the left of the painting, the Confederate attackers on the right. Note the rifle propped against the wall, inviting the viewer to pick it up and join the fight.

of dead men; and when the eye, sickened with the confusion and turmoil of the fight in the distance, drops upon the near images, it is caught and horrified by the sight of so much death."[4]

When it was first unveiled, in December 1870, the painting was met with enthusiasm. The *Philadelphia Press* reported that "the applause was unbounded, wild for a minute and then the thronged audience subsided into a deathlike stillness, every eye devouring the picture in its entirety and in its details."[5] There were some eyebrows raised about the marginalization of the officers who had patiently sat for the artist, but the state officials who had commissioned it appeared satisfied that Rothermel had fulfilled his brief to produce an artwork valorizing the manhood and bravery of the Pennsylvania defenders of the Union. Interestingly, although they are clearly losing ground, the rebels attacking from the right of the picture were no more savage, no less discernibly manly than the Union's defenders at the stone wall. And overall, the composition is almost symmetrical, with each side subject to the same unflinching gaze.

Five and half years later, in the summer of 1876, Rothermel's painting became the centerpiece of the American art section of the Centennial Exhibition in Philadelphia. But there, prominently displayed in the spectacular granite and marble Memorial Hall, its graphic depiction of violence proved newly controversial. To critics in 1876, Rothermel's painting posed the uncomfortable question of what kind of society could be built among the men on each side of the painting? The well-known art critic Clarence Cook could find no redeeming virtue in the depiction of the struggle. It is "not a picture of heroism," he complained. "It is a picture of blood and fury, of men—of brother-men, of fellow citizens—murdering one another in the lust of hate; of soldiers, brave men of the South and North, in the spasms of mortal agony; of dead men with blue faces and swollen hands—horrors piled on horrors."[6] The Centennial Exhibition was, after all, meant to showcase a reborn nation. Since the war could not be ignored, it ought to be turned into a positive, healing experience, a generator of technical innovation and economic growth, and, ideally, of renewed national purpose as well. Rothermel's reminder of its savagery struck a discordant note.

From one point of view, the brutality of the battle was the evidence of the scale of the existential challenge to the life of the nation which had been overcome. From this perspective, Rothermel's painting captured the necessity of reliving the gory as well as the glory. But viewed another way, the war was tragic evidence of the nation's continuing fragility. The priority was to build a stronger nation by binding up the nation's wounds. These perspectives—both elements of the Northern response to the end of the war—were not neatly represented by rival factions but coexisted as competing impulses, often within the same individuals. The varying responses to the violence in Rothermel's painting were a reflection of that reality.

* * *

For North and South alike, the unimaginable loss of life, the devastation of families and communities, the ongoing physical and emotional scars of those who had seen battle all demanded accounting. Meaning had to be found, and meaning was woven through collective memory: that endlessly contested process through which the past is represented in the present. In the immediate aftermath of the war everyone had their own personal experiences of those tumultuous four years. But as we all know when we reflect for a moment upon it, personal memories are never pure, nor unadulterated by the environment in which we live, and they shift as time goes by. The same is true of the officially sanctioned or generally agreed-upon ways of telling stories about the past.

Part of the problem for victorious Northerners in 1865, as they debated what lessons should be drawn from the war, was deciding what exactly they had won. The most obvious answer was that, by defeating the rebellion, they had saved the Union. But was reunion enough? What was needed to prevent a future rupture? Surely, the Union would have to be remade from stronger timbers, perhaps through a more powerful Federal government and a regenerated sense of national belonging. And then there was slavery: how did it fit into the story Northerners had to construct about the meaning of their sacrifices? In December 1865—eight months after the de facto end of the war—the Thirteenth Amendment to the Constitution was ratified, making chattel slavery illegal throughout the United States. But ending slavery was one thing; accepting those formerly enslaved people as equal citizens in the republic was quite another. For a dozen years after the end of the war, the dominant issue in US politics was how to "reconstruct" the Union. This was not just a question of when and on what conditions to readmit congressmen from former Confederate states and allow the South to take part in presidential elections, but also of what kind of society should be built in the post-war South—and specifically, what the place of Black people in that society would be.

Between 1866 and 1872, the Republican-dominated Congress in Washington passed a raft of legislations and two constitutional amendments with which Americans are still grappling today. The Reconstruction Acts placed the former Confederacy under (relatively light touch) military rule. The Fourteenth Amendment defined US citizenship to include African Americans, and then gave the Federal government the responsibility for ensuring that citizens should be treated equally under the law. The Fifteenth Amendment made it unconstitutional for state governments to disenfranchise anyone based on race. For a few extraordinary years, Southern politics was turned upside down. Former slaves served on juries, voted, and opened businesses. African Americans served as US congressmen and even, in a couple of cases, briefly as state governors. It was never true that, in the nineteenth-century phrase, "the bottom rail was on top," but it was more nearly true than it was to be again for a century; extraordinarily, in 1872 there were more Black officeholders in the South than there were to be again until 1970. This period of "radical Reconstruction" was, predictably, fiercely and violently opposed—and by Northerners as well as by Southerners. In the end it was overthrown by a combination of paramilitary violence in the

South and Northerners' recoil at the cost and divisiveness of the exertion of Federal power in the South. After a financial crisis in 1873, with rising industrial unrest and growing anxiety about how to integrate a new wave of immigration from Southern and Eastern Europe, most Northerners withdrew with distaste from the messy business of enforcing the notional constitutional rights of freedmen.

National politics shaped public meanings of the war. In the high period of Reconstruction—the years when Federal efforts to impose a new political settlement on the former Confederacy were strongest—a coalition including abolitionists, Union Army veterans, and Republican Party politicians fought to enshrine in national memory "the war of the rebellion" as a righteous triumph over wicked slaveholders.[7] One of the country's most prominent wartime proponents of Black rights, Congressman Thaddeus Stevens, whose factory had been burned by Lee's invading army, gave an electioneering address on the battlefield at Gettysburg in October 1865 in which he urged his fellow Pennsylvanians to see Reconstruction as a continuation of the war effort. But even at that early stage, with the detritus of battle still strewn across the field, Stevens had to combat the spirit of reconciliation. To speak of the war now, "among the thick graves of the immortal battle-field of Gettysburg" as a "family feud" as if it were but an amicable disagreement to be papered over, was "mockery to the loyal dead," Stevens warned. In his sights was the President, Andrew Johnson, a Tennessean who had succeeded to the presidency after Lincoln's assassination and who was busy conciliating the white South—"fraternizing with and embracing the murderers of [our] kindred," as Stevens put it.[8] But his eye, too, was on the rising romantic embrace of the idea that what must be remembered was not the politics but the bravery of ordinary soldiers.

The Reconstruction era saw the high tide of the movement to frame the war as being first and foremost about Black freedom. In 1866, Frederick Douglass warned that the battle now underway between President Johnson and Congress over Reconstruction policy "would decide whether the tremendous war so heroically fought and so victoriously ended shall pass into history a miserable failure, barren of permanent results... or whether, on the other hand, we shall, as the rightful reward of victory over treason, have a solid nation, entirely delivered from all contradictions and social antagonisms, based upon loyalty, liberty, and equality."[9] Douglass struggled indefatigably through the rest of his long life to keep emancipation at the center of the nation's vision. "I am not indifferent to the claims of a generous forgetfulness," he said on Decoration Day in 1894, "but whatever else I may forget, I shall never forget the difference between those who fought for liberty and those who fought for slavery; between those who fought to save the Republic and those who fought to destroy it."[10] Republicans like Douglass, fighting to diminish the continuing power of the old plantation elite and make real the promise of equal citizenship, framed the battle in terms that served their purpose. "The battle of Gettysburg was not more of a crisis than this," wrote one radical to the Massachusetts Senator Charles Sumner, encouraging him to continue his effort to resist President Johnson.[11] To compromise with the white South over Black rights, wrote a Pennsylvania congressman, would be to "consent that the cemetery at Gettysburg should be razed to the ground, and that the lamentation of the bereaved should give place to the lowing of the cattle."[12]

There were a few years in the late 1860s and early 1870s when this radical narrative was politically powerful. And even after it faded, it never disappeared. The segregated African American chapter of the Grand Army of the Republic in Baltimore, for example, organized annual excursions to the battlefield to commemorate the Emancipation Proclamation which continued into the 1890s despite their members facing surliness and occasional violence from Gettysburg residents. Many white Northerners who had been radicalized by the battle against slavery advocated for racial justice for the remainder of their lives. Even at the height of the "cult of reunion" in the early twentieth century, when Southern white stereotypes about contented slaves amid Spanish moss-clad plantations abounded, the idea of Gettysburg as a triumph for abolition persisted. For example, the playwright Percy MacKaye created the character of Link Tadbourne, an elderly Yankee veteran who spent his days drowsing in his wood-shed imagining the piles of logs and wood chips resembled the topography of Cemetery and Seminary Ridges. Dreamily, he talks through each phase of the battle and what was at stake. For him, this was not a place of sectional reconciliation, it was where the spirit of the martyred abolitionist John Brown triumphed and still lived. The play takes place on Decoration Day, and Link urges a seventeen-year-old school teacher called Polly not to forget why the war was fought. "Lord God, you ain't forgot the boys, have ye? the boys, how they come marchin' home to ye, live and dead, behind old Brown, a-singin' *Glory* to ye!"[13]

Even as the veterans in blue and gray sang "The Star Spangled Banner" on the field of Gettysburg, the story could be told in many ways and many morals drawn. For in truth, the motivations of those who had fought in the Union armies and supported them were far too complicated, the politics of this still-divided nation too cacophonous, for there to be any singular meaning attached to Gettysburg, even within the North. And just as antebellum anti-slavery politics had been as much about purifying the white republic as liberating the enslaved, remembering the war for the destruction of slavery was not necessarily the same as making it about Black people, still less creating a biracial democracy. Instead, the principal lesson of Gettysburg for many of those who spoke there in the immediate post-war decades was not, as it was for Douglass or the fictional Link Tadbourne, racial equality but the high stakes for the nation and the world of a battle against the believers in slavery.

To many victorious Northerners, the rebellion had represented a hideously corrupted version of the American republic in which enslavement and the aristocratic principles that sustained it would spread across the continent and beyond. Speaking at the 1869 dedication of the monument to fallen soldiers in the Soldier's National Cemetery on Cemetery Hill, the Indiana Republican Oliver P. Morton contrasted "steady Northern valor, animated by love of country" with the "boasted chivalry of the South fighting for slavery." The South, for Morton, was synonymous with the "false pride" and "vanity" of a "favored class, whose elevation is only seen by the depression of others." While such unrepublican ideas may "dazzle the eyes of the world" for a time, they cannot "long maintain a successful contest with truth, justice, and the strength of free institutions." The shallow, dashing Pickett was defeated by the unglamorous decency of Meade.[14] Morton's address, given at the height of radical Reconstruction, offered brutal clarity about the global stakes of the battle. Just as Lincoln had cast the war as a universal and transcendental conflict between democracy and tyranny, Morton drew a direct line between Lee's defeat in Pennsylvania and the bright "prospect of liberty throughout the world" in which, "in all civilized lands the grand armies of freedom are on their march."[15] Gettysburg was a battle between "two conflicting civilizations," one former general put it. The South had drawn their sword "to murder the State and establish a vast empire with slavery as its chief cornerstone" while "the great free north" girded its loins "for one more struggle for human liberty."[16] General Meade suggested that the bones of fallen Confederate soldiers be reburied not under a commemorative monument but with a simple stone noting that "below sleep the misguided men who fell in a battle for a cause over which we triumphed."[17] To this way of thinking the principal evil of slavery was not so much its impact on the enslaved but its threat to republican freedom.

The principal organization that helped create and sustain a self-conscious community of Union veterans was the Grand Army of the Republic (GAR), which grew by fits and starts into one of the most successful pressure groups in US history, and which kept alive this view of Gettysburg as the decisive nail in the coffin of the Slave Power, even if not the augury of a biracial democracy.[18] In the last quarter of the nineteenth century, the GAR successfully lobbied Congress for pensions and other benefits, creating in the process the United States' first Federal welfare state. The GAR leveraged the political capital accrued by the nineteenth century's "greatest generation" into vast fiscal transfers. By 1913, benefits to Union Army veterans accounted for a quarter of all Federal expenditure, greater than any other category other than servicing the interest on the national debt.[19] The GAR's success was based on a powerful story about the debt the nation owed to those who had fought to save it, which meant that it was essential to keep reminding post-war Americans of the political stakes. Thus, at a meeting of the Pennsylvania chapter of the GAR at Little Round Top in 1888, Brigadier General Gobin protested that he was "tired of [the] gush and pretense" that glorified rebel soldiers. "I want it to be distinctly understood, now and for all time, that the men who wore gray were everlastingly and eternally wrong."[20] And when it was proposed during the administration of Grover Cleveland (the first Democrat to be elected president since the war) to return a small number of captured Confederate battle flags there was implacable resistance. Ohio Governor Joseph B. Foraker threatened to invade Washington with the Ohio National Guard to prevent such "sacrilege,"[21] while National Commander Lucius Fairchild said the GAR would "rise as one man in solemn protest against any such disposition of the trophies won at such a fearful sacrifice of blood."[22]

* * *

The "glorification" of rebel soldiers that so irritated the GAR in the 1880s was a measure of the effective storytelling of their counterparts in the South: Confederate veterans and their wives, widows, and daughters. Because as soon as the war was over—indeed while it was still being waged—white Southerners weaved stories to provide balm for their grief and validation of their sacrifice. With Southern women in the vanguard, their status outside the formal political sphere giving them cover that men did not have, there was a huge collective effort to remake the war as a source of pride. It was said that Southerners had lost on the battlefield only because they had been overwhelmed by superior numbers, and if they no longer had a Southern nation state, they had everything else that made a nation. Beginning in the 1870s, former Confederate states were "redeemed" (the white supremacists' term) from "Black rule" (which actually meant the brief period after the Reconstruction Acts and the implementation of the Fourteenth Amendment in which African American men could vote). The overthrow of these Reconstruction governments was self-consciously a continuation of the war, the Ku Klux Klan's uniform of white sheets a ghastly evocation of the ghosts of the Confederate dead.

The myth of the Lost Cause, in other words, was a consciously created project propagated by poets and novels, and by journals like *The Land We Love* and *The Southern Review*. The Lost Cause myth enabled white Southerners to feel superior to the graceless, hypocritical Yankees who had defeated them in war despite lacking honor or martial virtue. Its core ideas were the claim that secession was constitutional and therefore the war was not a rebellion, and that the only reason the South lost their legitimate and noble fight was the imbalance in numbers and the brute strength of the Northern industrial machine. That and the perfidy or errors of Confederate commanders who failed to live up to the exalted standard of Lee. And, far from expiring with the end of the war, the self-serving paternalism that had coated white justifications for slavery was given new life. Poems imagined formerly enslaved people now "gaunt and wasted" by freedom and returning to their old master's home to die.[23]

Put simply, Gettysburg was the battle the white South could never get over. More than any other battle by far, white Southerners obsessed over Gettysburg, re-litigating tactical decisions, and dreaming of the might-have-beens. This reimagining of Gettysburg was a decades-long project, consuming countless pages of reminiscences and recriminations, making and ruining reputations in the process.

It began with the dead: the more than three thousand Confederate soldiers who had perished in the gently sloping fields of Pennsylvania who had received a rough burial in mass pits. In 1869, a group of Richmond, Virginia women began raising funds to set aside a section of the city's Hollywood Cemetery for the reburial of the Confederate war dead. The first of many efforts by Ladies Memorial Associations (LMAs) across the South to commemorate the war dead, the

Hollywood Memorial Association of Richmond set its sights on Gettysburg—the most prominent battle fought on Northern soil—and sought to bring the dead home.

In 1871, a few of the Confederate dead were reinterred on "Gettysburg Hill," as it was designated, in Hollywood Cemetery and more followed in succeeding years. In June 1872, 708 bodies were laid to rest in what the Richmond *Daily Dispatch* called "the most solemn and imposing demonstration of respect for the dead ever witnessed in Richmond." The coffins were carried on fifteen black-draped wagons through the city, escorted by a detachment from the First Virginia Regiment and a thousand Confederate veterans, many visibly maimed. "The sidewalks were thronged with people of all ages and sexes," reported the *Dispatch*. "Many eyes were filled with tears and many a soldier's widow and orphan turned away from the scene to hide emotion." The procession filed past Confederate flags and state flags at half-mast, and a banner with the inscription "They Died For Us." The marching Gettysburg veterans wore a lapel badge in the form of a miniature Confederate battle flag with the words "Gettysburg, July, 1863" upon it. And when they reached the burial place, the presiding minister, Reverend Hoge, intoned a prayer: "We thank Thee that we have been permitted to bring back from their graves among strangers all that is mortal of our sons and brothers, and that we have now laid them down on the bosom of their Mother."[24]

As with other memorial events, the language and symbolism of this procession strayed beyond the mere acknowledgment of loss. Evoking the idea that the Confederate dead of Gettysburg had not died in vain but for something greater and more enduring than themselves, it laid the groundwork for the Lost Cause myth. Hoge offered up a prayer that the "young men of our Commonwealth" might have engraved on their hearts the "remembrance of the patriotic valor, the loyalty to truth, to duty and to God, which characterized the heroes around whose remains we weep, and who surrendered only to the last enemy—Death."[25]

* * *

At stake for Southerners was "the truth of history," since "truth," as one former general noted, was "more precious to us than all the spoils of war which were captured by the sword."[26] And "truth" could not be captured by the enemy so easily as battle flags. The Southern Historical Society (SHS), founded first in New Orleans in 1869 but then finding a permanent home in Richmond, became the preeminent institutional means of waging this new war for the "truth" of the Lost Cause. The Society's purpose was "the collection, classification, preservation, and final publication, in some form to be hereafter determined, of all the documents and facts bearing upon the eventful history of the past few years, illustrating the nature of the struggle from which the country has just emerged, defining and vindicating the principles which lay beneath it, and marking the stages through which it was conducted to its issue." Through this careful archival work, the Society created an "arsenal from which the defender of our cause may draw any desired weapon."[27]

Lost Cause writers imagined Southerners having no choice but to secede in 1861 because the basis of the government they had helped establish in the 1770s and 1780s was being revolutionized by abolitionist fanatics. That is indeed how Southerners at the time had seen the situation and so it was natural that this was the central theme of the Lost Cause thesis. Southerners, despite fighting for independence, were the real patriots whose sacrifices had been for the values of free government and popular sovereignty to which even now Yankees made empty pledges of fealty. As an early address to the SHS in 1873, delivered in the midst of the violent resistance of many white Southerners to Reconstruction, warned: Southerners would be remembered "either as criminals—rebels or traitors . . . or as patriots defending our rights and vindicating the true principles of the government founded by our fathers."[28]

A "proper" sense of history also had instrumental value as Southerners rebuilt their society. It could "intensify the love of country and convert defeat and disaster into pillars of support for future manhood and noble womanhood," said former Confederate General John B.

Gordon in 1895. "Devotion to the glorious past is not only the surest guarantee of future progress and holiest bond of unity, but also is the strongest claim they can present to the conscience and respect to other sections of the Union."[29] In other words, understanding defeat as a "consecration" provided psychological bonds which could unify the South, the secret source of moral superiority that would enable them to participate in the United States with no stigma or hint of shame or regret. It was fairly openly a means of continuing the war by other means. As the leading light of the SHS, former General Jubal Early, put it, "Every now and then, I manage to land a bomb against the enemy, in the way of exploding some of their lies, and that affords me some consolation."[30]

Throughout the war, Southern clergymen and political leaders had assured their followers that the Confederacy was blessed by Providence. Their cause was God's. When there were reversals—as at Gettysburg—it was evidence that, in the familiar words of Hebrews Chapter 12, "for whom the Lord loveth he chasteneth." But a reversal was one thing, total defeat another. The Lost Cause project was designed, first and foremost, to assure Southerners that, notwithstanding their loss, their cause had still been blessed. Having failed to create an independent Southern nation, the enduring "values" for which the South had fought would yet triumph. And if the explanation for battlefield defeat did not, after all, lie in Providential design, then it must have been due to diabolical human error.

For Gettysburg raised in the most pressing form that most troubling question of all: How could Lee, that paragon of leadership, have lost? One early post-war Southern writer pointed out that Lee was outnumbered by Union troops who were "on their own soil, with their communication uninterrupted...while Lee was in hostile territory, a considerable distance from his base of supplies, and must, for that reason, either attack his adversary or retreat."[31] A veiled criticism of Lee was implicit in this analysis. Edward Pollard observed that "the failure of General Lee to follow up the victory [on the first day of the battle] enabled the enemy to take at leisure, and in full force, one of the strongest positions in any action of the war, and to turn the tables of the battle-field completely upon the Confederates."[32] James D. McCabe, a Confederate War Department official who wrote biographies of Lee and Stonewall Jackson not only regretted that Lee had not "stormed the heights before Hancock had succeeded in rallying his troops" on July 1, but went on to say that Lee's decision not to retreat before the disastrous assault on July 3 was a "strange error."[33]

Such tepid criticism was as strong as it ever got. Lee's death in 1870 elevated him to a God-like status. He became beyond reproach. If, as one Confederate officer wrote, "the divinity in [Lee's] bosom shone translucent through the man," it was hard to see how he could have erred.[34] If so, the defeat of Lee's army required a scapegoat among his subordinate officers, for every hero needs an antihero. There were various contenders for this role. Cavalry commander Jeb Stuart, who failed to remain in contact with Lee despite being his "eyes and ears," was one option. As the historian Thomas Desjardin has pointed out, the scapegoating of Stuart overlooked the stubborn fact that Lee had "significant cavalry forces, separate from those under Stuart's command, traveling with him throughout the campaign and that they also could have collected the information Stuart is supposed to have failed to supply."[35] Still, Stuart, being dead, was unable to answer his critics.

For his "failure" to take the heights south of Gettysburg on the evening of the first day when the Union Army was weakest, the sights were also often set on Richard Ewell. Much was made of Lee's order to Ewell to "carry the hill occupied by the enemy" if he found it "practicable," a less than clear-cut instruction that was nevertheless interpreted by Ewell's latter-day enemies as unambiguous.[36]

Yet even Ewell's alleged failings did not make him as tempting a target as James Longstreet. The charge sheet against Longstreet boiled down to the allegation that he deliberately dragged his feet, undermining through his laggard lack of faith what otherwise would have been a failsafe strategic operation by Lee. Specifically, the leading Lost Cause mythmakers Jubal Early, John Gordon, and Lee's nephew Fitzhugh all claimed that Longstreet had ignored a "dawn attack order" which Lee had supposedly issued on the morning of the second day, instead waiting for more reinforcements and marching his troops through an indirect route so that his assault on the southern end of the Union line only began late in the afternoon. Early recalled that Lee had met with him, Ewell, and Rodes on the evening of July 1 and "expressed his determination to assault the enemy's position at daylight on the next morning." He had "left us," Early claimed, "for the purpose of ordering up Longstreet's Corps in time to begin the attack at dawn the next morning" but "that corps was not in readiness to make the attack until four o'clock in the afternoon" and "by that time, Meade's whole army had arrived on the field and taken its position. Had the attack been made at daylight as contemplated, it must have resulted in a brilliant and decisive victory."[37] There is no other evidence that this meant that Lee had issued Longstreet with an order to attack at dawn, and the whole story was strongly rebutted by Longstreet and his allies, but it was a doggedly persistent myth. Other Confederate officers at Gettysburg, most of whom had decidedly patchy military reputations themselves, piled in. Artillery commander William N. Pendleton concluded his description of the battle by proclaiming that "never were General Lee's genius and power more signally displayed, and yet through errors of others [Pendleton himself excepted and Longstreet very much the target]...his admirably planned combinations failed of their effect." According to Pendleton, Longstreet's "disastrously tardy violation of explicit orders on an occasion of such supreme importance" led to Lee's "mental anguish at the fatal forfeiture of opportunity far surpassing anything of the kind ever elsewhere evinced by him."[38] Jefferson Davis got in on the act, concluding that "the plan and expectation of General Lee" was for a "concentrated attack at sunrise on the second day" which, had it occurred, we may "reasonable assume" that the "enemy would have been routed."[39]

Whether or not it was justified on military grounds, this scapegoating of Longstreet had an undertone of nastiness which had nothing to do with anything that happened in July 1863 and everything to do with post-war politics. In the eyes of the propagandists of the Lost Cause, James Longstreet's alleged tardiness at Gettysburg appeared in a new and possibly sinister light given his acceptance, by the late 1860s, of the reality and implications of Confederate defeat. Longstreet was far from a convert to the cause of Black citizenship, but in forthright remarks to the *New Orleans Times* in 1867, just as radical Reconstruction measures were beginning to bite, he urged his fellow white Southerners to accept the reality that they were a "conquered people" and "there can be no discredit to a conquered people for accepting the conditions offered by their Conquerors."[40] While Northerners and Southern Republicans praised him as "one of the most sagacious and efficient laborers in the work of reconstruction in the South," unreconstructed rebels sneered that his views were "too puerile and illogical to have effect on the course of any person" and his long-time friend D. H. Hill, publisher of *The Land We Love*, expressed hope that Longstreet was joking, and if he wasn't either his "theology or his loyalty is at fault."[41] As if confronting defeated Confederates with reality wasn't provocative enough, Longstreet followed his words with actions, commanding the forces that resisted an attempted coup d'état in Louisiana in 1874. At the so-called "Battle of Liberty Place," Longstreet, as Adjutant General of the state militia, attempted to fight off between five and eight thousand armed men of the "White League," most of them Confederate veterans. The state troops Longstreet commanded were outnumbered and outgunned, but, even so, in military terms, this was not Longstreet's finest hour. He was pulled off his horse, wounded, and held captive.[42]

Longstreet fought back in print against the allegations that his failings at Gettysburg had cost the Confederacy the battle, and thus the war, but given his pariah status it was never likely that he was going to win back many friends. If anything, he made his task even harder for himself by deflecting blame away from himself and on to the sainted Lee. The fundamental problem, in Longstreet's view, was that the entire Gettysburg campaign had been misconceived: by pushing so far into Pennsylvania, Lee left his army dangerously exposed.

But on top of that, Longstreet painted a picture of a commander who made a series of unforced errors. Allowing Stuart to leave the general line of march was a mistake. Lee should have pushed home the Confederates' advantage on the evening of July 1 (the fault here being Lee's and not Ewell's given the vague nature of Lee's "if practicable" order). On July 2, there should have been more cooperation between the assault he led on the Union left and that being launched at Culp's Hill on the Union right. The rebel forces should have moved position on the night of July 2 to the other side of Gettysburg so that they stood between Meade's forces and Washington. And, finally, capping off this long indictment, Lee should—of course—not have ordered Pickett's futile assault on July 3. Lee's (alleged) "remark, made just after the battle, 'It is all my fault,' meant just what it said," wrote Longstreet. "It adds to the nobility and magnificence of the remark, when we reflect that it was the utterance of a deep-felt truth, rather than a mere sentiment."[43]

Longstreet's self-defense catalyzed the Lost Cause writers into an even more fervent defense of Lee and pushed them into an ever-narrower explanation of Confederate loss, turning on the betrayal or failings of a few. For most Confederates, Lee's "It's all my fault" was not evidence of his tactical culpability but of humility. Lee, explained J. William Jones, editor of the *Southern Historical Society Papers*, was willing to "crucify, on self-erected cross, his own illustrious name, and make that reputation, more precious than life itself, vicarious sacrifice for his lieutenants and his men."[44] Meanwhile, for Jubal Early, Lee's offensive strategy in the Gettysburg campaign was essential and unavoidable, given the situation the Confederacy faced in the spring of 1863. "Unless we could break through the cordon closing and tightening around us, we must infallibly be crushed as a victim in the coils of a boaconstrictor [*sic*]."[45]

While some Lost Cause writers continued to blame Ewell and Stuart, Early was unwavering in focusing his fire on Longstreet. He did so with the help of an alleged quote by Lee himself, who was reported to have said, "Longstreet is a very good fighter when he gets in position and gets everything ready, but he is *so slow*." "Our failure to carry the position at Gettysburg was not due so much to the superior fighting of Meade's army," Early insisted, but to "the failure to support, according to General Lee's instruction, the several attacks made on the 2d and 3d, and the delay in making those attacks." Longstreet's "constitutional inertia" had "delayed his readiness to fight" with fatal consequences.[46]

Rarely far below the surface in this battle to take credit for the noble failure of Gettysburg was interstate rivalry. Many of the leading Lost Cause writers were Virginians and their state chauvinism was all too evident. In his tear-jerking description of Pickett's charge, Edward Pollard (of Richmond, Virginia), concluded that "the name of Virginia was that day baptized in fire, and illuminated forever in the temple of History."[47] North Carolinians, who liked to think of themselves (as the old saying goes) as a valley of humility between the two mountains of conceit of Virginia and South Carolina, were irritated by the appropriation by the Virginian Pickett of the "glorious" failed assault on the third day of the battle, but what really annoyed them was the tacit effort to add North Carolina troops to the unhappy roster of Southerners whose pusillanimity betrayed the Confederate cause. Pickett's men sometimes blamed the failure of the assault on a lack of support from Isaac Trimble's and J. J. Pettigrew's North Carolina divisions, who one Virginian claimed ran "like sheep."[48] "Steadily and grandly did the Virginians cross the valley of death," wrote one Virginian, while Pettigrew's men "wavered and broke under terrible fire."[49]

Whatever its basis in truth, the narrative that Pickett's division advanced steadily into a hail of gunfire while the North Carolinians flailed and fled was stubbornly advanced by the first wave of writers and Lost Cause publicists. It even became the standard account among Northern writers like William Swinton, who, in *The Twelve Decisive Battles of the War* (1871), told his readers that Pettigrew's division "showed such trepidation that they were jeered by the reserves that lay behind."[50] In 1888, William R. Bond, a native North Carolinian who had been severely wounded at Gettysburg, published a short book that took on the "myth" of Pettigrew's division faltering as an "example of the trash which passes for Southern history" and a "libel containing so much ignorance, narrowness and prejudice."[51] Bond was among those who resorted to attack as the best form of defense, insinuating that the much-lauded Pickett might not even have been on the field at all but behind the lines at a "whiskey wagon."[52]

The Lost Cause project was inherently introspective, celebrating, re-litigating, and generally obsessing over everything Confederates did on the battlefield, bleaching the Union Army of agency. Yet, when asked why Lee's army was defeated, Pickett himself was supposed to have drawled, "I always thought the Yankees had something to do with it."[53] If he ever said it, Pickett's sardonic remark hinted at an uncomfortable thought—if the Yankees were so strong that the South was doomed to fail, then was the sacrifice really worth it? Deified as he was, Lee's farewell address to his army at Appomattox (we have been "compelled to yield to overwhelming numbers and resources")[54] carried the uncomfortable implication that the war had been futile. Dying for a noble cause could be admirable; dying for a noble cause that was doomed from the start verged on foolishness. So, there was a balance to be struck by the Lost Cause project. On the one hand, the Yankees always held the advantage, but on the other, since God was on the side of the South, a plucky victory by the underdog must have been possible—hence the need to find scapegoats.

* * *

So, in the post-war decades, Northerners told a story of the battle as an apocalyptic confrontation between democracy and serfdom, while Southerners saw it as the tragic climax of their fight for freedom. But at the same time, discomfort with Rothermel's depiction of unrestrained violence at the 1876 Centennial pointed to another way of thinking about the battle, which was to see in it the seeds of sectional reconciliation. If Gettysburg was the greatest battle of the war, it was the litmus test of the capacity of former enemies to bury their enmity. It helped that the armies fighting at Gettysburg entirely consisted of white soldiers since it followed that reconciliation need only involve white Americans.

At its most saccharine and sentimental, the "cult of reunion" bled the battle dry of any political meaning. But in the early post-war decades, the impulse for reconciliation was not inimical to other political frameworks for understanding the battle. Southerners could celebrate the righteousness of their Lost Cause while acknowledging the bravery of the Yankees, and so long as they felt they were being accorded sufficient respect in the new post-war order, they could extend a fraternal hand of friendship to their former foes. Similarly, there was no fundamental reason why it was not possible for Northerners to conceptualize the battle as an apocalyptic struggle for freedom against the barbarism of the Slave Power while also recognizing the wisdom of building bridges to the defeated South.

Indeed, if the primary challenge facing the United States after the war was creating a stable polity, it was hard to see how that could be done without some measure of reconciliation. The alternative was to treat white Southerners in the way that Americans had treated other groups defeated in war—native peoples, Mexicans, or even the British—by defining the nation in opposition to them. If the Confederacy represented the antithesis of American democracy, perhaps its adherents should be forever marked as outside the pale, their defeat and humiliation endlessly replayed. Some radicals in the North took this uncompromising line. But in the end, numbers and politics made it an unfeasible strategy. There were simply too many white Southerners for them all, even metaphorically, to be bayoneted as they lay wounded. And, critically, the two sides were far too entangled, with their shared family, history, race, and religion, for them to be entirely dehumanized in the way that was possible in other wars. There were always limits to how far Southerners could successfully racialize "Yankees" as an alien species, as was later done, for example, to Germans in World War I. Nor could Northerners entirely disassociate themselves from their enemies as culturally and morally degraded, as they did in the war against Mexico in the 1840s. Both sides, instead, found sub-elements of the other that they could successfully demonize while holding out the possibility of redemption for the rest. So, for the South, the real enemy were Jacobinical abolitionists, foreign immigrants, and Black troops, while Northerners often saw their enemy as being the leaders of the Slave Power, allowing ordinary white Southerners to be the objects as much of pity as of contempt.

All this helps explain the emotional power of reconciliation even at the height of Reconstruction. In 1868, the Republicans nominated General Grant for president and fought the election as if the Democratic candidate, Horatio Seymour of New York, was an unreconstructed Confederate. Pro-Grant campaign literature described the election as a rerun of Gettysburg. "The cause" for which Seymour now allegedly stood had been "in peril" in 1863 when "our noble soldiers...paralyzed the rebellion and gave freedom new life upon the bloody fields of Gettysburg."[55] Yet also in that campaign, the path to reconciliation was signaled by the slogan "Let Us Have Peace." Like all effective political slogans, this was both startlingly clear, and fundamentally ambiguous. It implied that the war had not yet been won—or at least that the "fruits of victory" had not yet been secured. But it also promised final resolution rather than enduring enmity. Everyone wanted peace; the question was on what terms. And meanwhile, some who had been forthright wartime radicals were by the end of the decade reframing the war as a morality tale in which fault was equally shared between each section. The idiosyncratic *New York Tribune* editor Horace Greeley had pushed hard for emancipation early in the war (before later calling for negotiations when the death rate soared in 1864). By 1868, however, he mildly observed that the war had happened "because the North and South failed to understand each other."[56] Four years after that he was running for president endorsed by the Democrats on a platform opposing Reconstruction.

The first historians of the battle were mostly Northerners. Almost all wrote both with a clear view that the right side won while also wanting to smooth the path to reconciliation. An example is Jacob Hoke, a resident of Chambersburg, whose book *The Great Invasion*

(1887) was based in part on his own diaries from June and July 1863. But despite his personal stake in the events he described, Hoke made a point of writing in the third person and explained that "for those who arrayed themselves on the opposite side, he has but feelings of kindness."[57] Similarly, James T. Long, a captain in the Army of the Potomac and author of a battlefield guide, *Gettysburg: How the Battle was Fought* (1891), emphasized that his aim was simply to describe impartially "the decisive battle of the war," avoiding anything "that might mar the feelings of a single individual."[58] Writing as one who had been there, he declared that "the men who fought on the field of Gettysburg were among the bravest that ever faced the cannon's mouth" and "Unionists and Confederates alike may join hands in honest pride."[59]

An early sign of the willingness of Northerners to embrace reconciliation came in the extraordinary public response to the death in 1870 of General Lee. The man who at least in military terms was more responsible than anyone else for the resilience of the rebellion was lauded by Northerners almost as much as Southerners. The rapidity with which Lee, with glorious but telling paradox, was turned into an *American* icon was a function of three factors. The first was, essentially, the image of Lee as a man of gentleness and "nobility"—an image so well grounded because it was so assiduously cultivated by his champions and supporters before and during the war as well as after it. It enabled Lee to be presented as an exemplar of the Christian virtues and therefore in a fundamental sense as *passive*. He had not wished his state to secede, and yet, so it was imagined, in the force of circumstances his loyalty to home led him to accept the role of a Confederate commander despite the oath of loyalty to the Constitution he had sworn as an army officer. He was the military leader so lacking in venom for his enemies that he was said to simply refer to the Union Army as "those people." In this way, Lee's patriotism remained curiously unscathed.

The second factor was Lee's own conduct from the moment he surrendered his pitifully malnourished and poorly supplied Army of Northern Virginia at Appomattox. Thanking his men for their service, he nevertheless urged them to return to private life and become, once more, loyal citizens of the republic. He then followed his own advice, avoiding politics and retiring to the presidency of a small Virginia college. Never disavowing the cause for which he fought, nor doubting the valor of his men, Lee gave the appearance of having gracefully accepted fate. And the third factor that ensured Lee's honored status even in the North was the admiration for his military "genius." Douglass acerbically remarked that it would seem that "the soldier who kills the most in battle, even in a bad cause, is the greatest Christian, and entitled to the highest place in heaven."[60]

Part of the explanation for the phenomenon Douglass was observing was that the scale of the killing between 1861 and 1865 did little to dent the romantic allure of military combat, while a generation of men whose formative experience was in arms laid the foundations for a society in which military experience and acumen was held in the highest esteem. Although the sardonic writing of Ambrose Bierce foreshadowed modernist anti-war revulsion, what most characterized the post-war North was the endurance of the ideal of heroic warfare.

The same, incidentally, was true in Britain, where the American war was regarded with a mixture of horror and fascination. In a speech to military cadets in Woolwich not long after Appomattox, the artist and critic John Ruskin, who needless to say had never seen a shot fired in anger, argued that in war "the natural restlessness and love of contest among men are disciplined, by consent, into beautiful—though it may be fatal—play." Out of war, Ruskin asserted, came "all the highest sanctities and virtues of humanity" including art.[61] (If Ruskin ever saw Rothermel's painting, which he did not, he might have approved of the artistic ambition, but it is less certain that it would have justified his confidence that art, like war, built the moral foundations of society.) It was in this context that Lee and Jackson became celebrated figures in Britain. Of the two, Jackson was the more romantic—a statue of Stonewall in Richmond, Virginia, was paid for by a group of (mainly Conservative party-supporting) British admirers and John Greenleaf Whittier's famous poem about Barbara Frietchie—the old lady who defiantly hung out a Stars and Stripes when the "rebel tread, Stonewall Jackson riding ahead" rode down her street—became a staple of school poetry recitations.[62] Jackson is in the enemy camp in that poem, but he's a hero nonetheless: "Who touches a hair of yon gray head / Dies like a dog! March on!" he said. Yet it was Lee's gray-eyed dignity that made him—even more than Stonewall—the beau ideal of a military leader, while his supposed tactical audacity cast him as a genius in the art of war. Even though he was on the losing side, Lee, in death at least, was woven into a new self-image of the United States as a nation defined by military prowess. Before the Civil War, Americans fetishized France as the fountainhead of military wisdom; afterward they fetishized only themselves.

The valorization of Lee did not indicate that Northerners were succumbing en masse to a neo-Confederate narrative of the war. Far from it. By paying emotionally charged respects to a foe whom they had always admired—indeed, until Gettysburg, feared—they were reinforcing their own military achievement in beating him. It suited both their own sense of achievement and the goal of post-war national unity to imagine the late conflict as an epic test of martial strength among men of honor and virtue. The post-war "cult of reunion" was powerful, but it embraced rather than supplanted other political frameworks for understanding the meaning of Gettysburg and the war in general.

*   *   *

It is sometimes said that the American Civil War disproves the maxim that the winners write the history, but this is not really true. The white South's Lost Cause narrative was a potent way of portraying themselves as the true victims of the war, and victimhood, when appropriately garbed with heroic struggle, has a strong psychological allure. But ultimately the meaning of the war—and thus of Gettysburg's significance—was framed more by white Northerners than any other group. The impulse for reconciliation, and therefore the recasting of former foes as chivalrous warriors, was not a political concession so much as a strategic reincorporation of Southern elites back into the national fold. If the price of national stability and expansion was to marginalize the memory of emancipation and to romanticize the gentlemanly qualities of Robert E. Lee, that, to increasing numbers of writers and opinion formers by the 1870s and 1880s, was a price they were eager to pay.

It was, quite rightly, enraging to Frederick Douglass and like-minded fighters for racial justice, including many Union veterans, that the political cost of the romanticization of the war was the effective abandonment by the Federal government of any serious attempt to regulate race relations in the South. By the 1890s, Supreme Court decisions and the exigencies of party politics had left the Fourteenth and Fifteenth Amendments as little more than paper promises. A new "Jim Crow" South was emerging, in which hard racial segregation was legally imposed.

As this was happening, Gettysburg was being elevated higher and higher as, in the words of the early historian of the battle, Jacob Hoke, "the nation's shrine."[63] A guidebook by Jacob Wert, a Gettysburg resident who was an eyewitness to the battle, called it a "National Mecca." Christianizing his metaphor, Wert enthused that visitors to the battlefield would be walking over "the most consecrated ground this world contains, except the path of the Savior of the world as He ascended the rugged heights of Calvary."[64] Some of Hoke's and Wert's Northern readers were doubtless depressed by the betrayal of the "freedmen" after the end of Reconstruction, yet they surely would have unhesitatingly agreed that the most important "fruits of victory" had nevertheless been secured. After all, slavery, and with it the threat to democracy and global freedom, had been definitively destroyed. If former slaves were being denied their equal rights as citizens, such Northerners might muse, that was regretful, even disgraceful, but it did not change the fact that Northern victory had wrought the uncompensated expropriation of millions of dollars of "property" and therefore the permanent destruction of the Slave

Power. Moreover, the formal re-establishment of white supremacy in the former Confederacy did not change the most important fact on the ground, which was that the nation was reunited. In this most fundamental respect, Northerners conceded not one iota to the defeated white South. Whatever the ongoing capacity of Lost Cause writers to inflect dominant narratives of the war, Gettysburg's meaning was more shaped by a nationalism grounded in a faith that America was God's chosen nation.

Women were prominent in this Christian nationalist framing of the meaning of Gettysburg. An early example was *Idyls of Gettysburg,* a collection of poems published in 1872 by Miss E. Latimer, a former schoolteacher from Shippensburg, Pennsylvania. The profits from the sale of her slim volume benefited the National Orphans' Home, established in Gettysburg for the children of fallen Union soldiers.[65] Miss Latimer's aim, she stated, was to remind readers of the "pointed moral...lesson" of Gettysburg.[66] This was that slavery had fueled a shameful rebellion against law and right. At the repulse of Pickett's Charge, "the last rivet had fallen from the shackles of the slave," she wrote.[67] But the poems do not dwell on the lives or fate of enslaved people. Emancipation is crucial but is enfolded into a larger narrative of national rebirth. The main theme of the idyls is the imagery of redemption through sacrifice: "In death a nation's new-born life / Where peace was made thro' fiercest strife."[68]

Miss Latimer's idyls mourned and vindicated the death of soldiers, but it was the battle's only known civilian and only known female casualty who became perhaps its best-known embodiment of Christian virtue. Mary Virginia ("Jennie") Wade, killed in her house on Baltimore Street on the morning of July 3 by a stray bullet while (according to legend) she was kneading dough. Written in 1864, a poem by Mary Henderson Eastman about "the heroine, sweet Jenny Wade" became widely known after the war, reproduced in periodicals aimed at women, and in children's primers. The poem ended:

> For you poured out her bosom's tide
> For you, dear land, she died!
> Well may you weep!
>   But her loved name
> Will every patriot heart inflame—
> Will every coward bosom shame!
> Ne'er from this country's altar's fade
> The memory of Jenny Wade![69]

It is a salutary reminder of the danger of imposing political labels on people that the author Mary Eastman had acquired fame before the Civil War as a defender of slavery. Her first novel was a pro-slavery tract satirizing *Uncle Tom's Cabin*. But she was horrified by secession, and her Unionism compelled her to support emancipation. Eastman was far from the only writer to alight on the death of Jennie Wade, but her poem has good claim to be the creative work that first highlighted the story. Wade was a virtuous woman killed instantly in a domestic setting, the innocent casualty of fratricidal strife. In Eastman's telling, Wade's death answered the question about the "meaning" of Gettysburg. It did so not by blurring the distinction between the two sides but by turning Gettysburg into the moment of national rebirth through sacrifice. The triumph of the Union through blood sacrifice was a lesson in how self-sacrifice and discipline could forge a society founded on moral order. In this telling, ending slavery was unquestionably righteous but had no necessary implications for the ordering of a post-emancipation society. Or at least not any on which most people needed to trouble themselves for too long.

The miraculous healing waters of Gettysburg eventually dried up, at least as a revenue source. After a brief period of commercial success in the 1870s and 1880s, the Springs Hotel went bankrupt. And in 1913, half a century after the battle, the building was destroyed by fire.[70] But Gettysburg did not need spring water to attract visitors. The town's promoters—the local business owners, the historians, and the veterans who wanted their struggle to be meaningful—had known all along the reason why Gettysburg mattered: because it was here that the war, with the fate of human liberty in the balance, was determined.

7

Gettysburg as the Nation's "Turning Point," *c.*1880–1933

It is a key concept in the Gettysburg story: the idea of the battle as the "turning-point." As the Dickens scholar Robert Douglas-Fairhurst has pointed out, in Victorian Anglo-American culture it was a much-discussed term, almost always written with a hyphen, which served to focus attention on the point of rotation, as on the pin of a compass.[1] When it came to Gettysburg, the point of that compass was focused on a precise time and place—the spot in the Union line on July 3 where Confederate attackers briefly broke through and then were repulsed. As James T. Long wrote in 1891, summarizing the consensus among Civil War writers of that era, "It was at Gettysburg where the cursed rebellion reached its high-water mark. It was at Gettysburg where, beyond a doubt, it received its death blow at the stone wall of the bloody angle, where Pickett's charge terminated, where the battle of Gettysburg ended, where the heroism of the men of the Union Army kept our glorious country undivided."[2] Many people, from both North and South, helped to make Gettysburg the turning point of the war, from local town boosters to foreign writers, but critical to the story were the state and Federal governments, which provided funds, and (from 1895 when the Gettysburg National Military Park was created by Act of Congress) direct ownership and regulation of the battlefield. National politicians, many of whom, in the late nineteenth century were veterans, came to Gettysburg and wanted to be seen there, reinforcing the symbolic connection between the battle and the nation that had been articulated by Lincoln.

To emphasize the turning point was also to reflect on the role of Providence, which, Victorian Americans imagined, had bestowed upon Gettysburg a special significance in American and therefore in world history. Whatever the mistakes of mortals, the divine must have been at play. In 1872, the Reverend Frederick Arnold published a two-volume work reflecting on "'turning-points' both in the history of the race and in the history of the individual."[3] For Arnold, the "turning-points" were not "mere accidents." They had a "moral significance" and were "fraught with special lessons."[4] For Arnold, "turning-points" were ultimately the work of Providence. Since "the world is the appointed theatre for the exercise of [man's] intelligence and his energies," we may expect that "the providence of God will interpose at critical conjunctures to favour the ends which He designed."[5] In a phrase that was especially relevant to the fascination with Gettysburg as a turning point, Arnold observed, *If something had happened which did not happen, what would have happened afterwards? is a kind of speculation which is now much in fashion." But enjoyable as such speculation may be, his key point was that nations, like individuals, were subject to God's "sword of judgment" and might be diverted, at a turning point, "from error" and be "led back to truth."[6] This was an argument developed by a late nineteenth-century popular author, Henry Mann, whose didactic output included works with titles like *Handbook for American Citizens, Or Things Every Patriot Should Know* (1895). In a book called *Turning Points in the World's History* (1897), Mann saw Gettysburg as the culmination of a series of turning points beginning with "the birth of the savior." Gettysburg, he wrote, was "universally regarded as the decisive conflict of the Rebellion." After it, a "new spirit" animated Union troops who saw "that they could defeat the Confederates under the ablest Confederate commander, and the depression of former disasters was lifted from the breasts of our soldiers." For Mann, the significance of this "Providential" battle was its role in national consolidation. Had the Confederates won it would have temporarily stayed the inexorable tide of destiny, much as Bannockburn delayed but could not halt the Union of England and Scotland.[7] Gettysburg was "the culminating point in the great struggle,"[8] "the supreme crisis,"[9] "the great event of the century."[10] A common refrain among nineteenth-century writers was to compare Gettysburg not just with Waterloo but also with Marathon.[11] The Battle of Marathon in 490BC, in which an Athenian army defeated the invading Persians, was the first of the "fifteen battles" deemed by Sir Edward Creasy in his popular work to have been the "most decisive" in human history. And like Henry Mann or most of the other weavers of the idea of Gettysburg as the turning point, Creasy's theory of historical development ultimately rested on Providence. Although his criteria for decisiveness rested on a secular judgment about "cause and effect" and although his descriptions dwelt much on the decisions of commanders and on what appeared to be "mere" chance, Creasy sonorously declared that in all "we recognize emphatically the wisdom and power of the Supreme Lawgiver, the Design of the Designer."[12]

Among the American writers eager to add Gettysburg to Creasy's roster of great battles was John Watts De Peyster, a writer on "the art of war," best known for his trenchant defense of Dan Sickles' Gettysburg adventurism.[13] Although De Peyster gave honorable mentions to Shiloh, Antietam, Stone River, and Nashville, he was in no doubt about Gettysburg's preeminence as the moment when, had things gone differently, the South could have won the war. De Peyster, a board member of the Gettysburg Battlefield Memorial Association, was unusual, not to say perverse, in arguing that Lee's mistake in the Pennsylvania campaign was not that he was too rash but that he was too cautious.[14] Lee's true target, De Peyster argued, should have been Philadelphia, just as Napoleon's was Vienna. Instead of emulating Napoleon in 1805 by focusing on his true target, Lee instead emulated Sweden's Gustavus Adolphus, who, after the Battle of Breitenfeld in 1631 during the Thirty Years' War, chose not to march directly on Vienna and so missed the opportunity to dictate terms in the enemy's capital. Lee "should have crossed the Susquehanna" and "tried for

Philadelphia," De Peyster wrote, blithely disregarding the fact that Lee tried to do exactly that and was foiled by the destruction of the Columbia Bridge.[15]

For the white South, the narrative function of Gettysburg was as the turning point when all was lost. If one were to ask why it was that Southerners commemorated their defeat at Gettysburg more than they did their many victories in the Virginia theater—at Chancellorsville, Fredericksburg, or Second Manassas for example—the answer would surely be that since, in the end, Confederate armies were undeniably defeated, it was emotionally necessary to identify a single pivotal moment when all was lost. The glorious, plucky victories were the clinching evidence of Southerners' military prowess, even against long odds. But since the cause was lost, the narrative required a moment of catastrophic reversal. The alternatives were to recognize systemic failings, a far less romantic endeavor, or, still worse, to question whether secession (and therefore war) had been a mistake in the first place, which was literally unthinkable to most white Southerners since it would invalidate their enormous sacrifice.

In the immediate aftermath of Gettysburg, there is no evidence that the soldiers of Lee's army thought they had just fought the battle that would determine the war. But the notion took hold as soon as the first drafts of Lost Cause histories were written including by the man who coined the phrase, Edward A. Pollard. A young man in a hurry who was to die in 1872 at the age of 41, Pollard spent the war as an editor of the influential *Richmond Examiner*, churning out several best-selling books charting the war's course from a Confederate point of view. In 1866, he published his most influential work, *The Lost Cause: A New Southern History of the War of the Confederates*. Gettysburg looms large. It was then and there that the Confederates came closest to peace on their terms. The "moral effect of defeating Meade's army" would have been profound: New York, Philadelphia, and Washington would have been "uncovered" while "the vitals of the Confederacy were untouched."[16] In even more purple prose, John Esten Cooke, who served with Jeb Stuart, was convinced that at Gettysburg, "not only was the most precious blood of the South poured out like water—here the fate of her great sovereignties was decided. Gettysburg determined, for long years to come, at least, the destiny of the North American Continent. Here was the real end of the great struggle, not at Appomattox."[17] It was "one of those great contests which sum up and terminate an epoch."[18] But if Gettysburg was therefore the "American Waterloo," there was a twist. To commemorate Wellington's epochal victory over Napoleon, a mound was constructed on the battlefield surmounted by a British lion. But Cooke wryly warned Northerners that "the world" would say that at Gettysburg the monument should be to Lee.[19] This was the sly rhetorical maneuver that summed up the white South's creation of the Lost Cause. Even a battle so devastating that it could be dubbed the "American Waterloo" was ultimately a tribute to Southern valor. So, to the defeated, in this case, came the spoils.

* * *

The story of how Gettysburg became *the* turning point of the war takes us back to the battlefield itself. The landscape which in Lincoln's words had been "hallowed" and "consecrated" by the men who fell has been literally shaped by successive waves of veterans' groups, town boosters, entrepreneurs, and bureaucrats. Every generation has reinvented the battlefield, pulling down visitor attractions and building new ones, creating new sensations and disparaging the old, all the while doing so in the interests of honoring the dead and bringing the tourist dollars into what would otherwise be just another rural town in the pretty rolling hills of South Central Pennsylvania.

It was helpful that Gettysburg was relatively accessible by rail to the big cities of the Northeast. The Springs Hotel was just one of many new businesses set up to cater to the tourist trade. And, under the leadership of the lawyer and town booster David McConaughy, the Gettysburg Battlefield Memorial Association (GBMA) set out to design the stage set of the battlefield. The GBMA was a pioneering organization, the first to set out systematically a vision for commemoration on a battlefield site.[20] McConaughy envisioned formal carriage drives along the main lines of battle, and an observation tower on Little Round Top.[21] But unlike some later custodians of the battlefield, the GBMA under McConaughy's leadership prioritized landscape preservation, aiming to "hold and preserve the battlegrounds of Gettysburg...with the natural and artificial defenses, such as they were at the time of said battle." The early blueprint envisioned "such memorial structures as a generous and patriotic people may aid to erect, to commemorate the heroic deeds, the struggles and triumphs of their brave defenders," but imagined those memorials to be few and discreet—a far cry from the memorial park that Gettysburg was to become.[22] The first markers on the battlefield, placed in the late 1870s, were informational rather than formally commemorative. One was placed on Little Round Top to show where Colonel Strong Vincent had fallen, for example, while in 1879 the 2nd Massachusetts erected a tablet listing their unit's positions.[23] Others quickly followed on the assumption that the deeds of those who had visible markers would predominate in the imaginative reconstruction of the battle by future generations. Before too long, however, regiments and, by the mid-1880s, state legislators, were erecting grandiose monuments rather than merely descriptive markers.

The GBMA lost momentum when state appropriations dried up after the economic crash of 1873, but was revitalized in 1880 when the organization of Union veterans, the Grand Army of the Republic (GAR), purchased a controlling interest, paid off the Association's debts, and ousted McConaughy. Under the GAR's leadership, and with the recession of the 1870s over, state governments began to make significant donations, beginning with Massachusetts and Pennsylvania. In 1884, the GBMA established a "Committee on Legislation" to lobby state governments for funding and, within five years, every Northern state represented in the battle had made an appropriation, totaling over half a million dollars.[24] This public funding, supplemented by philanthropy from wealthy veterans, financed the growing array of state monuments, the purchase of more land, and the development of grand avenues, the first being along Cemetery Ridge.[25] Visitors could view the battlefield from their carriages as if it were a parkland—with the topography maintained as it had been in 1863, but the hedges and fences mostly gone, the mess and detritus of battle replaced by neatly mown grass, and brand-new finely engraved marble monuments marking the positions of Union troops. Memorials both sacralized the landscape and attracted visitors. A veteran who visited in 1893 compared the monuments to the ancient Greeks' commitment to teaching their children the names of those who had fallen at the Battle of Thermopylae. The monuments, he wrote, are "silent sentinels to watch over the ground of the pivotal point in the great struggle, and...an object lesson to future generations."[26] Object lesson, in this sense, had a literal meaning: the monuments were the material focus, intended to encode meaning for successive generations. The lessons to be drawn were of the heroism of individuals and of regiments. And in large part thanks to the encouragement and organizational power of the GAR, Gettysburg became the preeminent place for regimental reunions, providing veterans and their families with new experiences to overlay their memories of the battle.

After the GAR took control of the GBMA, the role of Gettysburg's principal interpreter and promoter passed from McConaughy to a commercial artist and irrepressible self-promoter called John Badger Bachelder. Just days after the battle ended, the thirty-eight-year-old Bachelder had arrived in the town and spent several weeks interviewing wounded soldiers in hospitals, sketching the sights, and mapping every fence and road. He then obtained permission from General Meade to travel to the Army of the Potomac in Virginia where he ingratiated himself with the officers and conducted interviews, from which he compiled trunk-loads of notes. "From the information thus obtained," Bachelder wrote with breathtaking hubris, "I have traced the movements of *every regiment and battery* from the commencement to the close of the engagement."[27] On the basis of this research, he produced an extraordinarily detailed "isometric" map of the battlefield, a panorama of the battle, as if seen from a "balloon two miles east of

Figure 7.1. John Bachelder's "isometric map" of the Gettysburg battlefield, showing topography and troop positions.

GREAT BATTLES

Gettysburg," topographically detailed and precisely calibrated to convey a sense of the movement of troops, color-coded to show the positions of regiments and batteries in each of the three days.[28]

Although he was often styled "Colonel" due to his appointment as Lieutenant Colonel of the Pennsylvania state militia, Bachelder had never seen active combat. But he spent the next three decades making Gettysburg both his obsession and his livelihood. Copies of his isometric map became hot property. Never shy about soliciting compliments, Bachelder sought, and received, endorsements from dozens of distinguished figures whether or not they were present at the battle.[29] After the war, Confederates bought copies, too; even Robert E. Lee was said to have owned one. As the historian Jim Weeks has written, the map "transformed the monstrous conflict into an edifying image appropriate for the parlor."[30]

But the map was only the start of Bachelder's Gettysburg work. Having created a lithograph-printing business, he commissioned the well-known artist James Walker to produce a grand painting of Pickett's Charge, *The Repulse of Longstreet's Assault*, under Bachelder's strict supervision, and then sold lithographed copies for $50 each.[31] The painting is vast in scale and Bachelder took great pride in its "accuracy" although he made what seems to have been the cardinal error of trying to encompass within one painting the story of the whole battle. Some light is shed on what is going on if the viewer inspects the accompanying "key," but otherwise the painting appears to be nothing more than a bewildering mass of men facing in different directions. As the historian Edwin Coddington put it, with disarming bluntness, the painting is as "moving as a blueprint, but not as accurate."[32] Compared to Rothermel's painting, Walker's lacks emotion; compared to Bachelder's isometric map, it is just confusing. Nevertheless, Bachelder made money out of it. He toured the country with the painting, which measured 20 by 7½ feet, giving lectures.[33] He also wrote the first major tourist guide, published in 1873, a book that was both informative and lyrical: "The traveler now studies the towering eminences, the rocky ravines, the woody coverts, the open fields, the meandering waters, and all the vast region over which destruction and death held carnival for three long days, with an intensity of interest which the simple charms of nature never would have aroused."[34]

Bachelder devoted the rest of his life to making Gettysburg *the* decisive battle of the war. His career was invested in making those three days in July 1863 stand apart from all the other supposedly lesser confrontations. In 1869, Bachelder convened a gathering of more than a hundred officers of the Army of the Potomac. They stayed in the Springs Hotel, curing their ailments in between traversing the fields with Bachelder, answering his questions as he took copious notes (Confederate officers were invited but did not attend).[35] And in the following years, he walked the battlefield with hundreds of retired officers, identifying the positions of their units at various stages. Wherever you may stand on the battlefield today, Bachelder will have been there before you, his walrus moustache quivering as he interrogated veterans, or, increasingly, told them things they did not know. And before long, even those who had been there deferred to Bachelder's superior knowledge. "I therefore think you know as much about the location of my command as I do," Union General Joseph Carr told him.[36] It is probably fair to say that no single person worked harder and with more success to shape the meaning of the battle than Bachelder.

The Federal government endorsed Bachelder's work, giving him the status of, in effect, the battle's official historian. In 1880, Congress appropriated the enormous sum of $50,000 to pay him to use all the data he had collected to write a definitive, objective history of the battle, "illustrated by diagrams."[37] Bathetically, all Bachelder was able to produce was a compilation of documents, rendered obsolete by the production of the 108-volume *Official Record of the War of Rebellion*, which began publication in 1881. As he must have realized when he began to try and stitch together a coherent narrative, Bachelder's hundreds of first-person accounts provided a tangle of complicated and conflicting information. As one veteran wisely said to him, "What a herculean task, to separate the truth from the falsehood in the

GREAT BATTLES

multitude of reports that have rained down on you since 1863."[38] And as another tartly observed of Bachelder's oral histories, "Some of these accounts are simply silly. Some are false in statement. Some are false in inference. All in some respects are untrue."[39] The letters and transcripts collected by Bachelder remain essential reading for any serious student of the battle, but they are at least as interesting for what they tell us about the limits of individual memory—especially when there is much at stake—as they are about what actually happened. "It is difficult in the excitement of battle," wrote General Abner Doubleday to Bachelder in 1885, "to see every thing going on around us for each has his own part to play and that absorbs his attention to the exclusion of everything else. People are very much mistaken when they suppose because a man is in a battle, he knows all about it."[40] And yet, in the mountain of testimony Bachelder collected, two themes stand out: the impossibility of knowing what really happened, alongside a certainty that the correspondent himself had played an important role.[41]

So, Bachelder failed to write the definitive battle account, but he succeeded in something more important. It was he who almost single-handedly deserves the credit for inventing the most holy of holy places on the battlefield: the "high-water mark." For Bachelder, the key to the whole battle, and thus to the war and the whole fate of liberty, lay in the clump of trees near the center of Cemetery Ridge which had been one of the visual markers guiding the Confederate advance on the third day, and the point in the Union line where rebel troops temporarily broke through. Bachelder later cultivated an anecdote explaining how he had come to realize the importance of this spot. He had walked the battlefield in 1869 with Colonel Walter Harrison, who had been on Pickett's staff at the time of the fatal assault on the third day.

> We spent several hours under the shade cast by the Copse of Trees [Bachelder recalled], when [Harrison] explained to me what an important feature that copse of trees was at the time of the battle, and how it had been a landmark towards which Longstreet's assault of July 3d 1863 had

been directed. Impressed with its importance, I remarked, "Why, Colonel, as the battle of Gettysburg was the crowning event of this campaign, this copse of trees must have been the high water mark of the rebellion." To which he assented, and from that time on, I felt a reverence for those trees.... The thought of naming the copse of trees the "High Water Mark of the Rebellion," and the idea of perpetuating its memory by a monument, was mine.[42]

As the historian Thomas Desjardin has pointed out, "copse" is not a common word in American English. It is rarely used in the US other than for that particular spot. For this reason, "copse" helps to confer an ethereal quality on the magical centerpiece of the Confederate quest which, had they succeeded, would have yielded riches unbound. And in his published memoir, Walter Harrison played his own part in building up the significance of the "High Water Mark." Recalling his feelings as he waited for Pickett's Charge to begin, Harrison wrote, "The great question of that campaign, perhaps of the whole war, was hanging on the next few hours. Success or defeat to either side would be an almost final blow given and received."[43] It matters little whether this big claim is plausible. The point is that people wanted to believe it, and Bachelder, by inventing the "High Water Mark," gave them a visually memorable stage setting. Conveniently, the monument is near the geographic center of the battlefield, visible from afar, and with a commanding view.

In the pamphlet he wrote to accompany Walker's painting, Bachelder described "the copse of trees in the center of the picture, the 'High Water Mark' of the rebellion."[44] If Gettysburg was the "Waterloo of the Confederacy," then the "copse" that Bachelder identified was the exact spot where the Confederacy was repulsed, and the republic saved. In June 1892, with great ceremony, the "High Water Mark" monument was dedicated. Designed by Bachelder, it is an open bronze book symbolizing "the record of history," set on a granite altar-like plinth and base in front of the copse. It lists the units in Longstreet's assaulting force as well as the Union troops defending, the only monument on the battlefield to recognize specific units from both sides.[45]

Figure 7.2. The "High Water Mark of the Rebellion" Monument, situated near the spot on Cemetery Ridge where Confederate attackers briefly broke through Union lines on July 3. The monument was the brainchild of John B. Bachelder, who invested most of his career in making Gettysburg the most important battle of the Civil War and perhaps of modern history. The monument was unveiled in 1892 and is notable for listing both the Confederate attacking units and the Union defending units. Almost all other Gettysburg monuments commemorate one or the other side.

Bachelder's official role with the GBMA in the 1880s was the "Superintendent of Tablets and Legends," a post which gave him immense power to shape how the battlefield appeared and was experienced by visitors. By 1890, the battlefield—or at least those portions of it under the ownership of the association—was a curated parkland dotted with three hundred pillars, statues, and granite slabs. When veterans or state legislatures wanted to erect a memorial, Bachelder had to approve the location, design, and inscription. Under his regime, a memorial had to be in "real bronze or granite" and the inscription had to avoid sectional antagonism.[46] The most important question, though, was not a monument's appearance but its location. The GBMA passed a resolution stating that markers should denote battle lines—in other words, where a unit started from rather than their furthest point of advance.[47] But "secondary" markers were also allowed to show the advance position of troops, which inevitably generated fierce competition about which unit had advanced furthest or had withstood enemy attacks for the longest time with each protesting that their motives were, as one retired Colonel put it, "simply to place the regiment in history where it belonged."[48]

Some of these spats were venomous. One especially fraught case was over the positioning of a monument to the 72nd Pennsylvania, which had played a role on July 3 defending the center of the Union line, though quite how important a role was a matter of dispute. Although the regiment unquestionably suffered significant casualties, accounts differed about precisely when they had entered the fray. Bachelder determined that the regimental monument should be placed 64 meters behind the Union front line, which outraged the regimental association. Fortunately for the veterans, a small parcel of land just in front of the stone wall was still in private hands. They bought it with the intention of erecting a second monument at what they claimed had been their forward position, only for the GBMA to argue that, under their 1863 state charter, they had the absolute right to determine the placement of monuments anywhere on the battlefield even on land they did not own. A court battle ensued, which the regimental association and its allies in the press, and with the support of Gettysburg veteran Pennsylvania Governor James A. Beaver, presented as a David and Goliath struggle pitting honest veterans against the "powerful corporation" that was the GBMA. The regiment won the case and eventually built their monument on the spot they wanted.[49] This and other battles forced Bachelder's resignation as Superintendent of Tablets and Legends, though he continued to seize every opportunity to influence the battlefield.

* * *

Up until the 1890s, Gettysburg was exclusively a Union shrine, with no Confederate memorials on the field, but Bachelder was one of many with a sentimental attachment to the project of reconciliation between the two sides. The core purpose of the GBMA remained to commemorate Union victory but, increasingly, the victors saw the advantages of including the defeated, if only in order to demonstrate through rituals of reconciliation how unthinkable it would be for the nation to break apart once again. In 1865, Bachelder invited Confederate veterans to help him locate and mark the positions of their units and did so again once he assumed his official position with the GBMA in the 1880s.[50] At first, he struggled to find Southerners who would cooperate. Walter Harrison's visit in 1869 was unusual. General Longstreet had agreed to be interviewed, but his pariah status probably made it even less likely that other general officers would do so.[51] General James L. Kemper grumpily refused a request for information on the grounds that any appearance of his command in a "northern version of the battle of Gettysburg" would "bear too much resemblance to the exhibition of the captives behind the triumphal car of The Roman Imperator to suit either my taste or my principles."[52]

Unsurprisingly, however, the early efforts at Confederate memorialization on the battlefield were fraught with difficulty. The first marker was placed on Culp's Hill in 1886 to a Maryland Infantry regiment who had fought there against Union troops from their own state.[53] But the Maryland Confederates wanted to place their monument at the point where they had broken through Union lines on July 2 while the GMBA, having hurriedly passed a resolution to this effect, insisted that it be situated at their battle line. The compromise was a monument at the foot of the hill on the battle line but also a position marker showing the extent of their advance, which seemed, in fact, like a win for the Confederates. The following year, survivors of Pickett's division asked for permission to erect a monument at the spot where General Lewis Armistead had fallen, inside Union lines near the "High Water Mark." This was too much for the GBMA who insisted that the association instead place their monument at the point from which the division had stepped off at the start of the assault on July 3, on the new avenue being constructed on Seminary Ridge. Bachelder told the Southerners that he had received "bushels of letters" from people "bitterly opposed" to the plan.[54] After a few weeks of tense correspondence, a compromise was found, for although Pickett's division's request for a monument on Cemetery Ridge was denied, Bachelder was more than happy to place a marker behind Union lines showing where Brigadier General Lewis Armistead fell.[55] For Bachelder, of course, a visual indicator of how far the Confederates had gotten before being repulsed reinforced the narrative importance of his "High Water Mark." As he told Congress in 1889, in a letter urging them to appropriate public money for the purpose, stones marking Confederate lines would "increase the value of Union monuments." No attempt had yet been made to mark the lines of the Army of Northern Virginia, Bachelder explained, and so the visitor must "depend entirely upon his imagination to locate them." Shall this knowledge "be preserved to history," Bachelder asked, "or shall it be allowed to be lost forever?"[56] For Northerners, emphasizing the strength of Pickett's Charge made the defense of their line more heroic; for Southerners it emphasized their valor in the face of overwhelming odds. But if the motivations of Northerners and Southerners in marking Confederate troop positions may have differed, they shared a commitment to the central idea of Gettysburg as the turning point of the war.

GREAT BATTLES

If erecting memorials to Confederate troops was still controversial in the 1880s, opposition was fading for reasons in addition to Bachelder's instrumental argument that they would enhance the achievements of Federal forces. One characteristic of the Civil War was that many participants expressed deeply ambivalent, often contradictory, feelings about the enemy. An example was Lieutenant Frank Haskell of Gibbon's brigade, who wrote a vivid account of the battle a few weeks after it had ended and sent it to his brother in Wisconsin. Haskell was killed at Cold Harbor in 1864, but his family had his account privately printed in 1878 and it became widely known when it was reprinted by his alma mater, Dartmouth College, in 1898, and then again by a veterans' association, the Loyal Legion, in 1908. Haskell was a natural storyteller. His description of Pickett's Charge, the dramatic high-water mark of the battle in his telling, bore more than an echo of Tennyson ("More than half a mile their front extends, more than a thousand yards the dull gray masses deploy"). But Haskell was one of many, even apparently in the midst of war, who respected the enemy's bravery, writing that Lee's men "showed a determination and valor worthy of a better cause" and that "their conduct in this battle even makes me proud of them as Americans."[57] From such wartime recognition grew the chauvinistic post-war celebration of fortitude of the nineteenth-century's "greatest generation."

Moreover, by the 1880s, the influence of Southern Lost Cause writers on national culture was being felt. There was a "hard core" Confederate ideological project, marinaded in continuing hatred of Yankee invaders and burnished by the ladies of the United Daughters of the Confederacy (UDC) long into the twentieth century, but there was also a much softer version, one that spun nostalgic stories about the antebellum South and the pre-modern plantation idyl.[58] This latter sentimental Southernism took the sting out of sectional enmity, making it possible for Northerners to feel a retrospective sense of respect for their vanquished enemy's cause. Culturally, this shift was not so dissimilar to the romantic portrayal of indigenous peoples as noble warriors on the wrong side of history. In both cases, such indulgence on the part of the victors was possible once the defeated parties represented no military threat and national stability was assured. So, there were clear limits to this "cult of reunion," but it was the essential cultural backdrop to the "Blue/Gray" reunions— meetings of veterans from both sides—which began at Gettysburg in the late 1880s.

There had been occasions before the formal reunions when Confederate and Union veterans had met together at Gettysburg. In 1886, for example, Confederate cavalry officers including Fitzhugh Lee and Wade Hampton attended a GAR encampment, though their participation was described by a reporter as being solely to help Bachelder "locate the points of action."[59] But the first time that a formal "reunion" took place with each side given equal billing was in 1887. The initiative did not come from the GBMA but from the Union veterans of the Philadelphia Brigade who extended a "warm" invitation to the members of the Pickett's Division Association (their "comrades and countrymen"). At first, the GBMA's denial of their favored location for their divisional monument caused Pickett's men to refuse the invitation; if they could not come on their own terms, they would not come at all.[60] But in the end, flattery and the offer to pay full expenses, changed their minds and about two hundred Confederate veterans made the journey by rail to Gettysburg. They were accompanied by General Pickett's glamorous young widow LaSalle, who, at the climax of the ceremony, was presented with flowers arranged in the form of the division's badge as a token of the men's "love and reverence" for the woman who "bears the credit of having been the first woman who welded the Blue and the Gray together."[61]

In correspondence with the Philadelphia Brigade, the Secretary of Pickett's Divisional Association expressed hope that "the day may come when all lines between the North and the South—the Blue and the Gray—shall have forever disappeared." He envisioned veterans from both armies meeting one day at Gettysburg to dedicate a "*Union* monument (not alone for what was once called the Union side) but a memorial to the gallant men of both sides, expressive of the true

American motto: 'A Large Country and a Warm Heart.'"[62] Sentiments like this—the heartfelt acceptance of national supremacy, albeit on terms which insisted on full respect and dignity being accorded to the white South—were the essential precondition for the joint veterans' reunions.[63] Emotionally, the reunions reinforced the self-image of veterans on both sides. The actual experience of combat may have been traumatic, but for most it was the most exciting and meaningful thing in their lives.

It was no accident that the 1887 reunion brought together some of the surviving attackers and defenders of Pickett's Charge. It was easy for Union veterans to gush, with complete sincerity, about the valor of their opponents in that particular action and the flattery made it possible for former Confederates to take part without a sense of shame. They had lost the battle and thus the war, but they could take heart from their former enemies' recognition of their manly courage.[64] It almost gave them a retrospective moral victory. The reports of the reunion flowed with high Victorian sentiment. "Manly tears dropped from manly eyes, as those wearing the Blue grasped the hands of those who wore the Gray," wrote one observer. As the band played "Dixie" (the 1850s minstrel song adopted by the Confederacy as an unofficial anthem), there was "such an exhibition of American patriotism and fraternity as had never before been witnessed."[65]

The culmination of the reunion was a meeting at the Bloody Angle, where "comrades," as they now described themselves, from the Philadelphia Brigade and Pickett's division, dressed not in uniforms but in suits and white pith helmets, clasped hands. The *Philadelphia Inquirer* celebrated the meeting of "brothers" and noted that, now, twenty-four years after the battle, it was once again possible to remember July 4 not as the day when "Lee was beaten back by Meade" but as the anniversary of a political rather than a military event: the Declaration of Independence, the "greatest in the world's annals," which "declared the supremacy of the people over kingship" and "gave to the world the first enduring government of the people, by the people, for the people." The historical function of Gettysburg was therefore to have

HAND CLASP
Comrades Philadelphia Brigade and Pickett's Division
"Bloody Angle," July 4, 1887.

Figure 7.3. The meeting at the stone wall at the Bloody Angle between veterans of the Philadelphia Brigade and Pickett's Division on July 4, 1887.

recovered, through battle, the true meaning of the Declaration, just as Lincoln had articulated.[66]

The following year, the twenty-fifth anniversary of the battle, saw an even larger reunion culminating in an even grander re-enactment of Pickett's Charge, which from then on became a standard part of

GREAT BATTLES

every Gettysburg Blue/Gray reunion. Bachelder was thrilled by the sight. No doubt he saw himself as an impresario bringing the warring sides together, their wounds healed as much by the curated display of national harmony on the field as by the water of the Gettysburg springs.

The terms of the GBMA's charter precluded it from spending money marking Southern troop positions, and Northern state governments had no interest in doing so, but under its GAR leadership, the association pressed Congress to step in. By 1890, more than half of all congressmen were Civil War veterans and many were determined that the battlefields should be "a monument to them" before they "left this world," as a congressional committee report put it. Battlefield preservation was too important to be left to private associations or spotty philanthropic efforts: "It must be done by the National Government or remain undone."[67] And if Gettysburg was the national shrine, surely the nation should own it, ran the argument. The government established what they called "National Military Parks" at Chattanooga and Chickamauga in the early 1890s—the term indicating their status as nationalized spaces, free from the petty jealousies and potential sectional animosities of veterans' associations and supposedly on a higher plane than the commercial interests who, at least at Gettysburg, had an eye only for a quick buck.

In 1890, a Pennsylvania Congressman and Gettysburg veteran, Henry H. Bingham, introduced a bill to "mark the lines of battle and the positions of troops of the Army of Northern Virginia."[68] Bingham was especially well positioned to do this since he had been the Union officer who had tended to General Armistead after he was mortally wounded and been entrusted with the Confederate's personal effects. Recognizing that the GMBA was not able to do the work, Bingham's bill argued that if all troop positions were not properly marked they would soon be "lost to history." Inevitably, the man envisioned by the bill's author as being given primary responsibility for identifying troop positions with "plain, enduring tablets" under the government's auspices was John B. Bachelder. Having accumulated enemies even beyond the incensed ranks of the 72nd Pennsylvania, objections to Bachelder's proposed role prevented the passage of the bill for two years, but in 1893, an amendment to a different piece of legislation was passed, establishing a commission charged with the work of mapping the Gettysburg battlefield. Bachelder did not get everything he wanted (it set a limit of $10 per day in fees as opposed to the $25,000 per year he was seeking), but he snagged a seat on the new commission anyway. The following year, however, Bachelder died. His passing was lamented by many who appreciated the vast knowledge he had obtained and the work he had done, but undoubtedly with him gone it was easier for Congress to pass a new bill formalizing their control of the battlefield by establishing Gettysburg as a National Military Park. General Dan Sickles, once more a congressman, stole the credit for the passage of the bill and relished the title "father of the park." The GMBA duly passed ownership of its lands to the government.[69]

Over the following decade, the battlefield, now designated a "military park" was developed under the control of a commission which included a former Confederate officer. New avenues were laid out and better facilities for visitors were built, including observation towers (which were extensively used by military students from the United States service academies and from abroad). Tensions with commercial operators remained a constant theme—the park had a long-running feud with the operators of an electric trolleybus which went all the way to the Supreme Court (the park won, establishing its eminent domain rights but the trolleybus continued to operate for several years anyway until it finally went bust).[70] But visitor numbers increased and local residents and congressmen alike regarded the new governance arrangements as a success. "All roads lead to Gettysburg" were the opening lines in a photographic history of the battle, published on the fiftieth anniversary. "Every American feels at some time in his life that he would like to make the journey to Gettysburg."[71] The commissioners, testified one newspaper reporter, should take the credit for "beautifying and converting into a grand picture this historic field, and of perpetuating it as a great patriotic lesson for all time"[72]—sentiments with which Bachelder would heartily have approved.

Bachelder's dominance and dogmatism had made him enemies, but he played a vital role in turning Gettysburg into the dramatic centerpiece of the Civil War in the public imagination. He had always been drawn to the battle for its human drama as well as for its political and strategic significance. Those acres of land made "sacred" by the fighting were a stage set, its heroic combatants the actors. In no small measure due to the colonel's indefatigable work, the battlefield became an intensely familiar stage set in American culture. The place names of Gettysburg—the Peach Orchard, Devil's Den, Culp's Hill, Little Round Top—instantly conjured images of valor. As the early battle historian Alfred E. Lee put it, comparing the topography of Gettysburg to a Greek amphitheater, "the arena in which it was fought was well adapted to its scenic grandeur."[73] Thanks to Bachelder, the "High Water Mark" was added to that list; in his hands, the landscape of Gettysburg was encoded with stories that fed the narrative that it was at Gettysburg in those July days that the fate of the nation was determined.

* * *

The greatest of all the reunions took place half a century after the battle when fifty-five thousand veterans returned to Gettysburg. Old men now, they traveled on free railroad passes provided by their home states. One of the returning veterans claimed to be 112, though the press reported this assertion with polite disbelief. Once young soldiers, they had become factory workers, lawyers, salesmen, shopkeepers, clerks, or farmers. A few had been politicians. But their shared identity was as veterans of a war that had shaped their world. A majority of those who returned had fought in the Union Army, but the presence of some Confederate veterans was essential to the way the reunion was presented. Fifty years on, the ex-rebels came back to Gettysburg with pride and were treated by Northern pressmen with a respect approaching awe. After all, if Lee's army could have won—were it not for Providence or perfidy—Gettysburg was far from a place of humiliation, as other battlefields might have been. Reporters eagerly recorded the stories of these old men and photographers pictured them smiling and waving their hats in their old uniforms, their medals proudly pinned to their chests. There were speeches and brass bands, the singing of old wartime songs, and much eating and drinking. For four nights, the veterans slept under canvas in a "great camp" constructed by the regular US Army, ate in a mess tent with meals catered by over two thousand staff, and were treated by the Red Cross for complaints including heat exhaustion (the temperature was over a hundred degrees), constipation, and excessive alcohol consumption. Nine deaths were recorded during the reunion, perhaps a surprisingly low figure given the heat and the attendees' average age.[74] Congress had appropriated $150,000 to support the event, and many states also made contributions.[75]

Dan Sickles was there. As the last surviving top Union general, he made the most of it. July 2, 1913, was described in the program as "Sickles Day" and the man himself was given free rein to quote now-dead comrades praising his valor and tactical genius. By 1913, Sickles was able to recall General Oliver O. Howard telling him, "Sickles, God surely must have inspired you in making that advance movement. Here you were, a volunteer soldier, not a West Pointer. You did the same thing which Wellington did at Waterloo; you threw out a force in front of your line and held on. That holding on probably saved us the field."[76] No matter that he had not "held on": what price reality when there were myths to be weaved? Howard, eight years in his grave, was unable to provide corroboration. Sickles was in any case entirely in tune with the spirit of reconciliation that the anniversary meeting was intended to promote. "There will be a lot of Jonny Rebs there for the anniversary," Sickles wrote in *The New York Sun*, "and I want to shake the hands of every one of them...it will be the most wonderful reunion in the history of the world. I believe it will do more to hasten the return of brotherly feeling between the North and the South than any other single event."[77] The tone was self-congratulatory, and the messaging was all about the triumph, through tragedy, of the white American republic. The whiteness of the event was not just a measure of how few African Americans were present (those there were mostly working as waiters or porters), but a reflection of how completely the context of slavery and emancipation had been erased.

The climax of the grand reunion was a re-enactment of Pickett's Charge. Around a hundred former rebel soldiers advanced once more up the gentle rise toward the stone wall on the crest of Cemetery Ridge. A group of Union veterans were waiting for them. When the old men in gray reached the stone wall, instead of a fusillade of bullets and shell, they were met with cheers and handshakes. Reporters duly filed heartwarming stories. One was about a veteran of Armistead's brigade, shot and wounded at the Bloody Angle, who recalled having been given a swig of water by an unexpectedly kind Yankee soldier. When a Union veteran was heard telling the same story quite separately reporters eagerly reunited them and "the two old foes fell into each other's arms embracing."[78] LaSalle Pickett was there, too, of course, and newspaper reporters fell over themselves to record her observations, which, naturally, promoted her husband as America's greatest romantic hero.[79]

By 1913, harmony among the former foes was seen as the bedrock of the United States' ongoing capacity to advance human progress. "It matters little to you or me now, my comrades, what the causes were that provoked the war," the chairman of the Pennsylvania Anniversary Commission assured the assembled veterans at Gettysburg.[80] After five decades of rapid growth and transformation, after a low-cost, high-yield war against Spain and the creation of European-style overseas colonies, with US financial and military power having destroyed the resistance of indigenous people in the West and with new infrastructure binding the country from ocean to ocean, it now seemed unimaginable to most Americans that they had once killed each other and that their nationhood had faced an existential threat. But fifty years on, with the largest economy in the world, Americans had no reason to doubt their nation's global position. This story of national

Figure 7.4. The Fiftieth Anniversary Reunion, 1913: Union and Confederate veterans shake hands at the Bloody Angle, the point on the Union line where the attacking Confederates briefly broke through on July 3.

growth was an important theme in the language of reconciliation deployed in the run-up to the reunion. Commander-in-chief of the Union veterans' organization, the Grand Army of the Republic, promised his counterpart, the Commander-in-chief of the United Confederate Veterans, that at Gettysburg "all the wounds of our former strife [will] be healed" in order that "this people, as a united and vital force, may effectively and mightily solve the problems of our Nation's destiny in world affairs and human progress."[81]

In this context, it was pleasingly fitting, at least to white reporters, that President Woodrow Wilson was the first Southerner to hold that office since Reconstruction. In his Gettysburg address, fifty years after Lincoln's, President Wilson told the assembled veterans that the "quarrel" that led to the war was "forgotten"—indeed it was unmentioned and almost unimaginable. What was left was "the splendid valor, the manly devotion of the men then arrayed against one another, now grasping hands and smiling into each other's eyes."[82] Remarkable alchemy was surely at work here: one of the bloodiest conflicts in history, it turned out, had merely fused the warring parties together. "The great conflagration, which it was feared would consume our country," explained Secretary of War Lindley M. Garrison, "merely served to weld the different parts of it so firmly together and into such a perfect whole that no power can ever break it."[83] Here, gushed a celebratory 1913 history, "the two noblest armies in the history of mankind fought for principles which each believed to be just—only soon to meet on the same battlefield as a reunited people and clasp hands in loving brotherhood."[84]

The warm and celebratory tone of the 1913 reunion foregrounded soldiering as a test of heroic masculinity and obscured the politics that explained why the war was ever fought. A 1913 volume of photographs of the buildup and aftermath of the battle wove the images into a narrative of the cruelty of fate. A caption accompanying a photograph of a dead Confederate soldier in Devil's Den claimed that the photographer who took the picture returned to Gettysburg for the cemetery dedication in November and returned to the spot. There he found "the [soldier's] musket, rusted by many storms, still leaned against the rock; the remains of the boy soldier lay undisturbed within the moldering uniform."[85] These kinds of tragic vignettes helped create a sentimental and theatrical framing for the war. It celebrated the role of the individual amid the mass of modernity; it dwelt on contingency not structure. With segregation by now well entrenched and Black people effectively disenfranchised in almost all former Confederate states, an African American newspaper summarized the ideological work of the 1913 Gettysburg reunion as the effort to "cement the white man of the north and the white man of the south [even though] the south that enslaved the Negro once has re-enslaved him again."[86]

Among other things, the semi-centennial reunion provided a big boost to Gettysburg tourism. Tens of thousands flocked to see where the great battle had been fought, admired the craftsmanship of the

Figure 7.5. This photograph of a dead Confederate sharpshooter in Devil's Den was reprinted in Francis Trevelyan Miller, ed., *Gettysburg: A Journey to America's Greatest Battleground, in Photographs Taken by the World's First War Photographers While the Battle Was Being Fought. Official Presentation, Semi-Centennial* (New York: The Review of Reviews Company, 1913). The caption claimed that the photographer had returned to the site several months later to find the musket and the remains of the soldier still there, unburied and unmarked. Published at the time of the semi-centennial, the photographic history of the battle reinforced the common ground of shared valor and sacrifice on both sides.

bronze and marble statues, and were entertained in the evening in a town whose economy was now more dependent on tourism than on agriculture or manufacturing. In preparation for the influx of visitors, the Pennsylvania Railroad produced a booklet describing facilities in the town, explaining how to buy train tickets, and recounting the "movements of the Confederate and Union armies" with no commentary on the battle's "meaning" other than to reprint Lincoln's Gettysburg Address.[87] The most spectacular new visitor attraction was the installation of Paul Philippoteaux's cyclorama of Pickett's

Charge in a specially built round building on Baltimore Street. A 360-degree cylindrical painting, 42 by 377 feet, it was first displayed in Boston in 1884, one of a number of cycloramas of Civil War battles (other famous ones included Shiloh, Atlanta, and Vicksburg) that gave viewers an immersive battlefield experience without actually having to visit. Often the cycloramas would be displayed with three-dimensional objects in front—bushes, cannons, and the like—to intensify the experience. Ever since 1913, the Pickett's Charge cyclorama has been a fixture at Gettysburg (it was incorporated into the new Visitor Center in the early twenty-first century). The viewer of the cyclorama stands with Union defenders near the Bloody Angle on the afternoon of July 3. As they turn to view the scene from all angles, the viewer is enveloped in the place and the moment of the great turning point. By 1913, Gettysburg, both as a place and as the subject of storytelling, perfectly exemplified the entwined human impulses of war and play.

The US military retained a close association with Gettysburg. In the first decade of the twentieth century, the battlefield was used for summer encampments of the Pennsylvania National Guard. And since the War Department was in ultimate control of the battlefield, it was an obvious place for an infantry training camp after the US entered World War I in 1917, the camp commander assuring the chairman of the Gettysburg National Military Park commission that he regarded the battlefield as "sacred" and therefore troops would not "molest" the monuments. In 1918, the army's first training camp for tank warfare was established under the command of Dwight D. Eisenhower, then a captain in the army. Three thousand men were based there in the summer of 1918, together with some prototype tanks which fascinated the local population. And while the monuments may have been unmolested, when the camp was abandoned, the battlefield was left scarred by temporary roads and drains which was a source of irritation to the battlefield park authorities for several years after the war.[88]

* * *

It is a common feature of wars that the passing of the generation who fought led to a peak in efforts to commemorate the dead. In this instance the commemoration was one element in a ferocious political effort to maintain white supremacy by enacting "Jim Crow" laws that imposed racial segregation and disenfranchised African Americans. The performative patriotism of Confederate veterans—acknowledging their loyalty to the United States—was part of an implicit deal whereby their "cause" was acknowledged as just. Gettysburg served this purpose as did no other battle. While many Confederates willingly participated in the 1913 Gettysburg reunion, none wished to commemorate the fiftieth anniversary of Appomattox. When a proposal was put to Virginia Governor William Hodges Mann (a Confederate veteran) to hold a "peace reunion" in Richmond in 1915, he took to the pages of the *Confederate Veteran* to point out how sharply the proposed event would differ from that at Gettysburg. "The spirit of Gettysburg was of friendship and of kindly relations. It was not a celebration of victory or of defeat. It was an effort to bring the old soldiers together to cement kindly relations and to further the idea that all are American citizens," which was quite different from a "celebration of the passing and fall of a government."[89] In making this distinction, Confederates once again asserted their own present-day loyalty to the United States while also taking pride in their rebellion of the 1860s. Their paradoxical claim was that the Confederate cause was quintessentially an American cause; in fighting for the ideals of "states' rights" and "liberty" (as they claimed to have been doing), Confederates were not really rebels but true to the spirit of the Revolution of 1776. Through this alchemy, the Confederates were compelled to secede in defense of *American* values, and the reunified nation was all the better for the harsh lesson the South had given it in the importance of liberty.

In the early twentieth century, then, Northerners were more emotionally invested in romantic stories about reunion than were Southerners. The latter were often willing to take part in national ceremonies but, as the Civil War generation passed away, they retained a nagging anxiety that their cause was insufficiently respected by their erstwhile enemies. It was this impulse that explains the rapid growth in the first two decades of the twentieth century of the United Daughters of the Confederacy (UDC). It was (and remains) an ancestral organization, requiring members to be the direct lineal descendant of a Confederate soldier.[90] In 1907, the President-General of the UDC, Lizzie George Henderson, told the annual convention that "we [the daughters] are no accidental thing. God has brought us into existence for specific purposes."[91] Those purposes included defending the righteousness of white supremacy and the justice of the Confederate cause. While a rising generation of Southern politicians spoke of a "New South" which could attract Northern investment, the UDC co-founder Anna Raines denounced "the creed that there is no North or South, but one nation." No "true Southerner," she wrote, could "ever embrace this new religion."[92] No organization was ever as full-throated in its determination to transform military defeat into political and cultural victory. The UDC even appointed its own "historian general," Mildred Rutherford, a prolific writer and speaker who enchanted audiences with her lectures about the Old South, the beneficence of slavery, and the valor of Confederate troops. She was tireless in arguing that enslaved Africans were not "ill-treated," that secession was constitutional and therefore not a rebellion, that the North's coercion of the Confederacy was tyrannical and their abolition of slavery hypocritical and opportunist.[93] These "unbiased, impartial truths," Rutherford argued, were especially important as the ranks of the veterans thinned. The UDC and the United Confederate Veterans formed committees to "select and designate such proper and truthful history of the United States."[94] A "patriotic" young girl from Nashville, Mary Louise Morris, became a celebrity because she burned her school history book on the grounds that it "made the Yankees win all the battles." She was even invited to give an address to a United Confederate Veterans reunion, where she melted the hearts of the old soldiers by telling them that "though the flag be furled and mute be the drum, we your children shall ever teach, as we have been taught, that for all past as well as all future ages it is to the Confederate soldier that we look for the brightest and truest exemplar of courage, endurance, and patriotism."[95]

Some of this spirit of undying Confederate partisanship inspired the plan hatched by a group of Virginia veterans and politicians to erect on the field of Gettysburg a massive equestrian statue of General Lee. In 1908, the Virginia legislature appropriated money for the purpose.[96] However, even with the support of the War Department for the principle of a Lee statue on the field of his great defeat, the devil was in the details—or more precisely in the inscription. The original proposal from the Virginian Gettysburg Monument Commission were the words "They Fought for the Faith of their Fathers," which the chairman of the national park commission tartly declared to be "unquestionably in violation of the rule of the [War] Department" that monument inscriptions be without "censure, praise or blame." An increasingly irritable correspondence ensued, with the War Department man calling the chairman of the Virginia commission "particularly annoying."[97] In the end, the Virginians had to back down. But if the final inscription ("Virginia to Her Soldiers at Gettysburg") was suitably bland, the mere fact of creating a heroic statue to the rebel commander was statement enough, and if the War Department could exercise control over what was chiseled in granite, it had far less power to control the meanings bestowed on the monument at its unveiling. Eventually, in June 1917, just as the United States was entering another war, surviving veterans of the Army of Northern Virginia gathered on the battlefield not to play their role in a reunion pageant, as some of them had done four years earlier, but to proudly assert the righteousness of their Lost Cause. Mann's successor as Virginia governor, Henry Carter Stuart, was a wealthy businessman too young to have fought in the Civil War, but like so many of the second generation, he was, if anything, even more determined than his predecessor to make clear that the magnificent Lee statue was a statement of an unbowed South. The monument, Stuart said, was an "undying expression of the high ideals in which we of the South would this day sanctify." The war, Stuart asserted, was a quarrel over "divergent views of the Constitution of the United States, a battle between rival conceptions of sovereignty rather than one between a sovereign and its acknowledged citizens." The Confederates, therefore, were not "rebels," still less "traitors." The "ideals and the principles" for which they fought had given "life and strength" to the reunified nation now engaged in a European war under the leadership of Stuart's fellow second-generation Virginian, Woodrow Wilson.[98]

It was left to the Federal government's representative, Assistant Secretary of War, William M. Ingraham of Maine, the only Yankee amid a line-up of Virginians, to argue that the main lesson of Gettysburg was to validate American exceptionalism. "Nowhere in the civilized world can you find a similar case" in which only a generation after a great battle it "awakens no feelings of anger within the heart of any one." It was "truly characteristic of the American people" to be able to turn such savagery into unity.[99] Ingraham's repetition of Northerners' standard "reunion" line—that "we are not here to discuss the causes of the War or to comment on its results" but only "to pay a loving tribute to those who fell for a cause which *they believed* was just and right" struck a discordant note in the light of the speaker who followed him on to the podium, Leigh Robinson, a seventy-seven-year-old Confederate veteran and popular Lost Cause orator. Robinson was more than willing both to comment on the causes of the war and to assert that what he and his comrades had fought for was not just what they "believed" to be right but that "better proof could not be offered of the truth of a cause, than the truth to it before our eyes today." Nor, unlike many propagators of the Lost Cause, was Robinson reticent about talking of slavery ("the noblest melioration of an inferior race of which history can take note"). He told his audience that Lee had stood in "immortal protest" against the North's barbaric threat of servile insurrection. But most importantly, Robinson reasserted the most fundamental of all the Lost Cause project's claims: that the South had seceded because it was *more* American than the North, not less. The war, he claimed, had pitted "a tradition of free government" against a "chimera," a "sham." In the end, "the South did not desert the Union, the Union deserted the South."[100]

*   *   *

The most striking feature of the ceremonies for the Virginia monument, however, was not that die-hard Lost Cause discourse made an appearance but that it attracted relatively little controversy. The entire event took place under the auspices of the Federal government as the owners and regulators of the battlefield. With a Southern president in the White House, and Jim Crow laws having been given tacit approval by Federal courts, the US government no longer appeared to white Southerners as the enemy. The rapprochement was solidified even further in the 1920s. In that decade, the alignment of the white North and the white South, under the banner of Union, reached its peak. Lee's statue at Gettysburg was accepted and celebrated by the nation as a whole, as represented by the Federal government who owned the site, but in the 1920s the South formally accepted and celebrated Lincoln at the dedication of the Lincoln Memorial in Washington on May 30, 1922. An Associated Press reporter breathlessly described the "swelling tide of the humble people who waited for hours under a blazing sun to claim this temple of freedom." And while Southern newspapers devoted noticeably fewer column inches to the ceremonies than did Northern newspapers, the presence of Southern senators on the steps of the memorial was essential to the presentation of Lincoln as a unifying figure. "How it would comfort his great soul," President Warren Harding said in his speech, "to know that the states of the southland join sincerely in honoring him."[101]

In the 1920s, the white South was at the peak of its cultural cachet in the nation as a whole. Its mythic past of plantations and codes of honor provided ballast in a dizzying world of industrial capitalism and rapid technological change. Relatively poor and undeveloped, the former Confederacy punched far above its weight culturally. It was in this context that the Ku Klux Klan was recreated as a national organization dedicated to nativist politics. The 1920s version of the

Klan, which had its core strength not in the South but in the Midwest, was modeled as a secret society with passwords and secret handshakes, but with children's and women's wings that embedded it into respectable middle-class communities. For a few years in the mid-1920s, its mix of family-friendly activities with anti-Catholic and white supremacist politics and a widespread anxiety about immigrants, made the Klan seem almost mainstream. Wearing their outlandish costumes, Klan members marched down Pennsylvania Avenue in the nation's capital. Inevitably, they came to Gettysburg, too. In September 1925, more than ten thousand "Klansmen and Klanswomen and their children" arrived in the town, with "On to Gettysburg" stickers on their cars for a grand celebration addressed by the "Imperial Grand Wizard" Hiram Wesley Evans, a Texas-based dentist with a track record of brutality against Black people.[102] In order to ensure the Klan came again the following year, local Gettysburg businessmen contributed $1,200 to the organizing committee. It was probably an unwise investment on the part of local traders since the 1926 Gettysburg gathering attracted far fewer people than had come in 1925, perhaps a symptom of the decline in the Klan's national standing in the wake of a series of scandals.[103] The point was made, though: Gettysburg welcomed the Klan, and the Klan wanted to be at Gettysburg.

Other battlefields had their own attractions, but in the early twentieth century, Gettysburg's status as the preeminent Civil War site remained secure. Each visitor found their own meanings encoded in the landscape and the memorials, but almost all saw there the story of the Civil War in its entirety. Gettysburg had been turned into a microcosm of the Civil War and it was a version of the war that served the purposes of American nationalism in the early twentieth century.

8

Gettysburg and the Meaning of America, *c.*1930–1990

There were still twenty-five battle veterans able to travel to Gettysburg to mark the seventy-fifth anniversary in 1938. The cameras rolled as the old men, now in their nineties but gamely dressed in blue or gray, shook hands at the stone wall at the Angle in what had become the traditional fashion. President Roosevelt gave a speech opening the art deco Eternal Light Peace Memorial. Inscribed on this vast cenotaph-like structure, conceived after the 1913 reunion, were the words "Peace Eternal in a Nation United." Roosevelt quoted Lincoln's famous phrase from his second inaugural address—"with charity for all, with malice toward none"—and then two veterans, one from each side, lit the flame which, its designers intended, would burn for all eternity as a symbol of the hope of national peace (in fact the flame was turned off in World War II, and then again, this time permanently, during the oil crisis of 1974). In 1938, with the country still in the grip of the Great Depression, Roosevelt spoke about how Lincoln, having been commander-in-chief in war, had wanted more than anything to be "commander-in-chief of the new peace," and how he, Roosevelt, now facing a "conflict as fundamental as Lincoln's," was "seeking to save for our common country opportunity and security for citizens in a free society."[1]

Roosevelt's New Deal had a direct impact on the battlefield. In 1933, the President signed an executive order transferring control of the Gettysburg National Military Park from the War Department to the

National Park Service, which had been established seventeen years earlier, in 1916, primarily to preserve the big natural parks in the West like Yosemite. After that, the curation of the battlefield would be influenced by trends within the Park Service. And until philanthropic and corporate funding increased in the 1990s, much of what was possible at Gettysburg depended on Federal funding. In the 1930s, this all benefited the battlefield. The Public Works Administration spent 40 million dollars improving roads and trails in the National Parks. At Gettysburg, the avenues were improved, anachronistic metal fencing removed, and efforts were made to return the landscape to something like its 1863 appearance. For nine years between 1933 and 1942, the Civilian Conservation Corps (CCC), a New Deal initiative that provided work for unemployed men, provided manual labor on the battlefield. Men enrolled in the CCC lived together in army-style barracks, racially segregated as was standard practice for Federal initiatives. Two of the CCC camps at Gettysburg were for African Americans but were unusual because the supervisors were also Black. One of those supervisors, Dr. Louis King, held a PhD in anthropology from Columbia University and wrote several historical reports for the Park authorities. According to the leading authority on the history of the Gettysburg National Military Park, neither King's race—nor the highly visible presence of Black workers—aroused opposition, or even much comment, though it is likely that they faced petty discrimination in daily life in a town that was still overwhelmingly white.[2]

The 1938 reunion was the last echo of the era when Gettysburg's meaning had been primarily defined by veterans. The first National Park Service superintendent at Gettysburg, James R. McConaghie, refocused the Park's efforts away from the monuments which had dominated the life of the battlefield for the previous half-century. Accepting that they held a "particular meaning" to the people who erected them, McConaghie argued that for most visitors the memorials "merely exist." Under his direction, CCC laborers planted trees and bushes to screen the monuments carefully. With the veterans passing away, it was almost as if Gettysburg was losing its identity as the place

Figure 8.1. Postcard of the Eternal Light Peace Memorial at Gettysburg showing the gas flame which was intended to burn in perpetuity but which was turned off permanently in 1974 during the oil crisis. The Eternal Light Peace Memorial was a magnet for opponents of the war in Vietnam, for whom it represented the futility of war, and for white supremacists, for whom it marked the reconciliation of the white South and the white North. Both groups had a point.

where the nation looked to understand itself. The Eternal Peace Memorial had been planned back in 1913. It was the culmination of the reconciliationist impulse that helped shape Gettysburg's meaning and memory from the 1880s into the twentieth century. Still, by the time it was dedicated it was almost as if it were no longer needed. In 1938, the United States had other problems that the Civil War no longer defined.

* * *

Yet, as the United States entered the world war and the Cold War, Gettysburg regained its meaning as a "shrine." No longer was it solely about the "reconciliation" of North and South—though the "High Water Mark" narrative continued to be the principal framing. Its meaning was even larger: as the battle which ensured American unity, Gettysburg was the essential foundation for the global struggle against fascism and communism. Gettysburg—both the address and the battle—became an obvious source for publicists wanting to articulate the United States' status as the leader of the free world. In a typical example of the genre, Lincoln's words, editorialized the *Baltimore Sun* in 1945, "suddenly come alive as applicable to events today... Once again, our generation is undergoing the ordeal to which Lincoln's generation was subjected."[3] The "pregnant words" of the Gettysburg Address, wrote a contributor to a Scranton, Pennsylvania newspaper, "never had such painful immediacy as they seem to have in our own anxious era."[4] As victory in the war came closer, the global meaning of Gettysburg came into sharper focus. "From the old conception of a free *country*," wrote one columnist, "we rise slowly but surely to the conception of a free *world*, in which all nations and races shall have a fair chance to live and flourish."[5] After all, as a Methodist minister wrote in a Michigan newspaper, "when Lincoln said that freedom shall not perish from the earth, he meant the earth, not just America."[6]

World War II affected the battlefield just as the Great War had done: German POWs were housed in an old CCC camp west of the "High Water Mark," with the prisoners hired out to local farmers as fruit pickers.[7] And in a larger sense, the war transformed Gettysburg's meaning by generating intense public interest in the American past.[8] The cynicism and moral relativism of the interwar sensibility seemed woefully inadequate after 1941. The struggle against fascism and then against communism demanded a traditional idealism instead. Gettysburg met that need, and not just for Americans.

It wasn't just in America that the war revived the relevance of Gettysburg as a turning point in human history and Lincoln's address as the capstone explanation of what it all meant. In 1941, the UK Ministry of Information released a film called *Words for Battle* directed by Humphrey Jennings, a pioneer documentary maker, designed to inspire popular support for the war at a frightening time when a German invasion was still widely feared. Behind images of clouded hills, factories, and London buses, Laurence Olivier reads extracts from great English authors—Milton, Shakespeare, Blake—until the climax, when the camera comes to rest on a statue of Lincoln in front of the Houses of Parliament and Olivier reads the final sentence of the Gettysburg Address with one small but significant alteration: "*this* nation" becomes the more universal "*the* nation." When he reaches the final line ("government of the people, by the people, and for the people, shall not perish from the earth"), the film cuts to a shot of ordinary Londoners hurrying past the statue on their way to work as tanks and military vehicles roll by.[9] If Blake and Milton evoked a tradition of English liberty, Kipling and Browning spoke of the English character, and Churchill offered defiance, it was the American Lincoln who expressed the idea that it was also the ordinary man and woman—not rulers or landscape or beautiful buildings—for whom Britain was fighting. Jennings' film set the tone for the increasing invocation of the Gettysburg Address in wartime Britain, where the phrase "new birth of freedom"—almost always directly attributed to Lincoln—came to sum up post-war hope. On Lincoln's birthday in 1944, the BBC mounted a technically ambitious radio broadcast combining Vice President Wallace's Lincoln Day address from Springfield, Illinois, with a sermon on Lincoln's legacy by the Archbishop of Canterbury (who quoted the Gettysburg Address) in Westminster Abbey, and, from beside the Lincoln statue in Parliament Square, a talk about Lincoln, democracy, and the cause of freedom by the young Tory MP Quintin Hogg in which, once again, the Gettysburg Address was the central feature.[10]

As the Gettysburg Address loomed large in the national and global imagination, the battlefield itself assumed new importance. Just after the surrender of Japan, a local Pennsylvania newspaper made a case for battlefield preservation. While it may have "cost our nation many millions of dollars" and "from a purely monetary point of view" was "an expensive enterprise with no tangible profits coming out of it," nevertheless "it is as important to our national life as the Congress itself. It reminds us of the price of our nationhood, without which Congress would be meaningless."[11] In the reflected light of this new international relevance, the battlefield entered a new post-veteran era as the place where Americans could go to find the patriotic inspiration—perhaps even the moral grounding—needed for leadership of the "free world."

The National Park Service (NPS) embraced this new sense of mission. Beginning a new program of instruction for guides in the 1950s, the bible for the Park Service leadership was the agenda-setting 1957 book *Interpreting our Heritage* by Freeman Tilden, a novelist and lover of national parks. Tilden's classic formulation was: "Information was not interpretation. Interpretation is revelation based on information." The key was the word "revelation," with its quasi-religious overtones and its conviction that the experience should transform the visitor. Whereas in the War Department era, the Military Park Commission had followed a policy of only providing dry "factual" information boards, under the aegis of the National Park Service, Gettysburg's mission was now quite explicitly to provoke and inspire, to inculcate patriotism through "revelation." The National Park's function, according to a 1960 "masterplan," was to "assist the visitor to convert the Park's resources, the battlefield and its monuments, and the National Cemetery, into meaningful concepts."[12] As NPS historian Frederick Tilberg explained the authorities' thinking, Gettysburg "served as a place for the nation's youth to learn to understand and appreciate their great American heritage of history."[13] The landscape of the battlefield was a historical artifact of immense cultural power.

The visitors came in ever greater numbers: a million a year by the end of the 1950s, peaking at seven million in the early 1970s. This was the boom time for family vacations. Driving along the new interstate highways, with cheap gas in their Chevrolet Corvettes or Ford Thunderbirds, the father behind the wheel and the two kids in the backseats, American families traveled hundreds of miles a year for leisure. The Park Service guides did their best to engage vacationing fathers and sons with the details of the ammunition used back in the 1860s and the mothers and daughters with moving tales of the civilians caught up in the conflict. (A whole museum opened about the experience of the battle's most famous civilian casualty, Jennie Wade.)

That historical sites like Gettysburg were firmly placed in the category of a wholesome family destination is an aspect of the larger story of the post-war development of the "heritage phenomenon." The leading historian of American memory, Michael Kammen, has argued that post-war Americans experienced a "pronounced sense of discontinuity between past and the present" which fed directly into a search for a commodified, consumable "past" as an anchor against the anxieties of the age.[14] There were many other places that Americans could go to experience their "heritage" in these years, from Colonial Williamsburg to Disneyland (where the historical section featured "Main Street USA," a recreation of a turn-of-the-century scene complete with a Civil War memorial obelisk), but Gettysburg was the real deal. Nowhere in America was freighted with more historical significance.

Tourism entrepreneurs had made money at Gettysburg since 1863 in ways that made purists despair. If families came to Gettysburg on a "pilgrimage"—the word often used at the time—to recharge their patriotism, they stayed because they had fun. In the post-war years, as visitor numbers grew, the entertainment industry moved up a gear. Some of these were marketed as fun ways of understanding the battle and its larger meaning. There was a wax museum featuring a dramatization of the Gettysburg Address and the hanging corpse of John Brown, a "Hall of Presidents" museum offering "the story of America," and TV comedian Cliff Arquette's "Cliff Arquette's Soldiers Museum," the centerpiece of which was his collection of toy soldiers. Others were geared to families worn out by the history, including an "Indian Village" complete with "real Indians" and "Fantasyland," which, among highlights, allegedly included the world's tallest Mother Goose.[15]

As had always been the case, some decried commercialization as a desecration of a national shrine. A 1961 article in *Parade*, a weekend magazine with a circulation in the millions, drew national attention to the apparent threat to the integrity of the battlefield, noting that 700 acres of land deemed essential to battle interpretation by the

GREAT BATTLES

NPS were still in private hands and in danger of being built on. Letters poured in from around the country to the *Gettysburg Times*, a representative example arguing that "the land may be in Adams County, but the battlefield belongs to the nation."[16] In 1959, the Gettysburg Battlefield Preservation Association was created to prevent commercial interests from buying up portions of the battlefield. Its honorary chairman was Cliff Arquette, who, in his famous persona as the homespun Charlie Weaver, led a national campaign to get people to donate money to purchase threatened battlefield land to "save it" for the nation.[17] In 1962, the Gettysburg Battlefield Preservation Association donated its first land purchase to the NPS.

The truth, however, was that the clash between high-minded "preservationists" and money-making commercial interests could usually be compromised. The two impulses were, after all, mutually dependent. The NPS itself wanted both to preserve the battlefield and increase visitor numbers. And what, in any case, did preservation mean? Did it mean the restoration of some version of an 1863 landscape or maintaining the status quo? Since the early nineteenth century, the self-appointed caretakers of historical sites in Western Europe and North America have debated both means and ends—not only the purpose of preservation (its patriotic or "civilizing" functions) but also how this should be done. In the case of Gettysburg, when the NPS took over in 1933, they inherited a carefully cultivated monument park, covering two and half thousand acres—a lot, but only a tiny portion of the area where the sprawling battle had taken place. The first Park superintendent, James McConaghie—the man who wanted to "screen" the monuments—was keen on promoting the battlefield's natural appearance, encouraging visitors to come and enjoy the redbuds and dogwoods in the springtime.

Consequently, trees and shrubs grew up the slopes of Little Round Top, on Oak Hill, and in many other parts of the battlefield which had been rocky or under cultivation in the 1860s. The nineteenth-century "woodlots"—tracts of trees grown for firewood where grazing livestock kept the undergrowth to a minimum—had become thickly

228

vegetated. By the end of the 1930s, it was hard for someone who wanted to visualize the battle to work out what could be seen from where, or what kinds of natural obstacles the soldiers of 1863 had to confront. If the NPS's philosophy was entirely to be expected from an agency that primarily existed to preserve the great national parks like Yosemite, it did not go down well with everyone. R. L. Jones, a historian (or "historical technician" as he was known in that age of bureaucratic systemization) employed by the Park Service in its early years, complained that Gettysburg was "ceasing to be a military park and becoming a mere spot of scenic beauty." Jones protested that "the nation as a whole is not and never can be interested in the Park as a scenic or recreational spot." It was "hallowed" ground, and "we should not desecrate it by encouraging picnics, even with a few rustic tables."[18]

By the 1950s efforts were being made by the NPS to create an "authentic" 1863 landscape, insofar as that was even imaginable given the number of family cars and the commercial development along the roads into the town, not to mention steel observation towers on the battlefield. No longer a monument park for the performance of veteran-centered rites, Gettysburg, in the Cold War era, was a place for visitors to "experience" a great historical event. Its perceived authenticity was becoming critical to its cultural power and thus its commercial success. Visitors came because they wanted to "experience" another time—now beyond the memory of even the oldest visitor—in which even warfare was on a human scale, testing men's courage and willingness to sacrifice themselves for the greater good. From the perspective of the nuclear age, the 1860s seemed dramatic and, in essential ways, simpler.

By the time of the Civil War centennial, the NPS had, with some reluctance, allowed battle re-enactment, and so was born a new era of entertainment in which crowds watched men dressed as Civil War soldiers firing blanks. The emergence of re-enacting as a mass hobby in the 1960s was a product of many social and cultural factors, including increased leisure time and disposable income. It was also, fundamentally, a reflection of the romantic allure of the past and, in particular, of the Civil War in American culture. This was the era in which toy stores were filled with model soldiers, Civil War board games, and "Cowboy and Indian" dressing-up kits, and families watched TV shows like "The Gray Ghost" about the Confederate cavalry raider John S. Mosby. The centennial of the Civil War, with the surrounding hoopla, pageants, and TV coverage, was a major stimulus to re-enacting. A Confederate re-enactment group, the Southern Skirmish Association, was even formed in the UK, by men who, for the most part, had never been to America but knew all about the Civil War from films and TV.[19]

For this new generation of Civil War "buffs," as with previous generations, Gettysburg was the lynchpin of the whole story. The story of those three July days was epic enough to make it a satisfying challenge to follow the narrative, yet contained enough to be manageable. Almost all the Civil War "stars" familiar from history lessons and Hollywood were there, from Lee to Lincoln. Only Stonewall Jackson was missing, but even he was part of the story because of the dire implications for Lee of having to fight his first battle without his right-hand man! Gettysburg's cultural power was rooted both in a perception of its current-day relevance and also, paradoxically perhaps, in the remoteness of the world of 1863.

The death toll at Gettysburg was still a somber reality, but at least the dead were imagined to be soldiers fighting for "noble causes," not civilians incinerated in an apocalyptic nuclear nightmare. No one who came to Gettysburg any longer mourned the loss of a loved one in a real sense—although some performed mourning rites anyway, and a growing interest in family history provided an important personal connection for many visitors. But the re-enactors tidied up the brutal reality of battle. The bayonet fights never resulted in gouged eyes or severed throats. The dead got up and walked away. In this sense, the Gettysburg battlefield at times became to the Civil War what Disney's "Main Street USA" was to corporate capitalism. Both responded to (and monetized) a widespread reaction against the anonymity of twentieth-century global forces and the powerlessness of individuals as automatons in offices. To Gettysburg's visitors, Civil War soldiers paradoxically seemed like masters of their own fate, tied into tangible, living communities. The performance of battle wounds—and even (in grisly re-enactments of field hospitals) amputations—could be horrifying, but at the end of the day, it was theater. What drew visitors was spectacle: the flags, guns, and escapism.

Nostalgia and historical understanding have a curious relationship. As a cultural impulse, the search for a comforting past requires amnesia as well as memory. The whole point is to provide an escape from the turbulence of the present with stories that make people feel better about themselves and their nation. The twentieth-century United States was simultaneously a highly diverse society yet also one with a very strong national culture. This meant that there were always multiple and clashing historical memories and a strong impulse to create a unified story about the national past. Gettysburg could offer visitors a bespoke story about their Irish or German ancestors. It could also, of course, tell a story to white Southerners and the descendants of Yankees. But these differing strands were encompassed within a story of the battle as an American turning point.

* * *

The Park Services' self-conscious "revelation" of Gettysburg's patriotic meaning was aided by the frequent presence there of President Eisenhower, who, with his wife Mamie, bought a run-down farm adjacent to the battlefield in 1950 as a weekend retreat. He recuperated there for six weeks in 1955 after a heart attack, signing bills and receiving cabinet members and congressional leaders. It was at Gettysburg, in July 1956, that Eisenhower's spokesman "casually" confirmed to "the White House correspondents leaning on the farm rails" that, notwithstanding the President's serious health issues, he would run for a second term that November.[20] In 1959, Eisenhower told an audience at Gettysburg College that "a free America...can exist only as part of a free world." Although "times and situations have changed," the ideals which Abraham Lincoln expounded endured, the President said, and there was no place where he was more aware of this "than when I am home at our farm near Gettysburg."[21] In September of that year, he brought Soviet premier Nikita Khrushchev to the battlefield as a break from talks at nearby Camp David. Khrushchev was reportedly equally delighted to meet both Eisenhower's grandchildren and his prize cows.

More than for any other president since Lincoln, Ike found Gettysburg a useful stage set. Being photographed on Little Round Top or at the "High Water Mark" reinforced his Lincolnian image as the martial defender of American freedoms at the height of the Cold War. But on at least one occasion, in 1957, Eisenhower's Gettysburg connection inadvertently triggered some of the still-simmering tensions over the place of the battle in American memory. The trouble was created by the President's old World War II sparring partner, the notoriously impolitic Field Marshal Bernard Montgomery, who by then had been ennobled as Viscount Montgomery of Alamein and was serving as deputy commander of NATO. The two generals had discussed the Battle of Gettysburg during World War II, and when he arrived in America in May 1957, Monty told reporters that he was looking forward to seeing the famous battlefield with the President. He then offered an unsolicited opinion which caused a frenzy in the press. He had read a great deal about the Battle of Gettysburg, Monty explained, and he thought that both Lee and Meade should have been fired afterward for the way they mishandled their forces. "Lee did not press his advantage," Monty explained somewhat imperiously, "and made a mistake in launching his strongest thrust against the strongest Union position," whereas Meade "did not keep his forces under adequate control."[22] Eisenhower, whose relationship with his former deputy had always been strained, was reportedly furious at the news reports—though that may have been as much because of Monty's criticisms of US policy in the Suez Crisis. Still, the President kept his commitment and hosted Montgomery at his farm, showing him over the battlefield with press reporters scurrying after them from viewpoint to viewpoint, trying to listen to as much of the conversation as possible. Standing in front of the Virginia Memorial on Seminary

Ridge—the huge equestrian statue of Lee erected in 1917—the two men looked across to Cemetery Ridge and pondered Pickett's Charge. "Why he would have gone across that field, I don't know," the President was heard to say. "The man must have got so darned mad he wanted to hit them with a brick." Montgomery then said, "It was a monstrous thing to launch this charge. A monstrous thing."[23] When asked by the reporters what he would have done if he were in charge of the Army of Northern Virginia, the British commander didn't hesitate. "Oh, I would have thrown a right hook around Little Round Top where you had plenty of cover. I would have used a little feint here to draw the Union's attention." But Meade also did a bad job in letting "that guy get away."

Figure 8.2. President Eisenhower and Field Marshall Montgomery tour the Gettysburg battlefield in 1957. Monty's flippant responses to questions and his breezy willingness to say that he thought Lee should have been sacked for his performance in the battle created a furor in the South, which the press dubbed "the Second Battle of Gettysburg."

Monty's breezy, rather flippant manner and willingness to keep repeating that he thought both Meade and Lee did a terrible job in a voice designed to carry to the press corps was evidently profoundly irritating to Ike. "I was resentful of Monty's lack of good taste," Eisenhower told a friend.[24] As a writer in *Time* magazine dryly commented, Montgomery had clearly not understood that "one of the few ground rules observed with equal fervor by editorial writers and politicians [in the United States] is that the Civil War is about as amenable to levity as motherhood." When reporters pressed the President on whether he agreed with Monty about Lee and Meade's mistakes, Eisenhower gave an evasive answer, blaming Jeb Stuart for Lee's problems. He turned to Montgomery and said: "If some of the generals who fought here were alive today, they probably would have criticized the way we fought." Montgomery nodded.

Unfortunately for Eisenhower, this was not enough to distance himself from Monty's dismissal of Lee (no one worried about his dismissal of Meade). The newspapers had a field day, outraged at the insult to the Civil War generals. "SOUTHERN BLOOD BOILS!" cried the Jackson, Mississippi *News*. "The Second Battle of Gettysburg Rages in the South!" proclaimed the Richmond, Virginia *News-Ledger*. The Montgomery, Alabama *Advertiser* reported that local citizens wanted to remove Montgomery's honorary citizenship of his namesake city. Mrs. Pickett Smith, United Daughters of the Confederacy President in Alabama and a distant relative of General Pickett, was quoted as saying, "I think President Eisenhower should apologize for making such a slur on our beloved Southern general," while the President of the Atlanta Ladies' Memorial Association called the comments "uncouth."[25]

The furor, coming in the wake of the Montgomery Bus Boycott and a few months before the violent confrontation in Little Rock over school integration, was another reminder of how important a Lost Cause interpretation of Gettysburg was to white Southern identity. Old tropes about Longstreet's culpability resurfaced, while Lee—"the greatest human being since Jesus Christ," according to one Alabama citizen—remained beyond all criticism. Senator Sam Ervin of Georgia, one of several prominent Southern politicians who spoke out in the wake of the Gettysburg tour, believed that Lee had ably demonstrated "that he was a greater general than either the President or Montgomery. The whole episode did not do Eisenhower's reputation in the former Confederacy any good. "The President must have lost his mind," spluttered a North Carolina editor. "Not only did he have the audacity to criticize our greatest military mind, but he did it in front of a Redcoat General! These two things are certain to ruin Ike in the South."[26]

* * *

The reaction of white Southerners to Field Marshal Montgomery's Gettysburg visit was a preamble to the crisis triggered by the collision of the Civil War centennial with the Civil Rights Movement. The planners, who had started planning in the mid-1950s, intended a rolling national celebration of American unity. In the words of the leading historian of the centennial, it was to be a "popular heritage bonanza" that would be a "weapon in the cultural Cold War," but it turned into a "train crash waiting to happen." Under the slogan "A Nation United," the overarching theme was the "brave deeds and deeply held values" of the men who fought on both sides.[27] But with America riven by the struggle for racial equality, a tone of self-congratulation was impossible to sustain, and before long, profoundly different visions of the meaning of the Civil War came into sharp conflict. At one extreme were pro-segregationist Southerners who hewed to the die-hard Lost Cause myth. At the other were the leaders of the Civil Rights Movement and their allies who saw the centennial as an opportunity to call for a Lincolnian new birth of freedom, as Martin Luther King did in his speech at the march on Washington in August 1963. King told friends he wanted his speech at the Lincoln Memorial to be a "sort of Gettysburg Address."[28] He made this clear in the Gettysburg echo of his opening line: "Five score years ago, a great American in whose symbolic shadow we stand today, signed the

Emancipation Proclamation." Just as Lincoln had premised the Gettysburg Address on his interpretation of the ongoing meaning of the Declaration of Independence, so King made his case for racial equality on the basis of Lincoln's emancipationist vision of the meaning of American nationality. And then, there was the Cold War Liberal establishment who saw the Civil War's outcome as the validation of the moral superiority of democracy. Seizing on the publicity surrounding the centennial, the State Department published comic books in various languages about Lincoln's life, quoting extensively from the Gettysburg Address, and mailed out fifty thousand copies of the address to "state department grantees and other exchange visitors to the United States who had returned to their home countries."[29] Liberals such as President John F. Kennedy were quite willing to embrace a narrative of racial progress—not least to bolster the United States' Cold War credentials—but were terrified by the prospect of political instability.

The Federal government had invested a lot of public money in supporting events and had to navigate the inevitable clashes. In 1961, for example, when African American members of the Federal Civil War Centennial Commission were barred from a Charleston, South Carolina hotel, a complete breakdown was avoided only by moving the commission's meeting to a desegregated US military base. Because the centenary was a rolling series of events, commemorating each element of the Civil War in turn, from the creation of the Confederacy through to its final destruction, it was easier for white Southerners to be enthusiastic about events in 1961 than they were to be later. The centenary of the formation of the Confederacy became a jamboree for pro-segregation politicians.[30] But by the summer of 1963, when the focus shifted to Gettysburg, Southern triumphalism faced a trial. Would the anniversary of the Confederacy's "High Water Mark" also be the high-water mark of their attempt to preserve formal racial discrimination in the old Confederacy?

While racial tensions shot through every aspect of the centennial celebrations, the high profile of the war in popular culture brought visitors to Gettysburg in unprecedented numbers. The centenary of other battles had attracted little attention other than the negative reaction to the amateur re-enactors who cavorted in store-bought gray costumes at the anniversary of the first Battle of Bull Run. The centennial of the Battle of Antietam in September 1962 largely passed unnoticed and produced only a modest uptick in visitor numbers at the battlefield.[31] But Gettysburg was a different matter entirely. In preparation for the expected surge in visitor numbers in 1963, the Park Service opened the first purpose-built visitor center on the battlefield. It incorporated the cyclorama with its dramatic rendering of Pickett's Charge, which perfectly fitted the "turning point of the war" theme of the other exhibits, including a fifteen-minute introductory slide show in which Gettysburg was presented as "the supreme battle of the Civil War."[32]

The Pennsylvania State Centennial Commission decided early on that its focus would be Gettysburg, both because the battle was "the turning point of the war" and because of the Address—"an eloquent and enduring expression of these United States."[33] Just as in 1913, the tone emphasized reconciliation and the valor of both sides. Local Gettysburg businesses paid tribute to the "South and the North and their acts of bravery and courage." The Five Star Restaurant offered a "salute to the Blue and the Gray...heroic men proud in victory, gallant in defeat," while the Veterans of Foreign Wars local chapter celebrated the centennial with a statement asserting that "never a war was marked by more deeds of noble kindness between men."[34] A special centenary edition of the local paper dripped with the rhetoric of the cult of reunion. Lee was "universally revered by friend and foe alike," and, despite his evident treason, "a symbol of the true spirit of America. Talented, generous, devoted to duty; persevering...he belongs to all of us."[35] The crux of the case for why Americans should plan a vacation to Gettysburg in 1963 was to see where "a strong nation dedicated to the cause of Peace and Unity" was born.[36]

Anyone who recalled the 1913 commemoration would have found the tone familiar. Echoing the coverage from fifty years earlier,

GREAT BATTLES

reporters lapped up evidence of Blue–Gray harmony, such as a sighting of North Carolina Governor Terry Sanford and Minnesota Governor Karl Rolvaag eating grits in the Hotel Gettysburg (the grits had been temporarily added to the menu as a tribute to the South).[37] There were no veterans now (the last man whose claim to have served was undisputed was Albert Woolson, a Union veteran who died in 1956). Still, Pickett's Charge was re-enacted anyway, this time with cannon and musket fire blasted from loudspeakers and accompanied by a portentous running commentary. Around one and a half thousand re-enactors took part, watched by some forty thousand spectators. "This is high tide for the Army of Northern Virginia," intoned the commentator. Although the Park Service had promised that the events would be somber and respectful, the mood was festive until the re-enactors playing the assaulting rebels came close to the stone wall. At that point, they froze, put down their weapons and shook hands with the Union re-enactors while the marine band played the national anthem. Reportedly, many in the crowd and among the re-enactors had tears in their eyes. The message was clear: only by overcoming its divisions was the United States able, in 1963, to confront the evil of Soviet communism.

The "head mogul" for the four-day ceremony (in the somewhat jaundiced words of James I. Robertson, Jr, a military historian and the young executive director of the Civil War Centennial Commission) was Adele Nathan. A New York producer previously responsible for the "Mr. Lincoln Goes to Gettysburg" pageant for the Western Maryland Railway in 1952 (an event celebrating its centennial), she cheerfully told reporters that the pageant was not history but show business.[38] And by the measure of tourist income and visitor satisfaction, the Gettysburg centennial was a triumph. The restaurants and motels were packed, there was an air of festive cheer, and the unintentionally ironic Civil War Centennial Commission's slogan of "A Nation United" provided a frame which, in theory at least, tied the battle to America's Cold War challenges. The summer commemorations began on June 30 with a speech by former President Eisenhower

238

encouraging his listeners to "ponder" the implications of Lincoln's words for the Cold War. Those words, Eisenhower said, "apply today as profoundly as they did on that November day when they were first spoken." They charted the path toward a global victory for American freedom.[39]

The July 1 ceremonies focused on the Eternal Light Peace Memorial, including the dedication of a "torch of peace," and on July 2, a two-hour parade through the town was entitled "Strength Through Unity."[40] The loudest cheers from the crowd that day were reportedly for Robert E. Lee IV, the great-grandson of the Confederate general, who rode through the town waving to the public from an army jeep.[41]

All the same, the centennial showed that, compared to 1913, it was now far less plausible to frame the battle purely in terms of a quarrel among noble, patriotic Americans. Unsurprisingly, there were few non-white faces among the crowds on the battlefield in July 1963. African Americans were less likely to enjoy all-American Cold War-era vacation experiences because they were less likely to have the money and time. Still, in Gettysburg de facto racial discrimination no doubt also played a role. Although Pennsylvania did not have Jim Crow laws on the statute book and Black people could and did vote and serve on juries, Gettysburg was only a half-hour drive from the Mason-Dixon line, a town dependent on the tourist economy with businessmen quick to explain that they practiced racial discrimination in their hotels or restaurants not because they were themselves racist—heaven forbid!—but because their valued Southern customers expected it. In the early 1950s, one study found that only three of the town's fourteen restaurants would serve Black people, while the most prominent hotel would only serve them if they were "nationally recognized or associated with a predominantly white group." There was de facto residential segregation in the town as well. Other than live-in domestic servants, all the African American residents of mid-twentieth-century Gettysburg lived in a single neighborhood.

Local ministers formed a group to encourage better race relations during the run-up to the battle centennial. At the same time, a state body, the Pennsylvania Human Rights Commission, visited local Gettysburg businesses to remind them that racial discrimination was illegal and encouraged them to post signs welcoming people of color. Reportedly, only one business owner refused to do so. The knowledge that national and international attention would be focused on Gettysburg in July 1963 spurred a campaign to present the town as welcoming to all. Businessmen anxious about civil rights campaigners using the centennial to stage demonstrations in the town were assured by the Reverend Joseph Haggler, a prominent Black pastor, that they would not do so, so long as the local motels and restaurants "treated patrons of color fairly."[42]

Even so, Gettysburg in 1963 was a comfortable destination for those for whom the Civil War was a refuge from the struggles of the Civil Rights Movement. Most visitors revered Lee and Lincoln in equal measure and tended to think that Confederates fought for noble reasons even as they celebrated a century of reunion. Many of them (the men, anyway, since interest in war has always been highly gendered) were "buffs," fascinated by the details of weapons and tactics, more interested in the military history of Gettysburg, as opposed to its causes and consequences. The reconciliationist narrative of the war, emphasizing the valor of both sides and ignoring the causes of the conflict, provided a comforting balm in troubled times.[43]

President Kennedy visited the battlefield with his wife and daughter Caroline in March 1963, driving the tour route in his convertible, but he declined the invitation to deliver an address on July 4, perhaps wanting to avoid directly having to engage the civil rights themes that were by now engulfing the centennial in the national media.[44] Local businesses and the Centennial Commission wanted Gettysburg removed from the racial politics of the present, yet the centennial unavoidably brought the politics of race to the surface.[45] In 1963 Vice President Johnson came to Gettysburg on Memorial Day to make a case for civil rights legislation (at that point held up in Congress by conservative Southern Democrats) as the unfinished business of the battle. Although he was a Texan, Johnson specifically invoked the sacrifice only of those who had died "on their native soil"—Northerners, or perhaps Pennsylvanians specifically—in calling for a "new birth of freedom." "Our nation found its soul in honor on those fields of Gettysburg one hundred years ago," Johnson proclaimed. "We must not lose that soul in dishonor now on the fields of hate."[46]

The "A Nation United" celebration exposed in raw form what had always been true, but had hitherto been hidden, which was that the "reconciliationist" view of the war was a gift to the defenders of segregation. The evidence of this was emerging in marble and bronze on Seminary Ridge, where, stimulated by the centennial, a new wave of Confederate memorialization was underway, funded, for the most part, by Southern state governments. Every Confederate monument in these years provoked some concern within the Park Service over the imagery and especially over the wording of the plaques. But the 1960s gatekeepers of the battlefield's appearance lacked John Bachelder's power, or at least his willingness, to go into battle, and almost every time, the result was that the Southerners got most of what they wanted. When the Mississippians wrote to the hard-pressed Park Superintendent informing him that their monument would include an inscription to "our brave sires [who] fought for their righteous cause," an internal Park Service memo gently demurred (if we allow it, we will "have to revise American history"). However the Mississippians got their way.[47] A rare example of the Park Service successfully vetoing a proposal was when the South Carolinians, who unveiled a monument in 1963, wanted to refer to the "Confederate War Centenary."[48]

A Union divided beneath the veneer of Cold War patriotism was inadvertently showcased by the *Gettysburg Times*. Someone at the local paper had the idea of inviting every state governor to send them a short piece reflecting on what Gettysburg meant to them. Unsurprisingly, Southern governors used the opportunity to restate their opposition to Federal interference. For example, Governor Ross Barnett of Mississippi was happy to endorse the slogan of "eternal peace," even while restating the case for states' rights. "We believe all Americans

GREAT BATTLES

should recognize legitimate differences in problems of the states," he wrote. Echoing the inscriptions being carved into Southern state monuments, Barnett proclaimed the "blood of our ancestors was shed on the battlefield of Gettysburg in a hopeless, though dedicated, cause."[49]

Governor George C. Wallace of Alabama, basking in international publicity for his stand in the "schoolhouse door" opposing the desegregation of the University of Alabama and on the verge of a run for president which would see him pile up votes among Northern white working-class voters as well as in the Deep South, relished the opportunity to come to Gettysburg for the re-enactment of Pickett's Charge. In the absence of the President, Wallace stole the limelight, surrounded everywhere he went by a press pack. He was surrounded by crowds of well-wishers asking him to autograph their centenary programs. In an interview with the *Gettysburg Times*, Wallace emphasized that his stand in the schoolhouse door was not intended to deny African Americans an education but was about opposing Federal interference. And seizing on an issue where he had plenty of local support in places like Adams County, Pennsylvania, he highlighted his opposition to the 1962 US Supreme Court's *Engel v Vitale* decision that state governments could not require prayers in public schools. "The Federal government may send troops in and arrest us for praying," he said, "but we're going keep right on doing it."[50] In the spirit of the centennial's celebration of American freedom, Wallace insisted his political crusade was necessary to "save the country from centralized socialist government." There were rebel yells from the crowd as Wallace came forward to speak at the Eternal Light Peace Memorial on July 1. "We stand with the descendants of brave men who fought for North and South, and we still stand for defense of the Constitution," Wallace told the crowd, to cheers.[51] "I think I'm safer here than at home," Wallace crowed. "I've got political enemies in Alabama, but I haven't any here."[52] By all accounts, he certainly had no enemies in the encampment of Confederate re-enactors, who treated him as if he was the second coming of General Lee himself.

"I don't know when I have ever enjoyed anything more," Wallace told a friend.[53]

In the *Gettysburg Times*, progressive governors made a very different case for Gettysburg, echoing the message of Vice President Johnson that the fruits of the Union victory in July 1863 would be secured only when there was racial justice in America. For Governor Pat Brown of California, for example, Gettysburg mattered because it was the beginning of a "Great Social Revolution in the history of the free world," a march toward equality that had still not been achieved. "All of us," Brown wrote, "share the responsibility to fulfill the promise of this country's founding pledge that 'all men' are created equal."[54] And Wallace did not have it all his own way on the battlefield. At the Eternal Peace Light Memorial event on July 1, the President of the University of Notre Dame, Reverend Theodore M. Hesburgh, argued that there could be no lasting peace without justice, and he urged his listeners to commit themselves to fight for racial justice so that those who had fallen at Gettysburg did not die in vain. New Jersey Senator Richard Hughes told the centennial crowds, "The Civil War was not fought to preserve the Union 'lily white' or 'Jim Crow,' it was fought for liberty and justice for all." It was a "shame" that "the full benefits of freedom are not the possessions of all Americans a full century after the war which was fought to save America's soul."[55]

There were more calls for racial justice at Gettysburg in November 1963 when the national cemetery was rededicated. President Kennedy again refused an invitation—opting instead to go to Dallas—so the starring role went to local resident, former President Eisenhower. But the proceedings also featured some prominent African American figures, including the singer Marion Anderson and E. Washington Rhodes, publisher of *The Philadelphia Tribune*, one of the most influential Black newspapers in the country. Evoking the final sentence of the Gettysburg Address, Rhodes closed his speech by warning that "unless men of substance and creative minds take positive action, move forward with alertness and stout hearts to remove [the] injustice [of second-class citizenship], I fear that government of the

GREAT BATTLES

people, by the people and for the people, will soon be endangered beyond repair."[56]

The tone of the November centennial ceremonies—focusing on Lincoln's address rather than the "drums and trumpets" story of the battle—was markedly different from the pageant of July. But it did not mark a fundamental shift in the interpretative focus of the battlefield, nor the wider cultural significance of Gettysburg. As both a place and as an idea, Gettysburg continued to be associated more with the romance of the "turning-point" than Lincoln's "new birth of freedom." Affirming the old Confederacy's determination to impose its presence on the battlefield, in 1971, the Louisiana State Memorial was dedicated. In a (literally) crowded field, it is probably the most directly pro-Confederate memorial at Gettysburg. It features a sculpture of two figures. One is a recumbent male described by the sculptor Donald De Lue, as "a young Confederate soldier from the Washington Artillery who has paid the full price of his devotion to the cause." The other is a woman in a floaty dress playing a trumpet "representing the spiritual idea of peace and memory" and "a resurgent Confederacy, strong, confident and prosperous." The memorial, De Lue wrote, "proclaims that generations unborn at the time of Gettysburg, over one hundred seven years ago, have seen fit not to forget their gallant men and that their memory shall endure for thousands of years."[57]

Donald De Lue also created the Mississippi monument, dedicated in 1973, which shows a fallen color bearer and an infantryman using his musket as a club to defend the flag, and the 1965 Memorial to the Soldiers and Sailors of the Confederacy. But the Boston-born De Lue, trained in Boston and Paris, was a pure Yankee.[58] De Lue's Gettysburg monuments are strikingly emotional and energetic compared to the generally somber tone of the nineteenth-century and early twentieth-century memorials, but the artist's heartfelt tributes to the loss of Southern white lives were not the product of a life marinaded in Southern struggles over race. They were, to him, entirely consistent with a mainstream, patriotic narrative of American history as a heroic struggle for freedom—even when, as between 1861 and 1865, two

244

understandings of freedom collided. De Lue was also the creator of the "American Youth Rising from the Waves" statue at the Normandy American cemetery in Colleville-sur-Mer, with an inscription which alludes to the Gettysburg Address: "To these, we owe the high resolve that the cause for which they died shall live." And perhaps his most famous work was a statue of George Washington at prayer at Valley Forge. To many white Southerners in the 1960s and 1970s, De Lue's sculptures were weapons in the cultural and political war they were waging against the advocates of racial equality. But to many other people, including, in all probability, the artist himself, they were the apotheosis of the fusion of the Confederate cause with the nation. Far from being jarring signals of renewed rebellion (as, no doubt, Northerners of the 1860s and 1870s would have seen them), the memorials appeared to be natural additions to the memorial landscape of Gettysburg. This place embodied, more than anywhere else, the providentially inspired story of the American nation.

This was a sentiment expressed by nationally syndicated columnist Max Freedman on July 4, 1963. There was "honor enough for everyone" at Gettysburg, he wrote. The battles in the West may have had a "deeper military significance," but, at the time and ever since, they did not touch "the conscience and compassion of the divided nation" as Gettysburg did. The battle still had a special place in the imagination of Americans in 1963, Freedman argued, because it was a reminder of a time when men mattered more than machines, and because there, more than anywhere else, "in the presence of the remembered dead," there is no "room for sectional boasting, no justification for words of division."[59] It was a message that emphasized American exceptionalism, downplaying internal division over racial injustice but emphasizing the nation's global role, fighting for a new birth of freedom in the world.

Neither Donald De Lue nor Max Freedman were from the South, yet were able to reconcile honoring the Confederacy with the democratic values of Cold War-era America. Others found this harder. By the time of the centennial, the most popular historian of the Civil War, Bruce

Catton, was expressing concern that the romance of the war was obscuring the "deep and tragic issues" that precipitated it. His own books, not least his three-volume *Centennial History of the Civil War*, played their part in drawing Cold War Americans into the exciting world of Stonewall Jackson and Robert E. Lee. Catton's riveting prose centered on the courage of ordinary soldiers, the tactical decisions of commanders, and the mutual respect each side developed for the other. He never lost his faith that the Lost Cause myth, including public admiration for Lee across the whole nation, not just in the South, had "been an asset to the entire country" by helping to bind it together, fitting it for the struggles against totalitarianism in the twentieth century.[60] Yet, as the historian Robert Cook has argued, Catton's increasing commitment to the Black freedom struggle created a tension in his thinking and writing about the place of the Civil War in American history.[61] The embrace of Confederate imagery and the die-hard version of the Lost Cause myth by hard-line segregationists and white supremacist vigilante groups jolted moderate liberal white Northerners like Catton into the recognition that unity and peace could only be meaningful if founded on justice. By 1967, Catton had changed his mind about the appropriateness of displaying the Confederate battle flag. As "a Northerner born and bred," he had "always looked on [the flag] as a valuable sentimental emblem speaking for Americans who endured much for a cause in which they deeply believed." But, he told a correspondent, "lately…the flag has been so misused by racist elements in various parts of the country" that it no longer belongs on a flagpole.[62]

Yet the sense persisted that Gettysburg had transcendent value. Eisenhower had used the battlefield to showcase American values, and in 1978 President Jimmy Carter hoped it had a universal appeal that might bring together Egypt's Anwar Sadat and Israel's Menachem Begin. Carter suspended negotiations at Camp David in order to helicopter the leaders and their entourages to the battlefield, inspecting the key sites with the war's great Southern chronicler Shelby Foote serving as a guide. Carter later claimed that he had insisted that no one mention the Middle East or indeed anything that had happened since 1865.[63] Sadat and the military staff on both sides knew the battle inside out, such was the utility of Gettysburg in British- and American-influenced military academies. Begin, however, knew nothing about the battle itself, and Carter felt a bit awkward on his behalf as the others exchanged views about the tactical decisions made in July 1863. But then they reached the national cemetery and, when they stood at the spot where Lincoln had delivered his address, Begin astonished the rest of the company by reciting it by heart.

So, was the Civil War a necessary response to the evil of slavery or a tragic misunderstanding among freedom-loving Americans? And was the lesson of Gettysburg that the nation must never again be divided, or that Americans needed to confront—with violence if necessary—those who would deny the equality of all men? Most visitors to the battlefield in the Cold War years, buying Catton's books in the gift shop along with packets of Civil War bullets and model soldiers in blue and gray, did not worry too much about such ethical dilemmas. For them, Gettysburg still meant the Confederate high tide and the romantic centerpiece of their nation's story. Yet at the same time, the racial reckoning of the 1960s had brought to the surface an older, abolitionist view of Gettysburg's meaning. While Donald De Lue's memorials were being dedicated, the battlefield remained isolated from the shifting currents of American public culture. But the tide was turning, nonetheless. And, as had been the case since 1863, Gettysburg's meaning was ceaselessly contested because what happened there—and what Lincoln said there—seemed, in some ineffable sense, to encapsulate what most mattered about America.

Epilogue

Gettysburg and American History

By the end of the twentieth century, Gettysburg—as both a place and an idea—seemed less salient in American culture than it had been at the height of the Cold War. After peaking in the late 1960s, the number of tourists visiting Gettysburg National Military Park declined during the 1970s and 1980s, but there were still more than one and a half million a year, which made it far and away the most popular Civil War site.[1] The town's economy remained as dependent as ever on tourist dollars, but toward the end of the Cold War period, its character gradually changed from a family vacation resort to a history buff's paradise. More Gettysburg restaurants adopted a faux 1860s décor and required their waiting staff to wear Civil War-era costumes; more stores catered to the re-enactor community, selling uniforms, replica weapons, and antiques. In the Cold War, Gettysburg had presented itself as the embodiment of American values; by the late 1990s, in a more fragmented, individualistic culture, visitors to Gettysburg came less for a civics lesson than to immerse themselves in a lost world, perhaps a simpler one. The modern re-enacting movement, which had begun with young men with toy guns and store-bought pants charging at each other during the centennial, had evolved into an expensive and time-consuming hobby for enthusiasts in pursuit of "authenticity"—and Gettysburg was the mecca for many of them.

By this time, the battlefield's appearance had altered considerably since the centennial, as the Gettysburg National Military Park implemented their vision "to restore, maintain, and perpetuate as closely as possible the historic scene and character that existed on this battlefield in July of 1863."[2] With a far more ambitious management plan than had been attempted by any previous generation, the Park Service sought to create an 1863 stage set on which the story of the battle (whatever that story might be) could be told. In the 1990s this even required park rangers to spend the night driving around the park with night vision glasses and rifles, killing the deer which destroyed the 1860s-style woodlots. In 1995, rangers killed more than five hundred of the beasts. History does not record the ultimate resting place of the carcasses.[3]

The 1990s was the decade of Ken Burns' PBS documentary series *The Civil War* and Ronald F. Maxwell's film *Gettysburg*, an adaptation of Michael Shaara's 1974 novel *The Killer Angels*. Both regenerated public interest in the Civil War, which had been gently sagging since the centennial. Visitor numbers to the Gettysburg battlefield rose by nearly 20 percent in 1994, and battlefield guides reported that Little Round Top had leapfrogged to the top spot of most popular battlefield sites due to the outsized role played in the Gettysburg movie by Jeff Daniels as Joshua Lawrence Chamberlain. *Gettysburg* buffed up the image of the battle as a noble fight among brave white men; just as scholars in university history departments were centering race in their understanding of American history, Hollywood doubled down on a war story that would have been familiar and comforting a generation earlier. Academics including the African American historian Barbara Fields were on screen in Burns' documentary series, but the star performer was the Southern novelist and historian Shelby Foote, interviewed in what appeared to be a graceful Southern home. Foote's uncanny and surely not coincidental resemblance to Robert E. Lee provided an additional dramatic layer to his sincere recounting of the trials of heroism and suffering of both sides, with a well-timed catch in his voice and an occasional tear in his eye. Interpretatively, Burns' documentary could not have been made before the Civil Rights Movement and the reevaluation of the meaning of the war in its wake. Even so, there were plenty of no doubt inadvertent Lost Cause notes. Ultimately, Confederates emerged from the documentary as wrong but romantic—entangled in forces beyond their control. Burns did not ignore Black people or the centrality of slavery to the war, yet slavery's narrative function was primarily to enable a redemptive national story to be told. "Between 1861 and 1865," the narrator David McCullough intones right at the start of the first episode, "Americans made war on each other and killed each other in great numbers if only to become the kind of nation that could no longer conceive of how that was possible." National unity, even a deep kind of consensus, was forged through the suffering of war— and that suffering was, in the spirit of Lincoln's Second Inaugural, atonement for the anomaly of slavery in a land of freedom. And Gettysburg, predictably, was the moral turning point of the story. "At Gettysburg in 1863," McCullough went on to say, "Abraham Lincoln said perhaps more than he knew: the war was about a new birth of freedom."

Visitors to Gettysburg in the 1990s, including those newly enthused by a fascination with the Civil War by Ken Burns, may well have subscribed to the general view that the war was a good thing—indeed a source of pride—because it ended slavery. But on the battlefield itself, slavery played no role at all. The Park Service focused on the challenges of "authentic" preservation, including the upkeep of monuments, while the town catered to Civil War buffs. In the last decade of the old century and the first of the present, the past was either "dusty" (in textbooks) or "alive" in re-enactments. In 2004 the *Gettysburg Times* reported on the 141st Gettysburg commemorations, which would "bring those dusty old history books back to life" with "all-day living history demonstrations of the Civil War period such as camp life, civil war music, and Ladies period dress." There were to be even more opportunities to buy "authentic" 1860s artifacts than was already the case in the tourist town because "the traveling salesman of the Civil War...will display and offer for sale an extensive array of authentic and high-quality period merchandise such as reproduction uniforms, dresses, clothing, weapons, sarsaparilla, molasses, cookies, furniture, artwork, collectables and other items."[4]

There was much less overt sermonizing on the "meaning" of Gettysburg in American public culture in these years than there had been either in the veterans' era or the Cold War years. But while the presence of so many middle-aged men in pseudo-Victorian military uniform would have bemused a time-traveling visitor from seventy years earlier, the implicit narrative that structured interpretation—the celebration of heroism and later reconciliation—would have been familiar. In the 1990s, a classic monument in the "reconciliationist" mode was unveiled. The "Friend to Friend" memorial in the National Cemetery, paid for by the Masons, features a touching exchange between the dying General Armistead, shot after breaking through at the "High Water Mark," and an aide who later went on to become the Pennsylvania congressman who introduced the first bill establishing Federal control over the battlefield. Both men, it transpired, were Freemasons—their fraternal bonds overcoming their political differences.

It was not until the 1990s that Congress, through the mechanism of including riders in legislation to revise and expand park boundaries, began to push the National Park Service to reframe its historical interpretation. For example, in 1991, in response to congressional pressure, the custodians of the Custer National Battlefield monument rewrote the information for visitors to dampen General Custer's heroism. It was also around then that the NPS opened new historic sites that directly addressed the United States' darker past. In 1998 the Park Service opened the Little Rock High School National Historic Site and in 2007 the Sand Creek Massacre National Historic Site was established near Denver on the land where, as Park Service archeologists had recently demonstrated, pro-Union Colorado regulars killed hundreds of native people in cold blood in 1864.

How, or whether, such a changing political climate would affect Gettysburg, as both a physical place and a cherished component in the American story, was far from clear. Academic historians, however, were increasingly making the case for change. In 1998, on behalf of the Organization of American Historians, three prominent Civil War scholars—James McPherson, Eric Foner, and Nina Silber—produced a report encouraging the Park Service to go beyond tactics and troop movements. "The museum ought to place the battle...in context," Foner wrote.[5] Happily, this was the direction of travel intended by Park Superintendent John Latschar. "Our interpretative programs had a pervasive, although unintended, southern sympathy," Latschar told a conference. "By...emphasizing the heroism of the soldiers, without discussing why they were fighting, we were presenting the reconciliationist memory of the Civil War...to the exclusion of the emancipationist vision."[6] In the early years of the twenty-first century, visitors could take special tours with battlefield guides that "emphasize[d] the causes of the war, the meaning of the Gettysburg address, the life of the common soldiers and the impact on the home front when the breadwinners left to fight."[7] Even though the creation of such tours revealed that the regular tours lacked all these things, traditionalists predictably condemned such innovations for "imposing a politically correct spin on the Civil War that makes race the central issue."[8] One veteran battlefield guide, James Tate, was quoted by a local newspaper complaining that "bringing in slavery and the array of other issues in the context of causes and consequences risks making the story largely academic and therefore boring." On the basis of his nearly five decades of experience as a guide, Tate bluntly pointed out that "the majority of people come here not to find out about the consequences of the Civil War...they're here for entertainment."[9]

The centerpiece of the NPS's twenty-first-century push to set the battle in context was opening a new visitor centre on April 14, 2008. The new building, made possible through private philanthropy, replaced the circular 1962 cyclorama building. It still housed the Philippoteaux painting—indeed, it was restored to its original splendor—but now visitors can only see it if they first watch a short film narrated by Morgan Freeman's mellifluous baritone. The film provides an interpretation of which historians Foner, McPherson, and Silber would approve—indeed all three are credited, along with many other academic historians. So, what had been at stake at Gettysburg? Morgan gives us the answer: "In the balance stands the future of slavery in this country and, therefore, the future of freedom." In this telling, the battle now mattered because it gave rise to Lincoln's speech, a point reinforced by the accompanying permanent exhibition entitled "New Birth of Freedom." The intent was clear: after decades of selling Gettysburg as the high tide of the Confederacy, the educational objective became for visitors to understand Gettysburg's place in the story of American slavery and freedom.

As in Ken Burns' Civil War documentary series, the message of the new visitor center troubled the old Lost Cause-inflected narrative but it was essentially comforting: the story was that an enormous evil had been overcome through struggle and heroism, validating the nation's promise. In 2013, to mark the 150th anniversary, Burns made a ninety-minute PBS documentary on the Gettysburg Address, followed by a campaign to encourage everyone in America to "video record themselves reading or reciting Abraham Lincoln's famous speech." Dozens of celebrities and five living presidents did so.[10] Of course, everyone who performed or reread the speech could inflect it with their own emphasis, just as had always been the case. Yet, with the first African American president in the White House, the overall effect was to reinforce the "new birth of freedom" meaning of Gettysburg. The address once again retrospectively recalibrated the battle in the public imagination. In 2013, Gettysburg was not as central to the American imagination as it had been a generation earlier, but it was fully incorporated into a progressive retelling of "the story of American freedom," to quote the title of a best-selling textbook by Eric Foner.

Even in 2013, however, most visitors to the battlefield did not bother to go to the exhibition (for which, in contrast to just visiting the site, you have to pay an entrance fee). Aside from school parties, visitors continued to skew white, male, and middle-aged. And the battlefield guides continued to focus, just as they always had, on strategy and tactics. Once the visitor had emerged blinking into the sunlight from

Morgan Freeman's authoritative presence, they were left with the battlefield, monuments, and heroism of those who fought.

In short, Gettysburg, as both a physical place and a site of the imagination, remained a contested space, just as it always had been. The late nineteenth-century Black visitors who faced open hostility to their attempts to claim Gettysburg as a site of emancipation would not have been surprised by the level of hostility generated by the Park Service's formal efforts to enshrine an emancipatory narrative in the new visitor center. Nor that the clashes over Gettysburg's current and future status have occasionally erupted into violence as the United States once again confronts the ongoing legacy of slavery. In 2015, a white supremacist gunman killed nine Black churchgoers during a Bible study class in Charleston, South Carolina. And after the election of Donald Trump a year later, the Civil War became more openly contested in the United States than at any time since Reconstruction. For the first time, there was a sustained effort to remove monuments to the Confederacy, many of which, as on the field of Gettysburg, were erected not by the generation who had fought and suffered but by their descendants in the 1950s and 1960s who saw in the celebration of their Confederate past a way of resisting the challenge to the racial order from the Civil Rights Movement. In an interview, one battlefield guide explained that, after President Trump came into office, more visitors than before felt able to express openly racist views. She recalled her profound discomfort at seeing people in her tour group wearing T-shirts with Confederate flags the morning after the violence generated by white supremacists in Charlottesville, Virginia, protesting the removal of a statue of General Lee.[11]

In 2019, there were more than two thousand monuments, place names, and other public symbols honoring the Confederacy across the United States.[12] But in 2020, in the context of intense public protests in response to the murder of George Floyd, a Black man, more than a hundred and sixty of these Confederate symbols had been removed.[13] By 2021, even the massive statue of Robert E. Lee on Monument Avenue in Richmond, Virginia, erected in 1890, had been taken down. It was as if a dam had burst; in months, decades of quiet toleration of the public celebration of the losing side in the war evaporated. It was a reminder that there are moments in history when, almost overnight, the unthinkable becomes the imperative. Like colonial Americans who, in less than two years, went from issuing loyal addresses to the King to melting down his statue in New York City to be fired as bullets against royal troops, the dramatic shift resulted from intense polarization. As recently as 2013, the reasonable "middle ground," perhaps even the basis of a new national consensus, had lain in the celebration of the Gettysburg Address's "new birth of freedom" narrative, and the narrator Morgan Freeman's assurance that the war reaffirmed American greatness through righting the nation with its ideals. But even in 2013, powerful voices challenged the comforting, even self-congratulatory, implications of this view of the war and emancipation. In *The Atlantic's* special issue on the Civil War sesquicentennial, Ta-Nehisi Coates pointedly asked why so few Black people studied the war and concluded, "The message is clear: the Civil War is a story for white people—acted out by white people, on white people's terms—in which blacks feature strictly as stock characters and props."[14] An example of what Coates was critiquing was Shelby Foote's opening line in Ken Burns' 1990s documentary, summarizing why the war came: "It was because we failed to do the thing we really have a genius for, which is compromise." White Americans in 2013, or any other time, would have been unlikely to have described the War of Independence as the result of a "failure of compromise," even though the issues at stake in the 1760s and 1770s were eminently more susceptible to compromise than those of the 1850s. The only possible consequence of white people compromising over slavery, after all, would have been for Black people's freedom to have been delayed. That self-evident truth was always the (sometimes unacknowledged) foundation of mainstream Civil War memory. It is harder to sustain in an era of a new racial reckoning, with calls for reparations for slavery even endorsed by conservative *New York Times* columnist David Brooks.[15]

The twenty-first-century radicalization of the public debate over the meaning of the Civil War was driven by a dynamic interaction between sides, as polarization always is. Donald Trump was more willing to embrace Confederate symbolism than any previous president. Woodrow Wilson was not so imprudent, given the sensitivity of his status as the first elected Southern president since the war. Grant would have been appalled. Even Warren Harding, happy to indulge the Ku Klux Klan in its 1920s heyday, did not so clumsily embrace the rebel battle flag, not least because of the lingering presence of a few Union veterans in his home state of Ohio. Richard Nixon left that sort of thing to George Wallace. But so intense was the loathing that progressive and centrist Americans felt for Trump that his blustering, hyperbolic defense of all commemorations of the Confederacy drove liberal opinion in the opposite direction. Donald Trump therefore inadvertently did more to remove Confederate symbols and advance the emancipationist memory of the war than any other leader since 1865.

Where did all this leave the field of Gettysburg with its proud line of Confederate monuments? Even as total visitor numbers decline, battlefield guides testify that visitors to Gettysburg are more eager to visit the Confederate monuments than ever before. And since 2017 there have been several incidents of violence on the battlefield. In 2017, around the time of the violence in Charlottesville, armed groups rallied on the battlefield avowedly to protect the Confederate monuments from what they imagined was an imminent threat of their removal. (In Pennsylvania in the early twenty-first century, you could be incarcerated for up to ninety days if the police caught you in public with an opened can of beer, but it was perfectly legal to carry a semi-automatic weapon.) One reporter quoted a woman named Jenny Lee, who claimed to be Robert E. Lee's third great-grandniece, congratulating the crowd on not bowing to the woke mob. "We must never back down or be intimidated by the antics of the ignorant," she was reported as arguing. "And all the safety-pin-wearing, easily offended, butt-hurt, temper-tantrum-throwing, vagina-hat-wearing, face-covered, commie fascists can kiss my ass."[16] Three years later, as another presidential election neared, the *Washington Post* reported that "nearly 160 years after a battle here helped turn the tide of the Civil War, Gettysburg is once again riven by conflict" as Trump fans clashed with Black Lives Matter protestors.[17] On July 4, 2020, "Trump trains"—cars festooned with Trump signs and Confederate flags—drove slowly through the town honking their horns while heavily armed men carrying Confederate flags occupied the National Cemetery where the bodies of Union soldiers rest. According to one battlefield guide, who later complained that the police had not removed the neo-Confederates, they shouted "racial epithets" and intimidated ordinary visitors to the cemetery. When they got into a confrontation with a man wearing a Black Lives Matter T-shirt, it was the BLM supporter who the police removed from the area.[18] A local resident was quoted in the *Washington Post* as saying that, unsurprisingly, in the circumstances, "very few Black people, in my experience, come to Gettysburg. It's not a very welcoming place, and the emphasis is on strategy rather than emancipation."[19]

If a visit to the battlefield becomes a political act, it is little wonder that the mom-and-pop tourist visits of yesteryear are becoming rarer and that Black visitation remains stubbornly low despite the best efforts of the Park Service. Even re-enactment, which in the 1990s floated the town's tourist economy, is in decline. Once, it was seen as the harmless eccentricity of baby boomers who wanted to carry on playing children's wargames; now, especially for those who put on Confederate uniforms, a shadow of suspected sympathy for the Confederacy is hard to shake off and may well explain—along with demographic change—the apparent decline of re-enacting since its 1990s peak.[20] Re-enactors have even been threatened with violence.[21] Many people now consider the pursuit of a patriotic past naïve at best and complicit with a racist order at worst. A 2019 essay for *Politico* magazine about the decline in popularity of historical landmarks like Gettysburg speculated that "older Americans who grew up on the American story, and felt its magic, now grieve for a lost sense of American exceptionalism."[22] Once, Gettysburg was the acme of exceptionalism, the shrine to America's past trials and its morally pure national purpose. If, in the age of Black Lives Matter and a widespread cynicism about the American project, even Morgan Freeman cannot rekindle the magic of Lincoln's commitment to a new birth of freedom, then Gettysburg's place in the American imagination is less secure than ever before.

Gettysburg may one day—perhaps very soon—be the last prominent place in America to honor the Confederacy through bronze and marble. That would be an ironic outcome given the original vision of the battlefield and cemetery as a monument to Union victory, and doubly ironic given the twenty-first-century efforts by the Park Service to shift the narrative frame in the visitor center.

The Civil War will matter in America for so long as race continues to be a source of division. There is sometimes a tendency on the left to invert traditional notions of American exceptionalism by implying that the United States' responsibility for slavery is somehow more profound and more enduring than that of the many other societies and polities over time that have enslaved people, brutalized them, and benefited from it. But it is probably true that the legacy of slavery is more visible in America than elsewhere. Even as the United States has been transformed in the last half-century by immigrants from Africa, Latin America, and Asia who did not have enslaved ancestors (or whose ancestors were not enslaved by white Americans anyway), the shame, alienation, and anger that are the long-term products of a mass system of race-based enslavement continue to fester. And so long as that is so, Gettysburg is unlikely to slip for long into the comfortable history buff niche occupied by other great battles in world history. Culloden and Waterloo altered the direction of nations and continents yet, for the most part, are no longer invoked in political debate. Not so with Gettysburg. When American presidential candidates have wanted to say that the nation's soul was at stake, they have done so by going to Gettysburg, and they still do.

In October 2020, Democratic candidate Joe Biden delivered his own "Gettysburg Address." The battlefield, he argued, was a reminder not of what happened when Americans forgot their well-honed skills at compromise (as Shelby Foote put it in the reconciliationist tradition) but of the price that had to be paid "when equal justice is denied, when anger and violence and division are left unchecked." For Lincoln, Biden claimed, the cause of the war was the "end of slavery", albeit (Biden would no doubt have silently added) on the presumption that emancipation could only be delivered in a consolidated nation-state. In the preceding four years, it had become a standard talking point among progressives that Donald Trump's brand of populist nationalism was morally and politically similar to the threat posed in the 1860s by the Confederacy (to be fair, Trump's defense of Confederate symbols made such an analogy painfully easy to sustain, at least superficially). Implicitly channeling this view that the United States of 2020 was facing a threat fundamentally similar to that of the United States of 1861, Biden concluded his Gettysburg address with the exhortation that it "cannot be that here and now in 2020, we will allow the government of the people, by the people, and for the people to perish from the earth...We owe it to the dead who were buried here at Gettysburg. We owe that to the living, and to future generations yet to be born."[23] Biden saw Gettysburg's significance as a test for the nation in which a Lincolnian ideal of equality was, if not vindicated, then at least kept alive for another day.

No doubt a part of Biden's purpose in going there was to provide a contrast to Trump, who had delivered a campaign speech there four years earlier, and who, in 2020, had wanted to announce his reelection bid on the battlefield. In 2016, Trump opened his speech on the battlefield by declaring that Gettysburg was "hallowed ground, where so many lives were given in service to Freedom...amazing place." He then discussed Lincoln, suggesting that "we could look at his example to heal the division we are living through right now" before explaining, inter alia, that "the system" was "totally rigged and broken" and that the women accusing him of sexual misconduct were "liars" who "will be sued after the election's over."[24] Donald Trump's second election in 2024, a triumphant popular vindication for him, will no more resolve the American battle over Gettysburg's meaning than did the apparent watershed of the election of the nation's first black president in 2008.

Traditionally, the challenge of history writing in the United States, a country where historians have almost always written self-consciously as citizens as well as scholars, is how to balance a "story of freedom" that might bind the nation with an acknowledgment of the oppression, violence, and inequality that have characterized the past of the United States as of any other country. The most common resolution—a very Lincolnian one—is to embed the oppression in a story of a nation striving to achieve its ideals, even as it falls short. This was the approach taken by Bruce Catton in his influential Cold War era histories—and Catton, like all thoughtful historians, often wrestled over how to strike a balance between optimism about the future and acknowledgment of how far the nation had fallen short. There have always been small numbers of Americans who have rejected that Whiggish premise and seen the entire edifice of the American state and society as so corrupted by white supremacy, complicity in enslavement, and capitalist exploitation that nothing short of revolution could bring true freedom. This radical tradition includes William Lloyd Garrison, who called the Constitution a "covenant with death," and the 1960s leftists who spelt Amerika with a "k" to imply a Nazi-style corruption. There are echoes of it among twenty-first-century scholars who argue that anti-Black racism is in the country's "DNA" and, thus, by implication, an indelible stain, there for as long as the country exists.[25] In such a telling, Gettysburg is at best an irrelevance, at worst emblematic of the problem, so hopelessly compromised by a century and a half of tales of white heroism that it has no possible utility to a progressive future.

In one possible future, Gettysburg becomes marginalized, the preserve only of those who mourn the loss of a national story in which they had once found comfort and a sense of purpose. But the slide into a backwater status seems unlikely if only because the pull of the American national myth remains so strong. The shocking violence of those July days in 1863 should be a source of meditation into how complex and contradictory human beings—and thus the nations they invent, sustain, and sometimes overthrow—can be. Nothing lasts forever. But so long as the United States of America retains its current political structure, and thus its need for founding myths and a sense of transcendent purpose, Gettysburg will matter; Americans will remain drawn to the most dramatic moment when their republic could have been rent apart and set on a very different course. Since that great, temporary rupture was fundamentally about slavery, and since the legacy of slavery remains one of the most apparent sources of inequality, the Gettysburg promise of a "new birth of freedom" will matter, too.

NOTES

Introduction

1. The case for Gettysburg as the principal site of American meaning is made powerfully in Garry Wills, *Lincoln at Gettysburg: The Words that Remade America* (New York: Simon & Schuster, 1992).
2. Norman Cousins, "Visit to Gettysburg," *Saturday Review*, July 11, 1964, 18.
3. Carol Reardon, "The Pickett's Charge Nobody Knows," in Gabor Boritt, ed., *The Gettysburg Nobody Knows* (New York: Oxford University Press, 1997), 126–7.
4. John M. Stone to Joseph R. Davis, March 1868, in David L. Ladd and Audrey J. Ladd, eds. *The Bachelder Papers: Gettysburg in their Own Words* (3 vols., Savas Beatie, El Dorado Hills, California: Savas Beatie, 2021), 1: 328.
5. Richard Holmes, *Acts of War: The Behaviour of Men in Battle* (London: Cassell, 2004), 175.
6. Frank A. Haskell, *The Battle of Gettysburg* (Madison: Wisconsin History Commission, 1908) [Hereafter *Gettysburg*], 181.
7. Thomas A. Desjardin, *These Honored Dead: How the Story of Gettysburg Shaped American Memory* (Cambridge, MA: Da Capo Press, 2003), 126.
8. Clare Makepeace, *Captives of War: British Prisoners of War in Europe in the Second World War* (Cambridge: Cambridge University Press, 2017), 24.
9. Schurz, Carl, Frederic Bancroft, and William Archibald Dunning, *The Reminiscences of Carl Schurz... Illustrated with Portraits and Original Drawings* (3 vols., Garden City, N.Y.: Doubleday, 1917) [Hereafter *Reminiscences*], vol. III, p. 31.
10. Bruce Catton, *Glory Road: The Bloody Route from Fredericksburg to Gettysburg* (London: White Lion Publishers, 1977), 314.
11. Ward Moore, *Bring the Jubilee* (New York: Ballantine Books, 1953).
12. Winston Churchill, "If Lee had not won the Battle of Gettysburg," *Scribner's Magazine* (Dec. 1930): 587–96.
13. General John C. Black, "The Battle's Lesson," speech delivered at Gettysburg on May 4, 1885, reprinted in the *National Tribune*, May 28, 1885.
14. Sir Edward Creasy, *Decisive Battles of the World, with a special introduction and supplementary chapters by John Gilmer Speed* (New York: Colonial Press, 1988), 406.

NOTES

15. William Faulkner, *Intruder in the Dust*. Vintage Book edn (New York: Vintage Press, 1972), 194–5.
16. John B. Bachelder, *Gettysburg: What to See and How to See It*, 9th edn (Boston: John B. Bachelder, 1889), 94.
17. Edward Everett, *Orations and Speeches on Various Occasions* (4 vols. Boston: Little, Brown, 1878–9), 4: 659.
18. J. R. R. Tolkien, "On Fairy-Stories," in C. S. Lewis, ed., *Essays Presented to Charles Williams* (London, 1947).
19. For various renderings of this quote and debate about its veracity, see: James M. McPherson, "American Victory, American Defeat," in Gabor S. Boritt, ed. *Why the Confederacy Lost* (New York: Oxford University Press, 1992), 19; George C. Rable, *God's Almost Chosen People: A Religious History of the American Civil War* (Chapel Hill: University of North Carolina Press, 2010), 397; Desjardin, *These Honored Dead*, 124.

Chapter 1

1. Quoted in Margaret S. Creighton, "Living on the Fault Line: African American Civilians and the Gettysburg Campaign," in Joan E. Cashin, ed., *The War Was You and Me: Civilians in the American Civil War* (Princeton: Princeton University Press, 2002), 214.
2. James C. Mohr, ed., *The Cormany Diaries: A Northern Family in the Civil War* (Pittsburgh: University of Pittsburgh Press, 1982), 328–30.
3. Diary of William Heyser, reproduced on Valley of the Shadow Project. https://valley.lib.virginia.edu/papers/FD1004.
4. Salome (Sallie) Myers Stewart Diary, entry for May 15, 1863, Robert Brake Collection, US Army Heritage and Education Center, Carlisle, PA.
5. David G. Smith, "Race and Retaliation: The Capture of African Americans During the Gettysburg Campaign," in Peter Wallenstein and Bertram Wyatt Brown, eds. *Virginia's Civil War* (Charlottesville: University of Virginia Press, 2004), 138; Peter C. Vermilyea, "The Effect of the Confederate Invasion on Gettysburg's African American Community," *Gettysburg Magazine* 24 (Jan. 2001): 112–28; Margaret Creighton, "Living on the Fault Line: African American Civilians and the Gettysburg Campaign," in Joan E. Cashin, ed. *The War Was You and Me* (Princeton: Princeton University Press, 2004), 209–36.
6. Smith, "Race and Retaliation," 146; Kent Masterson Brown, *Retreat from Gettysburg: Lee, Logistics and the Pennsylvania Campaign* (Chapel Hill: University of North Carolina Press, 2005), 27.
7. "General Orders, No. 73," June 27, 1863, Clifford Dowdey, ed., *The Wartime Papers of R. E. Lee* (Boston: Little, Brown, 1961), 533.
8. Alan Nolan, *Lee Considered: General Robert E. Lee and Civil War History* (Chapel Hill: University of North Carolina Press, 1991), 17.

NOTES

9. G. M. Sorrel to George Pickett, July 1, 1863, in *The War of the Rebellion: A Compilation of the Official Records of the Union and Confederate Armies* [Hereafter OR] 1 (51)2: 732–3.

10. Brown, *Retreat from Gettysburg*, 32.

11. Henry Cleveland, *Alexander H. Stephens, in Public and Private: With Letters and Speeches, Before, During, and Since the War* (Philadelphia, 1866), 717–29.

12. From Joseph T. Glatthaar, "A Tale of Two Armies: The Confederate Army of Northern Virginia and the Union Army of the Potomac and Their Cultures," *Journal of the Civil War Era* 6: 3 (Sept. 2016), 315–46.

13. Elizabeth Brown Pryor, *Reading the Man: A Portrait of Robert E. Lee Through his Private Letters* (New York: Viking, 2007).

14. *Declaration of the Immediate Causes Which Induce and Justify the Secession of South Carolina from the Federal Union*, Dec. 24, 1860. Avalon Project, Yale University. https://avalon.law.yale.edu/19th_century/csa_scarsec.asp.

15. Douglas L. Wilson and Rodney O. Davis, *Herndon's Informants: Letters, Interviews, and Statements About Abraham Lincoln* (Urbana: University of Illinois Press, 1998), 64.

16. *New York Times*, Aug. 28, 1860.

17. Roy P. Basler, *The Collected Works of Abraham Lincoln* (New Brunswick, NJ: Rutgers University Press, 1953), 8 vols., 2: 461.

18. *Declaration of the Immediate Causes Which Induce and Justify the Secession of South Carolina from the Federal Union*, Dec. 24, 1860. Avalon Project, Yale University. https://avalon.law.yale.edu/19th_century/csa_scarsec.asp.

19. W. S. V. Prentiss to S. S. Cox, Jan. 5, 1861, Samuel Sullivan Cox Papers, Ms 77.5, Brown University Library.

20. Abraham Lincoln to J. T. Hale, Jan. 11, 1861, *Collected Works of Abraham Lincoln* 4: 172.

21. *Collected Works of Abraham Lincoln* 4: 267–9; *New York Times*, March 5, 1861.

22. Joseph L. Harsh, *Confederate Tide Rising: Robert E. Lee and the Making of Southern Strategy, 1861–1862* (Kent, OH: Kent State University Press, 1998), 8.

23. James Buchanan to Lewis S. Coryell, Sept. 18, 1861, Coryell Papers, Historical Society of Pennsylvania.

24. Burlingame, *Lincoln*, 128.

25. Elizabeth Brown Pryor, "'Thou Knowest Not the Time of Thy Visitation': A Newly Discovered Letter Reveals Robert E. Lee's Lonely Struggle with Disunion," *The Virginia Magazine of History and Biography* 119, no. 3 (2011): 276–96.

26. *Adams Sentinel* (Gettysburg, PA), April 24, 1861.

27. *Adams Sentinel*, April 24, 1861.

28. Matilda Pierce, Battle of Gettysburg Civilian Accounts, Adams County Historical Society [Hereafter ACHS].

29. Memoirs of Henry Eyster Jacobs, "Notes on the Life of a Churchman," transcript in ACHS.

30. Jay Bellamy, "Brother vs Brother, Friend against Friend: A Story of Family, Friendship, Love, and War," *Prologue*, Spring 2013, 20–6; William A.

NOTES

Frassanito, *Early Photography at Gettysburg* (Gettysburg, PA: Thomas Publications, 1996), 124–8; Adams County Confederates File, *Pittsburgh Gazette Times*, Nov. 9, 1913, ACHS.

31. *New York Tribune*, July 28, 1863; *New Hampshire Statesman*, Sept. 6, 1862.
32. *New York Tribune*, Oct. 11, 1863.
33. James L. Morrison, *"The Best School in the World": West Point; The Pre–Civil War Years, 1833–1866* (Kent, OH: Kent State University Press, 1986).
34. Carol Reardon, *With a Sword in One Hand and Jomini in the Other: The Problem of Military Thought in the Civil War* (Chapel Hill: University of North Carolina Press, 2012); Archer Jones, "Jomini and the Strategy of the American Civil War," *Military Affairs* 38 (Dec. 1970): 127–31; T. Harry Williams, "The Military Leadership of North and South," in David H. Donald, ed., *Why the North Won the Civil War* (New York: Simon & Schuster, 1960).
35. Kevin Dougherty, *Civil War Leadership and Mexican War Experience* (Jackson: University of Mississippi Press, 2007), 64–8.
36. Reardon, *With a Sword in One Hand and Jomini in the Other*, 20.
37. Dunbar Rowland, ed., *Jefferson Davis, Constitutionalist: His Letters, Papers and Speeches* (Jackson, Mississippi: Printed for the Mississippi Department of Archives and History, 1923), 6: 386.
38. Grady McWhiney and Perry D. Jamieson, *Attack and Die: Civil War Military Tactics and the Southern Heritage* (University of Alabama Press, 1982).
39. Mark Wilson, *The Business of War: Military Mobilization and the State, 1861–1865* (Jackson: University Press of Mississippi, 2005); Allan Nevins, *The War for the Union: The Organized War, 1863–1864* (New York: Scribner's, 1971), 212–13.
40. Harsh, *Confederate Tide Rising*.
41. Henry Heth, "Why Lee Lost at Gettysburg," *Philadelphia Weekly Times*, Sept. 22, 1877.
42. R. E. Lee to John B. Hood, May 21, 1863, *Wartime Papers of R. E. Lee*, 490.
43. "The Revolt of the Generals," *Wartime Papers of R. E. Lee*; Bruce Tap, *Over Lincoln's Shoulder: The Committee on the Conduct of the War* (Lawrence: University Press of Kansas, 1998), 170.
44. Lincoln to Hooker, May 14, 1863, Abraham Lincoln, *Collected Works of Abraham Lincoln*, 6: 217.
45. Sears, *Lincoln's Lieutenants: The High Command of the Army of the Potomac* (Boston: Houghton Mifflin Harcourt, 2018), 527–30.
46. Lee to G. W. C. Lee, May 11, 1863, *Wartime Papers of R. E. Lee*, 484.
47. *Southern Historical Society Papers* [Hereafter SHSP] 4: 154.
48. Richard Rollins, "'The Ruling Ideas' of the Pennsylvania Campaign: James Longstreet's 1873 Letter to Lafayette McLaws," *Gettysburg Magazine*, 17 (1997), 7–16.
49. John J. Pettus to Jefferson Davis, May 8, 1863, OR 52.2: 468.
50. R. E. Lee to James A. Seddon, May 10, 1863, *Wartime Papers of R. E. Lee*, 482.
51. R. E. Lee to Jefferson Davis, May 11, 1863, *Wartime Papers of R. E. Lee*, 483.
52. R. E. Lee to Jefferson Davis, June 25, 1863, *Wartime Papers of R. E. Lee*, 531.
53. R. E. Lee to Gen. Samuel Cooper, Jan. 20, 1864, *Wartime Papers of R. E. Lee*, 569.

NOTES

54. R. E. Lee to Jefferson Davis, June 10, 1863, *Wartime Papers of R. E. Lee*, 508.
55. Arthur J. L. Fremantle, *The Fremantle Diary: Being the Journal of Lt. Col. Fremantle, Coldstream Guards, on His Three Months in the Southern States* (Boston: Little, Brown, 1954) 178.
56. R. E. Lee to Jefferson Davis, May 30, 1863, *Wartime Papers of R. E. Lee*, 495.
57. R. E. Lee to James A. Seddon, June 8, 1863, *Wartime Papers of R. E. Lee*, 504.
58. Allan, conversation with Lee, Feb. 19, 1870, in Gary W. Gallagher, ed., *Lee the Soldier* (Lincoln, NE: University of Nebraska Press, 1996), 17.
59. *Southern Historical Society Papers*, 4: 153. See https://en.wikisource.org/wiki/Southern_Historical_Society_Papers.
60. Davis to Lee, May 31, *Davis Papers*, 9: 201–2. There is some ambiguity about exactly what Davis thought he was authorizing. See Edwin B. Coddington, *The Gettysburg Campaign: A Study in Command* (1st edn Charles Scribner's Sons, 1968), 9.
61. William Swinton, *Campaigns of the Potomac, 1861–1865* (New York: Charles Scribner's Sons, 1882), 311, 372.
62. R. E. Lee to Gen. Samuel Cooper, Jan. 20, 1864, *Wartime Papers of R. E. Lee*, 569.
63. Coddington, *Gettysburg Campaign* 8–9.
64. James Longstreet, "Causes of Lee's Defeat at Gettysburg," *Philadelphia Times*, Nov. 3, 1877, reprinted in *SHSP* 4 (1877), 57.
65. Richard Rollins, "'The Ruling Ideas' of the Pennsylvania Campaign: James Longstreet's 1873 Letter to Lafayette McLaws," *Gettysburg Magazine*, 17 (1997), 7–16.

Chapter 2

1. Lee to Davis, May 20, 1863, *Wartime Papers of R. E. Lee*, 488.
2. Donald C. Pfanz, *Richard S. Ewell: A Soldier's Life* (Chapel Hill: University of North Carolina Press, 1998), 150.
3. In this book, I follow most military historians in referring to the corps of the Confederate Army of Northern Virginia by the name of their commander (e.g., Longstreet's Corps) or, less often, by their number (e.g., First Corps). In contrast, I refer to the Union Army of the Potomac's Corps by Roman numerals (e.g., I Corps).
4. US War Department, *OR* 1 (25)2: 849–50.
5. Gary W. Gallagher. *Fighting for the Confederacy: The Personal Recollections of General Edward Porter Alexander* (Chapel Hill: University of North Carolina Press, 1998), 221.
6. W. W. Blackford, *War Years with Jeb Stuart* (New York: Scribner's, 1946), 212.
7. R. E. Lee to Mrs. W. H. F. Lee, June 11, 1863, *Wartime Papers of R. E. Lee*, 512.
8. *Richmond Examiner*, quoted in Stephen W. Sears, *Gettysburg* (Boston: Houghton Mifflin, 2004), 73.
9. Coddington, *Gettysburg Campaign*, 258–9.
10. Lincoln to Hooker, June 5, *Collected Works of Abraham Lincoln* 6: 249–50.
11. Marsena R. Patrick, *Journal*, June 17, 19, 1863, Library of Congress.

NOTES

12. Sears, *Gettysburg*, 258.
13. Quoted in Brown, *Retreat from Gettysburg*, 27.
14. *Chambersburg Gazette*, quoted in *Baltimore Gazette*, July 25, 1863.
15. Stevens to Simon Stevens, Lancaster, July 6, 1863, Thaddeus Stevens Papers: Speeches and Writings File, Manuscripts Division, LIbrary of Congress.
16. John Edward Dooley, *John Dooley, Confederate Soldier, His War Journal*, Edited by Joseph T. Durkin, S. J., Foreword by Douglas Southall Freeman (District of Columbia: Georgetown University Press, 1945), 99.
17. Randolph H. McKim, "The Gettysburg Campaign," *SHSP* 40 (1915), 256.
18. Quoted in Glatthaar, "A Tale of Two Armies," 9.
19. Charles W. Ford, ed., *A Cycle of Adams Letters, 1861–1865* (Boston, 1920), 2: 55–6.
20. Barlow to his mother, July 7, 1863, Francis C. Barlow Papers, Massachusetts Historical Society (Coddington, *Gettysburg Campaign*, 24).
21. Emory Thomas, "Ambivalent Visions of Victory: Davis, Lee, and Confederate Grand Strategy," in Gabor S. Boritt, ed., *Jefferson Davis's Generals* (Oxford University Press, 2000), 44.
22. At this time, the Army of the Potomac's primary sub-division was into seven corps of infantry, often designated by Roman numerals as the I, II, III, V, VI, XI, XII, though sometimes as "First Corps," etc. There was also a Cavalry Corps. See Carol Reardon and Tom Vossler, *A Field Guide to Gettysburg: Experiencing the Battlefield through its History, Places, and People* (Chapel Hill: University of North Carolina Press, 2013), 10–12. Each Union corps was subdivided into divisions (either two or three), then brigades, regiments, and finally—the smallest unit of all—the company.
23. Charles E. Davis, Jr., *Three Years in the Army: The Story of the Thirteenth Massachusetts Volunteers* (Boston: Estes and Lauriat, 1894), 221, 223.
24. Edwin C. Fishel, *The Secret War for the Union: The Untold Story of Military Intelligence in the Civil War* (Boston: Houghton Mifflin, 1996), 416–18.
25. Catherine Mary White Foster, in David A. Murdoch, ed., *The Battle of Gettysburg: A Citizen's Eyewitness Account* manuscript in the Civilian Accounts File, ACHS.
26. Tillie Pierce, (*At Gettysburg, or, What a Girl Saw and Heard of the Battle. A True Narrative* (New York, W. Lake Borland, 1889). See also Pierce Account, Civilian Accounts File, ACHS.
27. John Charles Wills Account, Civilian Accounts File, ACHS.
28. OR 1 (27)2: 467.
29. Frederick Maurice, ed., *An Aide-de-camp of Lee, Being the Papers of Colonel Charles Marshall, Sometime Aide-de-camp, Military Secretary, and Assistant Adjutant General on the Staff of Robert E. Lee, 1862–1865* (Boston: Little, Brown, 1927), 218.
30. Randolph H. McKim, "The Gettysburg Campaign," *SHSP* vol. 40 (1915), 292.
31. Randolph H. McKim, "The Gettysburg Campaign," *SHSP* vol. 40 (1915), 254.
32. OR 1 (27)2: 3.
33. Polley, *Hood's Texas Brigade*, 149, quoted in Brown, *Retreat from Gettysburg*, 23.
34. Maurice, ed., *An Aide-de-camp of Lee*, 220.
35. Maurice, ed., *An Aide-de-camp of Lee*, 223, 229–30.

NOTES

36. Maurice, ed., *An Aide-de-camp of Lee*, 230.
37. A. L. Long, *Memoirs of Robert E. Lee: His Military and Personal History* (New York: J. M. Stoddart & Co., 1886), 275.
38. Sears, *Lincoln's Lieutenants*, 540.
39. Haskell, *Gettysburg*, 6.
40. OR 27(3): 415.
41. Davis, *Three Years in the Army*, 224.
42. Harry W. Pfanz, *Gettysburg, the First Day* (Chapel Hill, NC: University of North Carolina Press, 2010), 43.
43. OR 1 (27)3: 420.
44. Catton, *Glory Road*, 18.
45. Theodore Lyman, in George R. Agassiz, ed. *Meade's Headquarters, 1863–1865: Letters of Colonel Theodore Lyman from the Wilderness Campaign to the Appomattox* (Boston: Atlantic Monthly, 1922), 21.
46. Pfanz, *First Day*, 42.
47. Lydia Catherine Zeigler Clare Account, Civilian Accounts File, ACHS.
48. Walter Clark, ed., *Histories of the Several Regiments and Battalions from North Carolina in the Great War, 1861–'65* (5 vols. Raleigh, NC, 1901), 5: 116–17.
49. Troy D. Harman, *All Roads Lead to Gettysburg: A New Look at the Civil War's Pivotal Battle* (Mechanicsburg, PA: Stackpole, 2022).
50. Pfanz, *First Day*, 53.
51. OR 1 (27)1: 927. This was Buford's post hoc recollection at least and it is possible that he was more concerned, in the first instance, with defending the town.
52. Abner Doubleday, *Chancellorsville and Gettysburg* (New York: Charles Scribner's Sons, 1886), 122.

Chapter 3

1. Catherine Mary White Foster, in David A. Murdoch, ed., *Battle of Gettysburg: A Citizen's Account* manuscript in the Civilian Account File, ACHS.
2. Mary McAllister, Account of the Battle of Gettysburg, Civilian Accounts File, ACHS.
3. Sears, *Gettysburg*, 170.
4. Pfanz, *First Day*, 13.
5. Pfanz, *First Day*, 123–4.
6. Lydia Catherine Zeigler Clare Account, Civilian Accounts File, ACHS.
7. Quoted in Tom Huntington, *Maine Roads to Gettysburg: How Joshua Chamberlain, Oliver Howard, and 4,000 Men from the Pine Tree State Helped Win the Civil War's Bloodiest Battle* (Mechanicsburg, PA: Stackpole Books, 2018), 209.
8. Schurz et al., *Reminiscences III*: 5.
9. Warren C. Robinson, *Jeb Stuart and the Confederate Defeat at Gettysburg* (Lincoln: University of Nebraska Press, 2007) argues that Stuart was every bit as culpable as Lee seemed to think him. Stuart vaingloriously carried out his

NOTES

own independent campaign without reference to the rest of the army with the result that, when he eventually arrived, his horses and men were tired and less effective than they should have been.

10. John W. Busey and David G. Martin, *Regimental Strengths and Losses at Gettysburg* (Hightstown, NJ: Longstreet House Press, 2005), 298, 386.

11. Quotes from Rod Gragg, *Covered with Glory: The 26th North Carolina Infantry at Gettysburg* (Chapel Hill: University of North Carolina Press, 2010), 140, 146.

12. Mary McAllister, Civilian Accounts File, ACHS.

13. Annie Young, Civilian Accounts File, ACHS.

14. Gilbert Letter, Civilian Accounts File, ACHS. The identification of Emma from a letter written later by her granddaughter was made by Tim Smith of the ACHS.

15. Sallie Myers, Civilian Accounts File, ACHS.

16. Louisiana 6th Infantry Regt. Seymour diary, copied from the Clements Library, University of Michigan, Brake Collection.

17. Annie Young, Civilian Accounts File, ACHS.

18. Albertus McCreary, "Gettysburg: A Boy's Experience of the Battle," *McClure's Magazine* 33 (1909), 250.

19. Major E. P. Halstead, "Incidents of the First Day at Gettysburg," *Battles and Leaders* 3 (1888), 285.

20. Henry F. Hunt, "First Day at Gettysburg," *Battles and Leaders* 3 (1888), 283.

21. Tom Huntingdon, *Searching for George Gordon Meade: The Forgotten Victor at Gettysburg* (Mechanicsburg, PA: Stackpole Books, 2013), 160.

22. Letter from William Calder to Mother (First Lieutenant, Company K, 2nd North Carolina State Troops) in Brake Collection, US Army War College, Carlisle, PA.

23. Louisiana 6th Infantry Regt. Seymour diary, copied from the Clements Library, University of Michigan, Brake Collection.

24. Gallagher, *Fighting for the Confederacy,* 233.

25. Schurz, *Reminiscences,* III: 16.

26. OR 27(2): 446.

27. OR 27(2): 318; James Longstreet, "Lee's Right Wing at Gettysburg," *Battles and Leaders* 3(1888): 339–40; Harry W. Pfanz, *Gettysburg, the Second Day* (Chapel Hill, NC: University of North Carolina Press, 1987), 26.

28. James Longstreet, "Lee in Pennsylvania," in Alexander K. McClure, ed., *Annals of the Civil War by Leading Participants North and South* (Philadelphia: Times Publishing Co., 1879) [Hereafter "Lee in Pennsylvania"], 421. Longstreet offered a slightly different recollection of what was said in *From Manassas to Appomattox: Memoirs of the Civil War in America,* ed. James I. Robertson (Bloomington, IN: Indiana University Press 2020), 358.

29. OR 27(2): 308.

30. Longstreet, "Lee in Pennsylvania," 421.

31. SHSP 5 (1878), 92.

32. Arthur Fremantle, *Three Months in the Southern States: April–May 1863* (New York: J. Bradburn, 1864), 256.

33. Longstreet, "Lee in Pennsylvania," 427.

NOTES

34. James Longstreet to A. B. Longstreet (Uncle), July 24, 1863, in Longstreet, "Lee in Pennsylvania," 412.
35. Schurz, *Reminiscences,* III: 21.
36. Joshua Lawrence Chamberlain, "Through Blood and Fire at Gettysburg," *Hearst's Magazine* 3 (June 1913), 896.
37. Schurz, *Reminiscences,* III: 20.
38. Quoted in Sears, *Gettysburg,* 263.
39. John Gibbon, quoted in Huntingdon, *Searching for Meade,* 162.
40. Quoted in Sears, *Gettysburg,* 264.
41. General E. M. Law, "The Struggle for Round Top," *Battles and Leaders of the Civil War* (New York: Century, 1884), III, 324.
42. Quoted in Richard Wheeler, *Witness to Gettysburg* (Stackpole, 1987), 188.
43. Law, "The Struggle for Round Top."
44. Chamberlain, "Through Blood and Fire at Gettysburg," 899. As is usually the way with such recollected words, especially at dramatic moments, different sources record slightly different versions even when the source is written by the same author. Chamberlain elsewhere recalled Vincent telling him to hold the line at "all costs." Oliver W. Norton, *Strong Vincent and his Brigade at Gettysburg, July 2, 1863* (Chicago, 1909), 38.
45. Quoted in Alice Rains Trulock, *In the Hands of Providence: Joshua Lawrence Chamberlain and the American Civil War* (Chapel Hill: University of North Carolina Press, 1992), 8.
46. William C. Oates, *War Between the Union and Confederacy and Its Lost Opportunities* (New York: Neale, 1905), 213.
47. Norton, *Strong Vincent,* 39.
48. Joshua Lawrence Chamberlain, Address of Gen. Joshua L. Chamberlain at the Dedication of the Maine Monuments on the Battlefield of Gettysburg, October 3, 1893 (Augusta, ME: Maine Farmer's Almanac Press, 1895), 15.
49. Theodore Gerrish, *Army Life: A Private's Reminiscences of the War* (Portland, Maine: Hoty, Fogg and Donham, 1882), 69.
50. Chamberlain, "Through Blood and Fire at Gettysburg," 907.
51. Thomas A. Desjardin, *Stand Firm Ye Boys from Maine: The 20th Maine and the Gettysburg Campaign* (New York: Oxford University Press, 1995), 61.
52. Quoted in Desjardin, *Stand Firm,* 63.
53. Chamberlain, "Through Blood and Fire at Gettysburg," 906.
54. *OR* 27(1): 179.
55. Joshua Lawrence Chamberlain, *Address of Gen. Joshua L. Chamberlain at the Dedication of the Maine Monuments on the Battlefield of Gettysburg,* October 3, 1893 (Augusta, ME: Maine Farmer's Almanac Press, 1895), 15.
56. Quoted in Sears, *Gettysburg.*
57. Lieutenant William Lochren, speech at the dedication of the First Minnesota Monument at Gettysburg, July 2, 1897, reprinted in R. I. Holcombe, *History of the First Regiment Minnesota Volunteer Infantry, 1861–1864* (Stillwater, MN, 1916), 344.
58. Pfanz, *Second Day,* 430.

NOTES

59. Allan Nevins, ed., *A Diary of Battle: The Personal Journals of Colonel Charles S. Wainwright* (New York: Harcourt, Brace, 1962), 243.
60. Harry W. Pfanz, *Culp's Hill and Cemetery Hill* (Chapel Hill, NC: University of North Carolina Press, 1993), 221.
61. Nevins, ed., *A Diary of Battle*, 245.

Chapter 4

1. Troy D. Harmon, *Lee's Real Plan at Gettysburg* (Mechanicsburg, PA: Stackpole Books, 2003).
2. As with almost every known "fact" about the battle, the exact number of men participating in the assault is uncertain. Earl J. Hess, *Pickett's Charge: The Last Attack at Gettysburg* (Chapel Hill: University of North Carolina Press, 2001), estimates a total of 11,830 men engaged in the assault, revising downward Coddington's estimate of 13,500 and Sears' of 13,000. Some veterans claimed as many as 20,000 had participated.
3. Henry J. Hunt, "The Third Day at Gettysburg," *Century Magazine* v. 33 (1886–7), 453.
4. Diary of James Kirkpatrick (Company C, 16th Mississippi Infantry Regt.), Brake Collection.
5. Durkin, ed., *Dooley*, 103–4.
6. Peter S. Carmichael, "Every Map of the Field Cries Out About It: The Failure of Confederate Artillery at Pickett's Charge," 283.
7. Hess, *Pickett's Charge*, 165.
8. Hunt, "Third Day at Gettysburg," *Battles and Leaders*, 469.
9. Gary M. Kross, "'I do not believe that Pickett's Division would have reached our line': Henry J. Hunt and the Union Artillery on July 3, 1863," in Gallagher, ed., *Three Days at Gettysburg*, 287.
10. Captain Elijah Taft, quoted in Sears, *Gettysburg*.
11. Haskell, *Gettysburg*, 112–13.
12. Christopher Mead, Corporal in Co. H, 12th NJ Inf. to wife, July 6 in Brake Collection.
13. Christopher Mead, Corporal in Co. H, 12th NJ Inf. to wife, July 6 in Brake Collection.
14. William J. Burns Diary, July 3, 1863, US Military History Institute, Carlisle, quoted in Carole Reardon, *Pickett's Charge in History and Memory* (Chapel Hill: University of North Carolina Press, 1997), 21.
15. Schurz, *Reminiscences*, III: 31–2.
16. Ladd and Ladd, *Bachelder Papers* 3: 1398.
17. Ladd and Ladd, *Bachelder Papers* 2: 933–4.
18. Hess, *Pickett's Charge*, 265.
19. Coffin, *The Boys of '61*, 296.
20. Hess, *Pickett's Charge*, 333.
21. Durkin, ed., *Dooley*, 107.

NOTES

22. OR 27(2): 556–7.

23. Winfield Scott, "Pickett's Charge as Seen from the Front Line," in *Civil War Papers of the California Commandery and the Oregon Commandery of the Military Order of the Loyal Legion of the United States* (Wilmington, NC: Broadfoot Publishing Company, 1995), 14.

24. Bushrod Washington James, *Echoes of Battle* (Philadelphia: H. T. Coats, 1895), 11.

25. Michael J. Armstrong and Steven E. Sodergren, "Refighting Pickett's Charge: Mathematical Modeling of the Civil War Battlefield," *Social Science Quarterly,* 96(4) (Dec. 2015), 1153–68.

26. Coddington, *Gettysburg Campaign*, 463.

27. Wilbur Fisk, Emil Rosenblatt, and Ruth Rosenblatt, *Hard Marching Every Day: The Civil War Letters of Private Wilbur Fisk, 1861–1865* (Lawrence, KS: University Press of Kansas, 1992), 115.

28. George Gordon Meade, *The Life and Letters of George Gordon Meade, Major-General United States Army*, 2 vols. (New York, Charles Scribner's Sons, 1913) 2: 360.

29. Schurz, *Reminiscences*, III: 42.

30. *New York Herald*, July 14, 1863.

31. *New York Times*, July 8, 1863.

32. *Boston Journal*, July 6, 1863.

33. *Boston Journal*, July 6, 1863.

34. Brown, *Retreat from Gettysburg*, 384, 387.

35. *Collected Works of Abraham Lincoln* 6: 327–8.

36. *Collected Works of Abraham Lincoln* 6: 27–8.

37. Meade, *Life and Letters*, 2: 169.

38. *Richmond Daily Dispatch*, July 6, 1863, p. 1.

39. Quoted in Gallagher, "'Lee's Army has not lost any of its presitige' The Impact of Gettysburg on the Army of Northern Virginia and the Confederate Home Front" in Gallgher, ed., *The Third Day at Gettysburg and Beyond* (Chapel Hill: University of North Carolina Press, 1994), 5.

40. *Richmond Examiner*, July 21, 1863, p. 2.

41. *Raleigh Weekly Standard*, July 15, 1863.

42. Brown, *Retreat from Gettysburg*, 387.

Chapter 5

1. Quoted in Gregory A. Coco, *A Strange and Blighted Land: Gettysburg: The Aftermath of a Battle* (Havertown: Savas Publishing Company, 2017), 19. This appeared in the Franklin (PA) Repository, March 30, 1863.

2. Quoted in Coco, *Strange and Blighted Land*, 43.

3. Quoted in Coco, *Strange and Blighted Land*, 56.

4. Coco, *Strange and Blighted Land*, 60.

5. Gettysburg Battlefield Memorial Association, Announcement, 1863.

6. *The Adams Sentinel*, Sept. 15, 1863.

NOTES

7. Martin P. Johnson, *Writing the Gettysburg Address* (Lawrence: University Press of Kansas, 2013), 148.
8. Coco, *Strange and Blighted Land*, 350.
9. Quoted in Jim Weeks, *Gettysburg: Memory, Market, and an American Shrine* (Princeton: Princeton University Press, 2003), 29.
10. Weeks, *Gettysburg*, 13.
11. Coco, *Strange and Blighted Land*, 307–8.
12. *The Adams Sentinel*, Sept. 15, 1863.
13. *New York Herald*, July 24, 1863.
14. John F. Reynolds Monument Committee Papers, Civil War Papers (Collection 1546), Historical Society of Pennsylvania.
15. James Paradis, *African Americans and the Gettysburg Campaign* (Lanham, Md.: Scarecrow, 2005), 112.
16. Quoted in Coco, *Strange and Blighted Land*, 108.
17. John W. and Travis W. Busey, *Confederate Casualties at Gettysburg: A Comprehensive Record* (Jefferson: McFarland & Company, Incorporated Publishers, 2016), 1997.
18. Quoted in Coco, *Strange and Blighted Land*, 112.
19. John Russell Bartlett, *The Soldiers' national cemetery at Gettysburg: with the proceedings at its consecration, at the laying of the corner-stone of the monument, and at its dedication* (Providence, R.I.: Printed by the Providence Press Co. for the Board of Commissioners of the Soldiers' National Cemetery, 1874), 14.
20. John Russell Young, *Men and Memories; Personal Reminiscences, by John Russell Young; Ed. by His Wife, May D. Russell Young*, 2 vols, (New York (State): F.T. Neely, 1901), 1: 64.
21. Cleveland *Plain Dealer*, Nov. 23, 1863.
22. Quoted in Chuck Raasch, *Imperfect Union: A Father's Search for His Son in the Aftermath of the Battle of Gettysburg* (Stackpole Books, 2016).
23. Johnson, *Writing the Gettysburg Address*.
24. David Wills to Abraham Lincoln, Nov. 2, 1863, Lincoln Papers, Library of Congress.
25. Lincoln's close ally, the Pennsylvania editor John W. Forney, was probably briefed by the White House when he wrote on November 16 of the President's "deep interest in the dedication of the cemetery." Quoted in Johnson, *Writing the Gettysburg Address*, 29.
26. Quoted in Frank L. Klement, "Ward H. Lamon and the Dedication of the Soldiers' Cemetery at Gettysburg," *Civil War History* 31 (Dec. 1985), 299.
27. Johnson, *Writing the Gettysburg Address*.
28. Johnson, *Writing the Gettysburg Address*, 171, 172.
29. Thomas H. Stockton, *Prayer at the Dedication of the National Cemetery at Gettysburg, Thursday, November 19th, 1863* (W. S. & A. Martien, Booksellers, Philadelphia, Pennsylvania, 1863), Alfred Whittal Stern Collection of Lincolniana, Library of Congress.

NOTES

30. Matthew Mason, *Apostle of Union: A Political Biography of Edward Everett* (Chapel Hill: University of North Carolina Press, 2016).
31. Edward Everett, *Orations and Speeches on Various Occasions* (4 vols. Boston: Little, Brown, 1878–9), 4: 622–59.
32. Everett, *Orations and Speeches*, 4: 646.
33. Everett, *Orations and Speeches*, 4: 652.
34. This text is the final version of the Address, copied out by Lincoln sometime in 1864 in response to a request. *Collected Works of Abraham Lincoln* 7: 22–3. The speech as delivered may have been slightly different, but, if so, the differences were minor.
35. Johnson, *Writing the Gettysburg Address*, 164.
36. Gary Wills, *Lincoln at Gettysburg: The Words that Remade America* (New York: Simon & Schuster, 1992).
37. *Collected Works of Abraham Lincoln* 4: 426.
38. *Collected Works of Abraham Lincoln* 6: 269.
39. *Collected Works of Abraham Lincoln* 5: 527.
40. Nathaniel Hawthorne, "Chiefly About War-Matters," *Atlantic Monthly* 10 (July 1862), 64.
41. The word "did" was underlined by pencil in the text from which Lincoln probably read. See Johnson, *Writing the Gettysburg Address*, 199.
42. *Collected Works of Abraham Lincoln* 2: 533.
43. *Collected Works of Abraham Lincoln* 6: 409.
44. *Collected Works of Abraham Lincoln*. Message to Congress, Dec. 1863.
45. *Collected Works of Abraham Lincoln* 6: 357.
46. John Russell Young, *Men and Memories: Personal Reminiscences* (2 vols. New York: Neeley, 1901), 1: 65.
47. Young, *Men and Memories*, 2: 333; Clark E. Carr, *Lincoln at Gettysburg* (Chicago: A. C. McClurg, 1907), 52.
48. Young, *Men and Memories*, 1: 70.
49. Major Henry T. Lee, quoted in Johnson, *Writing the Gettysburg Address*, 197.
50. Philip Gerard, *The Last Battleground: The Civil War Comes to North Carolina* (Chapel Hill, 2019).
51. John B. Jones, *A Rebel War Clerk's Diary at the Confederate States Capital* (Pennsylvania: Lippincott, 1866), II: 50.
52. Quoted in Richard Shannon, *Gladstone: Peel's Inheritor, 1809–1865* (London: Penguin, 1982), 456.
53. H. C. G. Matthew, *Gladstone, 1809–1874* (Oxford University Press, 1986), 133.
54. OR 1 (44): 799.
55. Ibid., 190.
56. John F. Marszalek, David S. Nolen, and Louie P. Gallo, eds., *The Personal Memoirs of Ulysses S. Grant: The Complete Annotated Edition* (Cambridge, MA: Harvard University Press, 2017), 455.

NOTES

Chapter 6

1. *New York Times*, May 26, 1869. Local tradition holds that in fact the waters were discovered prior to the Civil War by the landowner but he failed to monetize his find.
2. Quoted in Edwin B. Coddington, "Rothermel's painting of the Battle of Gettysburg," *Pennsylvania History: A Journal of Mid-Atlantic Studies* 27, no. 1 (1960), p. 7.
3. My discussion of the politics of the painting draws on Edwin B. Coddington, "Rothermel's Painting of the Battle of Gettysburg," *Pennsylvania History: A Journal of Mid-Atlantic Studies* 27, no. 1 (1960): 1–27; Marc Thistlewaite, "'Magnificence and Terrible Truthfulness': Peter F. Rothermel's Battle of Gettysburg," in William Blair and William Pencak, eds., *Making and Remaking Pennsylvania's Civil War* (University Park: Pennsylvania State University Press, 2001), 211–42; and Susanna W. Gold, "'Fighting It Over Again': The Battle of Gettysburg at the 1876 Centennial Exhibition," *Civil War History* 54: 3 (2008). Quotation from Rothermel in Coddington, "Rothermel's Painting," 17.
4. Quoted in Susanna W. Gold, "'Fighting It Over Again'", 303.
5. Quoted in Gold, "Fighting It Over Again," 287.
6. Clarence Cook, *New York Tribune*, May 4, 1876, quoted in Gold, "Fighting It Over Again," 302–3.
7. A case made especially clearly by Robert J. Cook, *Civil War Memories: Contesting the Past in the United States Since 1865* (Baltimore: Johns Hopkins University Press, 2017); and Caroline E. Janney, *Remembering the Civil War: Reunion and the Limits of Reconciliation* (Chapel Hill: University of North Carolina Press, 2013).
8. Speech of Hon. Thaddeus Stevens, *Bedford Enquirer*, Oct. 27, 1865, p. 1.
9. "Reconstruction," *Atlantic Monthly*, vol. 18, no. 102 (Dec. 1866), pp. 761, 763.
10. Available at https://www.loc.gov/resource/mfd.27003/?sp=10.
11. Letter from P. R. Guiney, in Charles Sumner, *Charles Sumner: His Complete Works, with an introduction by George Frisbie Hoar* (Boston: Lee and Shepard, 1900), XII, 354.
12. Republican John Martin Broomhall (R-PA), *Congressional Globe* 39/1, p. 1264 (March 8, 1866).
13. Percy MacKaye, *Gettysburg* (New York: 1922).
14. "Oration of Governor O. P. Morton," in John Bartlett Russell, ed., *The Soldiers' National Cemetery at Gettysburg* (Providence: Providence Press Co., 1874), 89.
15. "Oration of Governor O. P. Morton," 92.
16. Gen L. S. Trowbridge, quoted in Caroline E. Janney, *Remembering the Civil War: Reunion and the Limits of Reconciliation* (Chapel Hill: University of North Carolina Press, 2013), 200.
17. "Oration of General Meade," in John Bartlett Russell, ed., *The Soldiers' National Cemetery at Gettysburg* (Providence: Providence Press Co., 1874).
18. Stuart McConnell, *Glorious Contentment: The Grand Army of the Republic, 1865–1900* (Chapel Hill: University of North Carolina Press, 1992).
19. Theda Skocpol, "America's First Social Security System: The Expansion of Benefits for Civil War Veterans," *Political Science Quarterly* 108, no. 1 (1993): 85–116.

NOTES

20. Quoted in Edward T. Linenthal, *Sacred Ground: Americans and their Battlefields* (Urbana: University of Illinois Press, 1991), 95.
21. John W. Frazier, *Reunion of the Blue and Gray: Philadelphia Brigade and Pickett's Division* (Philadelphia: Ware Bros, 1906), 41.
22. Quoted in Janney, *Remembering the Civil War*, 174–5.
23. "Poor Tom," *The Land We Love*, May 1868, 23–4.
24. "The Dead of Gettysburg," *Richmond Daily Dispatch*, June 21, 1872, p. 1.
25. "The Dead of Gettysburg," *Richmond Daily Dispatch*, June 21, 1872, p. 1.
26. Quoted in J. William Jones, *Army of Northern Virginia Memorial Volume. Compiled by Rev. J. William Jones… at the Request of the Virginia Division of the Army of Northern Virginia Association* (Virginia: J. W. Randolph & English, 1880), 31.
27. "Editorial Department," *SHSP* 1:1 (Jan 1876), pp. 41, 45.
28. *Proceedings of the Southern Historical Convention* (Baltimore: Turnbull Brothers, 1873), p. 27.
29. Quoted in Gaines Foster, *Ghosts of the Confederacy: Defeat, the Lost Cause, and the Emergence of the New South, 1865 to 1913* (New York: Oxford University Press, 1987), 125.
30. Quoted in David W. Blight, *Race and Reunion: The Civil War in American Memory* (Cambridge, MA: Belknap Press, 2001), 125, 262.
31. John Esten Cooke, *Hammer and Rapier* (New York: Carleton, 1870), 306.
32. Edward A. Pollard, *The Lost Cause: A New Southern History of the War of the Confederates* (1866), 406.
33. James D. McCabe, *The Life and Campaigns of General Robert E. Lee* (Atlanta: National Publishing Company, 1870).
34. John W. Daniel, quoted in Desjardin, *These Honored Dead*, 114.
35. Desjardin, *These Honored Dead*, 116.
36. OR 27(2): 317–18.
37. Jubal Anderson Early, *The Campaigns of Gen. Robert E. Lee. An Address by Lieut. General Jubal A. Early, before Washington and Lee University, January 19th, 1872.* (Maryland: J. Murphy, 1872), 30.
38. Pendleton, "Personal Recollections," 520, 523–4.
39. Jefferson Davis, *The Rise and Fall of the Confederate Government* (New York: D. Appleton and Company, 1, 3, and 5 Bond Street, 1881), II, 447–8.
40. *New Orleans Times*, March 19, 1867.
41. *New Orleans Republican*, June 11, 1867, p. 1; *New Orleans Picayune*, quoted in Richter, "Longstreet," 224; Hill quoted in Piston, 11.
42. Longstreet's post-war career is described in Elizabeth Varon, *Longstreet: The Confederate General Who Defied the South* (New York, 2023).
43. James Longstreet, "Lee in Pennsylvania," in Alexander McClure, ed., *The Annals of the Civil War: By Leading Participants North and South* (New York: Da Capo Press, 1994), 434.
44. J. William Jones, *Army of Northern Virginia*, 122.
45. "Causes of the Defeat of Gen. Lee's Army at the Battle of Gettysburg—Opinions of Leading Confederate Soldiers," *SHSP* 4:2 (Aug. 1877), 54.

NOTES

46. "Causes of the Defeat," 65.

47. Pollard, *Lost Cause*, 409.

48. Quoted in Reardon, *Pickett's Charge*, 32.

49. Albert Bledsoe, quoted in Reardon, *Pickett's Charge*, 76.

50. William Swinton, *Twelve Decisive Battles of the War* (New York: Dick & Fitzgerald, 1871), 344.

51. William R. Bond, *Pickett or Pettigrew? An Historical Essay* (Scotland Neck, NC: W. L. Hall, 1888), 10.

52. Reardon, *Pickett's Charge*, 156–7.

53. This quote is apocryphal but plausible since it reflects other comments Pickett made after the war. See James M. McPherson, *Drawn with the Sword: Reflections on the American Civil War* (New York: Oxford University Press, 1996), 115; Lesley J. Gordon *General George E. Pickett in life & Legend* (Chapel Hill: University of North Carolina Press, 1998).

54. Lee's "General Order No. 9", issued on April 10th, 1865, began: "After four years of arduous service marked by unsurpassed courage and fortitude, the Army of Northern Virginia has been compelled to yield to overwhelming numbers and resources." Lee, Robert Edward. *Recollections and Letters of General Robert E. Lee.* (Doubleday, Page & Company, 1904), p. 153.

55. Quoted in Blight, *Race and Reunion*, 125.

56. Speech by Senator James Warren Nye, July 10, 1868. Congressional Globe 40/2, p. 3909.

57. Jacob Hoke, *The Great Invasion of 1863, or, General Lee in Pennsylvania* (Dayton, OH: W. J. Shuey, 1887), 33, xxix, xxxi.

58. James T. Long, *Gettysburg: How the Battle was Fought* (Harrisburg, PA: E. K. Mayers, 1891). Long's account is, inter alia, notable for being one of the very few to emphasize the importance of the cavalry fight on July 3, arguing that, had Kirkpatrick's forces not compelled Stuart to retreat, the infantry "would have lost the battle at the angle" because Stuart's cavalry could attack from the rear.

59. James T. Long, *The Sixteenth Decisive Battle of the World: Gettysburg* (Gettysburg, PA: Gettysburg Compiler, 1906), 18.

60. Quoted in Gary W. Gallagher, *The Myth of the Lost Cause*, 44.

61. John Ruskin, "War," in Edward Tyas Cook and Alexander Wedderburn, eds. *The Works of John Ruskin* (Cambridge: Cambridge University Press, 2010), 18: 465.

62. Michael Turner, *Stonewall Jackson, Beresford Hope, and the Meaning of the American Civil War in Britain* (Baton Rouge: LSU Press, 2020).

63. Hoke, *The Great Invasion of 1863*, 3.

64. J. Howard Wert, *A Complete Hand-Book of the Monuments and Indications and Guide to the Positions on the Gettysburg Battle-Field* (Harrisburg, PA: R. M. Sturgeon & Co., 1886), 5, 212.

65. E. Latimer, *Idyls of Gettysburg* (Philadelphia: George McLean, 1872); Gettysburg *Star and Sentinel*, May 28, 1869; *Shippensburg News*, March 23, 1872.

NOTES

66. *The Evening Telegraph* [Philadelphia], Dec. 28, 1872.
67. Latimer, *Idyls of Gettysburg*, 41–2.
68. Latimer, *Idyls of Gettysburg*, 66.
69. Mary Henderson Eastman, *Jenny Wade of Gettysburg* (Philadelphia: Lippincott, 1864).
70. "Springs Hotel is the Subject of Presentation to 1776 AARP," *Gettysburg Times*, Oct. 20, 1984, 18.

Chapter 7

1. Robert Douglas-Fairhurst, *The Turning Point: A Year in the Life of Charles Dickens* (London: Jonathan Cape, 2021).
2. James T. Long, *Gettysburg: How the Battle was Fought* (Harrisburg, PA: E. K. Mayers, 1891), 5.
3. Frederick Arnold, *Turning-points in Life* (2 vols., London, 1873), vol. 1, p. 1.
4. Arnold, *Turning-points in Life*, vol. 1, p. 2.
5. Arnold, *Turning-points in Life*, vol. 1, p. 3.
6. Arnold, *Turning-points in Life*, vol. 2, p. 158.
7. Henry Mann, *Turning Points in the World's History* (New York: Christian Herald, 1897), 275, 280.
8. Anonymous preface to Latimer, *Idyls of Gettysburg*, 11.
9. Alfred E. Lee, *The Battle of Gettysburg* (Columbus, Ohio: A. H. Smyth, 1888), 97.
10. *The Evening Telegraph* [Philadelphia], Dec. 28, 1872.
11. Samuel P. Bates, *Battle of Gettysburg* (Philadelphia: T. H. Davis & Co., 1875). Similar points were made by other early historians of the battle, such as John S. C. Abbott, *History of the Civil War in America: Comprising a Full and Impartial Account of the Origin and Progress of the Rebellion* (New York: Henry Bill, 1866), and William Swinton, *Campaigns of the Army of the Potomac: Critical Operations in Virginia, Maryland and Pennsylvania from the Commencement to the Close of the War* (New York: Charles Scribner's Sons, 1882).
12. Edward Creasy, *The Fifteen Decisive Battles of the World: From Marathon to Waterloo* (1st edn, 2 vols., London: Richard Bentley, 1851), I: ix.
13. De Peyster, *Before, At, and After Gettysburg* (New York: C. H. Ludwig, 1887). On his role in the Meade–Sickles controversy, which began with an article De Peyster published in *The Volunteer* in 1869, see Richard A. Sauers, "Gettysburg: The Meade-Sickles Controversy," *Civil War History* 26:3 (1980), 205.
14. John M. Vanderslice, *Gettysburg Then and Now: The Field of American Valor, Where the Troops Fought and the Troops They Encountered* (New York: Dillingham and Co., 1897), 392.
15. De Peyster, *Before, At, and After Gettysburg*, 19.
16. Pollard, *Lost Cause*, 412.
17. Cooke, *Hammer and Rapier*, 197.

NOTES

18. Cooke, *Hammer and Rapier*, 198.
19. Cooke, *Hammer and Rapier*, 227.
20. Vanderslice, *Gettysburg Then and Now*, 363. The original minutes of the GMBA, and a manuscript transcription, are available in the Gettysburg National Military Park Library and Research Center.
21. Weeks, *Gettysburg*, 21.
22. Quoted in Edward T. Linenthal, *Sacred Ground: Americans and their Battlefields* (Urbana: University of Illinois Press, 1991), 90.
23. Timothy B. Smith, *Altogether Fitting and Proper: Civil War Battlefield Preservation in History, Memory and Policy, 1861–2015* (Knoxville: University of Tennessee Press, 2017), 27.
24. Vanderslice, *Gettysburg Then and Now*, 367, 400–71. State appropriations in the mid-1880s were listed by Vanderslice as follows: New Hampshire ($4,500); Maine ($30,300); Vermont ($17,953); Massachusetts ($30,000); Rhode Island ($3400); Connecticut ($5,700); New York ($244,825); New Jersey ($44,255); Pennsylvania ($121,500); Delaware ($2,000); Ohio ($40,000); Wisconsin ($3,000); Indiana ($3,000); Illinois ($6,000); Michigan ($20,000); Minnesota ($20,312).
25. Vanderslice, *Gettysburg Then and Now*, 363, 368, 372.
26. Ziba B. Graham, *On to Gettysburg: Ten Days from my diary of 1863*, reprinted in *War papers* read before the Michigan commandery of the Military order of the loyal legion of the United States (2 vols, Winn & Hammond, 1893), Vol. 1., p. 523.
27. John B. Bachelder, *Gettysburg: What to See and How to See It* (n.p., 1873), 51.
28. John B. Bachelder, *Key to Bachelder's Isometrical Drawing of the Gettysburg Battle-Field* (n.p., n.d.), 1.
29. Ladd and Ladd, *Bachelder Papers*, 1: 180–6.
30. Weeks, *Gettysburg*, 23.
31. Desjardin, *These Honored Dead*, 93.
32. Coddington, "Rothermel's Painting," 20.
33. Richard Sauers, "Introduction," in Ladd and Ladd, *Bachelder Papers* 1, p.10.
34. John B. Bachelder, *Gettysburg: What to See and How to See It* (n.p., 1873), 3.
35. Walter Harrison, *Pickett's Men: A Fragment of War History* (New York: Van Norstrand, 1870), 177.
36. Quoted in Desjardin, *These Honored Dead*, 90–1.
37. "The Gettysburg Battle-Field," House of Representatives Report No. 1632, 46th Congress, 2nd Session, 4 June 1880 in *Index to the Reports of Committees of the House of Representatives for the First and Second Sessions of the Forty-Sixth Congress*, 6 vols. (Washington: Government Printing Office, 1880), Harlan D. Unrau, *Administrative History: Valley Forge National Historical Park, Pennsylvania* (Denver, CO: US Department of the Interior, National Park Service, Northeast Team, Branch of Cultural Resources, Denver Service Center, 1985), 47–8.
38. Quoted in Desjardin, *These Honored Dead*, 89.
39. Quoted in Desjardin, *These Honored Dead*, 20.

NOTES

40. Quoted in Desjardin, *These Honored Dead*, 89.
41. An edited collection of his correspondence is Ladd and Ladd, *Bachelder Papers*.
42. Quoted in Desjardin, *These Honored Dead*, 95.
43. Harrison, *Pickett's Men*, 94.
44. Bachelder, *Key*, 9.
45. Martin, *Confederate Monuments*, 165–7.
46. Vanderslice, *Gettysburg Then and Now*, 375.
47. John M. Vanderslice, Gettysburg: *A History of the Gettysburg Battle-field Memorial Association, with an account of the battle, giving movements, positions, and losses of the commands engaged* (Philadelphia: Gettysburg Battlefield Memorial Association, 1897), 232–3.
48. R. A. Alger to General L. G. Estes, Feb. 12, 1897, Brake Collection, US Army College.
49. *Gettysburg Compiler*, July 6, 1889; *The Seventy-Second Regiment of Pennsylvania Volunteers at Bloody Angle*, Gettysburg (n.p., 1889); Unrau, *Administrative History*, 58–9; Vanderslice, *Gettysburg: A History*, 241–4.
50. Vanderslice, *Gettysburg Then and Now*, 215. Bachelder had invited Confederate officers to his 1869 gathering, hosted at the Springs Hotel. Harrison, *Pickett's Men*, 177.
51. Reardon, *Pickett's Charge*, 180: Ladd and Ladd, *Bachelder Papers*, 1: 372, 476.
52. Ladd and Ladd, *Bachelder Papers*, 1: 224.
53. David G. Martin, *Confederate Monuments at Gettysburg* (Combined Books, Pennsylvania, 1995), 9. Martin explains the confusing nomenclature of this regiment which is described on the monument as "1st Md, changed to 2nd Md. Infantry CSA."
54. John Tregaskis, *Souvenir of the Reunion of the Blue and the Gray on the Battlefield of Gettysburg, July 1, 2, 3 and 4, 1888: How to get there and What is to be done during the year* (New York: The American Graphic Co., 1888), 204.
55. Vanderslice, *Gettysburg: A History*, 231–3; Frazier, *Reunion*, 73–4; Tregaskis, *Souvenir*, 204; Reardon, *Pickett's Charge*, 94–5.
56. Quoted in Unrau, *Administrative History*, 61.
57. Haskell, *Gettysburg*, 187.
58. In their classic study, Thomas L. Connelly and Barbara L. Bellows, *God and General Longstreet: The Lost Cause and the Southern Mind* (Baton Rouge: Louisiana State University Press, 1982), identify a die-hard "inner" Lost Cause and a softer "national" Lost Cause, the latter of which demonstrated to Northerners the white South's place in American culture. See also Charles R. Wilson *Baptized in Blood: The Religion of the Lost Cause. 1865–1920* (Athens: University of Georgia Press, 1980); Gaines Foster, *Ghosts of the Confederacy*.
59. *National Tribune* July 8, 1886, quoted in Mary Munsell Abroe, "All the profound scenes: Federal preservation of Civil War battlefields," PhD diss., Loyola University, 1996, 135; Buck, *Road to Reunion*, 258.
60. Reardon, *Pickett's Charge*, 95; Tregaskis, *Souvenir*, 11.

NOTES

61. Anthony W. McDermott and John E. Reilly, *A Brief History of the Sixty-Ninth Regiment Pennsylvania Veteran Volunteers from its Formation Until Final Muster out of the United States Service, Also an Account of the Reunion of the Survivors of the Philadelphia Brigade and Pickett's Division of Confederate Soldiers and the Dedication of the Monument of the 69th Regiment Pennsylvania Infantry at Gettysburg, July 2nd and 3rd, 1887 and the Rededication, September 11, 1889* (Philadelphia: D. J. Gallagher and Co., 1889), 76; Tregaskis, *Souvenir*, 10.

62. Frazier, *Reunion*, 81.

63. The cultural production that seeded and sustained this form of sectional reconciliation has been documented by Nina Silber, *The Romance of Reunion, 1865–1900* (Chapel Hill: University of North Carolina Press, 1993)

64. This is an argument developed by Gerald Linderman, *Embattled Courage*.

65. Frazier, *Reunion*, 89.

66. *Philadelphia Inquirer*, July 4, 1887.

67. Quoted in Smith, *Altogether Fitting and Proper*, 35.

68. Kathleen George Harrison, "'Patriotic and Enduring Efforts': An Introduction to the Gettysburg Battlefield Commission," in *The Fourth Annual Gettysburg Seminar Gettysburg National Military Park, March 4, 1995*, Gettysburg National Military Park Library and Research Center.

69. The most complete account of the legislation establishing the Park Commission and then the National Military Park at Gettysburg is Unrau, *Administrative History*, 67–83.

70. Unrau, *Administrative History*, 75–7.

71. Francis Trevelyan Miller, ed., *Gettysburg: A Journey to America's Greatest Battleground, in Photographs Taken by the World's First War Photographers While the Battle Was Being Fought. Official Presentation, Semi-Centennial* (New York: The Review of Reviews Company, 1913), 17. I am immensely grateful to Mercy Ford for drawing my attention to this source.

72. "The Gettysburg Commission," *The Press* (Dec. 7, 1900), quoted in Harrison.

73. Lee, *Battle of Gettysburg*, 98.

74. *Fiftieth Anniversary of the Battle of Gettysburg: Report of the Pennsylvania Commission* (Harrisburg: n.p., 1913), 60.

75. Unrau, *Administrative History*, 110.

76. "Gettysburg's Fiftieth Anniversary," *New York Sun*, June 29, 1913, p. 4; Thomas Keneally, *American Scoundrel* (London: Viking, 2003).

77. "Gettysburg's Fiftieth Anniversary," *New York Sun*, June 29, 1913, p. 8.

78. Walter H. Blake, *Hand Grips: The Story of the Great Gettysburg Reunion, July, 1913* (Vineland: n.p., [c.1913]), 22–3.

79. Lesley J. Gordon, *General George E. Pickett in Life and Legend* (Chapel Hill: University of North Carolina Press, 1998).

80. *Fiftieth Anniversary of the Battle of Gettysburg: Report of the Pennsylvania Commission* (Harrisburg: n.p., 1913), 95.

NOTES

81. Trimble to UCV Commander in Chief C. Irvine Walker, March 4, 1912, in *Fiftieth Anniversary*, 15.

82. Available at: https://millercenter.org/the-presidency/presidential-speeches/july-4-1913-address-gettysburg.

83. "Garrison Welcomes the Blue and Gray," *New York Tribune*, July 2, 1913, p. 3.

84. Miller, ed., *Gettysburg*, 17.

85. Miller, ed., *Gettysburg*, 51.

86. *Washington Bee*, August 23, 1913.

87. Pennsylvania Railroad, *Gettysburg: The Story of the Battle of Gettysburg and the Field, Described as It Is on the Fiftieth Anniversary, 1863–1913* (Philadelphia, 1913).

88. Unrau, *Administrative History*, 116–20.

89. "Governor Mann," *Confederate Veteran*, 21:8 (Aug. 1913), 386.

90. Karen L. Cox, *Dixie's Daughters: The United Daughters of the Confederacy and the Preservation of Confederate Culture* (Gainesville: University Press of Florida, 2003), 50–1.

91. Quoted in Cox, *Dixie's Daughters*, 1.

92. Quoted in Cox, *Dixie's Daughters*, 141.

93. Mildred Rutherford, *Truths of history: a fair, unbiased, impartial, unprejudiced and conscientious study of history. Object: to secure a peaceful settlement of the many perplexing questions now causing contention between the North and the South* (n.p., 1920).

94. "Report of the History Committee," *Confederate Veteran* 6 (Oct 1898), 476.

95. "Delightful Reunion at Nashville," *Confederate Veteran* 4: 11 (Nov 1896), 362.

96. Message of Hon. Claude A. Swanson Governor of Virginia to the General Assembly Jan. 8, 1908 (Richmond: Davis Bottom, Superintendent of Public Printing, 1908), 10.

97. Thomas Smith to John P. Nicholson, March 29, 1912; Nicholson to L. L. Lomax, April 1, 1912; Nicholson to Smith, April 1, 1912; Nicholson to Lomax, April 11, 1912. Gettysburg National Military Park Library.

98. "Address at the Dedication of the Virginia Memorial at Gettysburg, Friday, June 8, 1917 By His Excellency Henry Carter Stuart, Governor of Virginia," *SHSP* (Sept. 1917) New Series, vol. 4, Old Series, vol. XLII.

99. Quoted in J. Christian Spielvogel, *Interpreting Sacred Ground: The Rhetoric of National Civil War Parks and Battlefields* (Tuscaloosa: University of Alabama Press, 2013), 94, 96.

100. "Address by Leigh Robinson," *SHSP* (Oct. 1917), New Series, vol. 4, Old Series, vol. XLII.

101. Greenville (South Carolina) *News*, May 31, 1922.

102. *Gettysburg Times*, Sept. 19, 1925.

103. *Gettysburg Times*, Sept. 30, Oct. 1, 2, 1926. The organizers blamed rain for the low attendance.

NOTES

Chapter 8

1. Speech of the President, July 3, 1938. https://www.battlefields.org/sites/default/files/atoms/files/fdr-gettysburg-speech2.pdf.
2. Jennifer M. Murray, *On a Great Battlefield: The Making, Management, and Memory of Gettysburg National Military Park, 1933–2013* (Knoxville: University of Tennessee Press, 2014), 19–24.
3. *The Baltimore Sun*, Baltimore, Maryland, Monday, Feb. 12, 1945.
4. *The Tribune*, Scranton, Pennsylvania, Monday, Nov. 19, 1945.
5. *Kenosha News*, Kenosha, Wisconsin, Friday, Jan. 12, 1945.
6. *The Times Herald*, Port Huron, Michigan, Thursday, Feb. 8, 1945.
7. Unrau, *Administrative History*, 219–21.
8. Philip Gleason, "Americans All: World War II and the Shaping of American Identity," *Review of Politics* 43 (1981): 483–581.
9. Copies of the film are held by the National Archives and by the British Film Institute and can be viewed online at http://www.screenonline.org.uk/film/id/727923/.
10. *Manchester Guardian*, Feb. 14, 1944; *The Times* (London), Feb. 14, 1944.
11. Duncannon Record, Duncannon, Pennsylvania, Thursday, Aug. 16, 1945.
12. Quoted in Murray, *On a Great Battlefield*, 83.
13. Quoted in Murray, *On a Great Battlefield*, 84.
14. Kammen, *Mystic Chords of Memory*, 537.
15. *Gettysburg Times* Visitors' Supplement, 1962, Tim Smith Collection, ACHS; Weeks, *Gettysburg*, 137–40.
16. Quoted in Jill Ogline Titus, *Gettysburg 1963: Civil Rights, Cold War Politics, and Historical Memory in America's Most Famous Small Town* (Chapel Hill: University of North Carolina Press, 2023) 34.
17. *Gettysburg Times*, Sept. 14, 1959.
18. Quoted in Murray, *On a Great Battlefield*, 31–2.
19. Adam I. P. Smith, "Re-enactors, National Identity and a 'Usable Past,'" in Robert Phillips and Helen Brocklehurst, eds. *History, Nationhood and the Question of Britain* (Basingstoke: Palgrave, 2004), 302–12.
20. The quote is from Alistair Cooke's report in the *Manchester Guardian*, July 12, 1956.
21. *The Gettysburg Times*, Gettysburg, Pennsylvania, Thursday, Nov. 19, 1959.
22. *New York Times*, May 11, 1957; Glenn La Fantasie, *Gettysburg Heroes*, 198.
23. There are slightly different versions of Eisenhower's remarks reported in the papers. See *New York Times*, May 13, 1957; *Gettysburg Times*, May 13, 1957; Louisville, Kentucky *Courier-Journal* May 13, 1957.
24. Quoted in La Fantasie, *Gettysburg Heroes*, 198. A Pathé News report of the visit can be viewed online at https://www.britishpathe.com/video/eisenhower-and-montgomery-see-the-civil-war-battle.

NOTES

25. "Gettysburg Refought," *Time*, May 27, 1957, p. 74; Richmond, Virginia, *Times-Ledger*, May 15, 1957; *New York Tribune*, May 13, 1957; *Washington Post*, May 14, 1957; *Atlanta Constitution*, May 13, 1957.

26. "Gettysburg Refought," *Time*, May 27, 1957, p. 74; Shelby, North Carolina, *Daily Star*, quoted in Richmond, Virginia, *Times-Ledger*, May 15, 1957.

27. Robert J. Cook, *Troubled Commemoration, The American Civil War Centennial, 1961–1965* (Baton Rouge, LA, 2007), 15.

28. Quoted in Jared Peatman, *The Long Shadow of Lincoln's Gettysburg Address* (Carbondale: Southern Illinois University Press, 2013), 175.

29. Peatman, *The Long Shadow*, 154.

30. Cook, *Troubled Commemoration*; Jon Weiner, "Civil War, Cold War, Civil Rights: The Civil War Centennial in Context, 1961–1965," in Alice Fahs and Joan Waugh, eds., *The Memory of the Civil War in American Culture* (Chapel Hill, NC, 2004), 237–57; Mary L. Dudziak, *Cold War Civil Rights: Race and the Image of American Democracy* (Princeton, NJ, 2000).

31. Murray, *On a Great Battlefield*, 99–100; Joan M. Zenzen, *Battling for Manassas: The Fifty Year Preservation Struggle at Manassas National Battlefield Park* (State College: Pennsylvania State University Press, 1998), 71.

32. Murray, *On a Great Battlefield*, 95–6.

33. Quoted in Brian Matthew Jordan, "'We Stand on the Same Battlefield': The Gettysburg Centenary and the Shadow of Race," *Pennsylvania Magazine of History and Biography*, 135:4 (Oct. 2011), 485.

34. *Gettysburg Times*, June 29, 1963, Section B p. 5, D:11, C:2.

35. *Gettysburg Times*, June 29, 1963, E:1 [Battle of Gettysburg Centennial Edition].

36. *Gettysburg Times*, June 29, 1963, EE.

37. Titus, *Gettysburg 1963*.

38. Robertson to Nevins in Nevins Papers, auoted in Peatman, *The Long Shadow*, 170.

39. *Gettysburg Times*, July 1, 1963.

40. Unrau, *Administrative History*, 262–3.

41. Murray, *On a Great Battlefield*, 102.

42. Jill Ogline Titus, *Gettysburg 1963: Civil Rights, Cold War Politics, and Historical Memory in America's Most Famous Small Town* (Chapel Hill: University of North Carolina Press, 2021).

43. Jim Weeks argues that the emergence of this new kind of hyper-informed war buff shifted the power balance at Gettysburg away from the Park Service as the gatekeepers of information and toward a new economy geared toward hobbyists and obsessives rather than the less informed general visitor. Weeks, *Gettysburg*, 166–7.

44. Titus, *Gettysburg*.

45. Jordan, "We Stand on the Same Battlefield," p. 483.

46. *Gettysburg Times*, May 31, 1963.

NOTES

47. George F. Emery to Ed D. Sturdivant, Oct 7, 1970; Tom P. Brady to George M. Emory, Oct. 21, 1971, Gettysburg National Miliary Park Library and Archives; Martin, *Confederate Monuments*, 33–4.
48. Acting Regional Director, Northeast Region to Director, Gettysburg Military Park, March 26, 1963.
49. *Gettysburg Times*, June 29, 1963, Section B, p. 11.
50. Titus, *Gettysburg 1963*.
51. *Montgomery Advertiser*, July 2, 1963, p. 2.
52. *Gettysburg Times*, July 3, 1963, p. 2.
53. Cook, *Troubled Commemoration*, 200.
54. *Gettysburg Times*, June 29, 1963, Section B, p. 9.
55. *Gettysburg Times*, July 2, 1963.
56. *Gettysburg Times*, Nov. 19, 1963.
57. Quoted in Martin, *Confederate Monuments*, 32–3.
58. Martin, *Confederate Monuments*, 47.
59. Max Freedman, "Gettysburg Has Unique Niche in US," *Fort Worth Star-Telegram*, July 4, 1963, p. 8.
60. David W. Blight, *American Oracle: The Civil War in the Civil Rights Era* (Cambridge, MA: Belknap Press of Harvard University Press, 2011), 123.
61. Robert Cook, "Bruce Catton, Middlebrow Culture, and the Liberal Search for Purpose in Cold War America," *Journal of American Studies* 47:1 (2013): 109–26.
62. Cook, "Bruce Catton," 125.
63. Remarks by President Carter, Oct. 25, 1998, at the University of Maryland, College Park. https://sadat.umd.edu/events/remarks-president-jimmy-carter.

Epilogue

1. Visitation statistics collected by the National Park Service are available at https://irma.nps.gov/Stats/SSRSReports.
2. US Department of the Interior, NPS, "(Draft) Resources Management Plan, GMNP (Natural Resources Management Plan)," Oct. 29, 1981, 1, DSC-TIC Files, GMNP Archives, quoted in Brian Black, "The Nature of Preservation: The Rise of Authenticity at Gettysburg," *Civil War History* 58, no. 3 (2012): 362.
3. Black, "The Nature of Preservation," 369.
4. *The Gettysburg Times*, Friday, May 7, 2004.
5. Quoted in Murray, *On a Great Battlefield*, 169.
6. Quoted in Weir, "Graying of Gettysburg," 72.
7. *The Baltimore Sun*, Sunday, May 14, 2000.
8. *York Sunday News* (York, PA), Sunday, June 25, 2000.
9. *York Sunday News* (York, PA), Sunday, June 25, 2000.

NOTES

10. Available at https://ushistoryscene.com/article/learn-the-address/. The author of the present work, although not American, also joined in. https://adamipsmith.com/2013/11/17/the-gettysburg-address-as-performance-art/.
11. Anonymous Battlefield Guide, interview with the author, March 2019.
12. According to a report by the Southern Poverty Law Center. https://www.splcenter.org/20190201/whose-heritage-public-symbols-confederacy.
13. Available at https://www.splcenter.org/presscenter/splc-reports-over-160-confederate-symbols-removed-2020.
14. Ta-Nehisi Coates, *The Atlantic Special Commemorative Issue on the Civil War*, 2013, 142.
15. David Brooks, "The Case for Reparations," *New York Times*, March 7, 2019.
16. Available at https://www.huffingtonpost.co.uk/entry/gettysburg-confederate-rally-kkk-antifa_n_59592bd8e4b05c37bb7f0ca4.
17. "In Gettysburg, Trump supporters clash with Black Lives Matter protesters as election nears," *Washington Post*, Oct. 30, 2020.
18. Bitt Isenberg, "Park Service and 'Patriots' failed the community last week," *Hannover Evening Sun*, July 8, 2020. https://eu.ydr.com/story/news/2020/07/06/gettysburg-park-expert-britt-isenberg-says-park-service-and-militia-both-failed/5384553002/.
19. "In Gettysburg, Trump supporters clash with Black Lives Matter protesters as election nears," *Washington Post*, Oct. 30, 2020.
20. Bryn Stole, "The Decline of the Civil War Reenactor," *New York Times*, July 28, 2018; Nick Sacco, "A statistical analysis of visitation to National Park Service Civil War Sites during the Sesquicentennial," Muster Blog, *Journal of the Civil War Era*, Jan. 9, 2018; John Coski, "Whither Public History?," *The Civil War Monitor*, June 25, 2018; Cameron McWhirter, "Civil War Battlefields Lose Ground as Tourist Draws," *Wall Street Journal*, May 25, 2019.
21. "'We wanted to send a message': Reenactors stage Civil War battle despite threat", *Washington Post*, Oct 15, 2017.
22. M. Scott Mahaskey and Peter Canellos, "Are Americans Falling Out of Love with their Landmarks?" *Politico*, July 4, 2019. https://www.politico.com/magazine/story/2019/07/04/are-americans-falling-out-of-love-with-their-landmarks-227258.
23. Available at https://edition.cnn.com/2020/10/06/opinions/biden-gettysburg-address-campaign-best-avlon/index.html.
24. Available at https://transcripts.cnn.com/show/cnr/date/2016-10-22/segment/03.
25. Nikole Hannah-Jones, "Our democracy's founding ideals were false when they were written. Black Americans have fought to make them true," *New York Times*, Aug. 14, 2019.

FURTHER READING

There are literally whole libraries full of nothing but books on the battle itself. In a crowded field, those I found especially useful were Edwin B. Coddington, *The Gettysburg Campaign: A Study in Command* (New York: Scribner, 1968); Stephen W. Sears, *Gettysburg* (Boston: Houghton Mifflin, 2004); Gary W. Gallagher, ed., *Three Days at Gettysburg: Essays on Confederate and Union Leadership* (Kent, Ohio: Kent State University Press, 1993); Earl J. Hess, *Pickett's Charge: The Last Attack at Gettysburg* (Chapel Hill: University of North Carolina Press, 2001); and Kent Masterson Brown, *Retreat from Gettysburg: Lee, Logistics, and the Pennsylvania Campaign* (Chapel Hill: University of North Carolina Press, 2005).

On the town in 1863 and subsequently, see Margaret S. Creighton, *The Colors of Courage: Gettysburg's Forgotten History, Immigrants, Women, and African Americans in the Civil War's Defining Battle* (New York: Basic Books, 2005) and Jill Ogline Titus, *Gettysburg 1963: Civil Rights, Cold War Politics, and Historical Memory in America's Most Famous Small Town* (Chapel Hill: The University of North Carolina Press, 2023).

On Lincoln's address, see Garry Wills, *Lincoln at Gettysburg: The Words that Remade America* (New York: Simon & Schuster, 1992); Martin P. Johnson, *Writing the Gettysburg Address* (Lawrence: University Press of Kansas, 2013); Sean Conant, ed., *The Gettysburg Address: Perspectives on Lincoln's Greatest Speech* (New York: Oxford University Press, 2015); and Jared Peatman, *The Long Shadow of Lincoln's Gettysburg Address* (Carbondale: Southern Illinois University Press, 2013).

There is a rich field of scholarship on Gettysburg's place in American memory. I particularly recommend Thomas Desjardin, *These Honored Dead: How the Story of Gettysburg Shaped American Memory* (Cambridge, Mass.: Da Capo Press, 2003); Jim Weeks, *Gettysburg: Memory, Market, and an American Shrine* (Princeton, NJ: Princeton University Press, 2003); Carole Reardon, *Pickett's Charge in History and Memory* (Chapel Hill: University of North Carolina Press, 1997); and Jennifer M. Murray, *On a Great Battlefield: The Making, Management, and Memory of Gettysburg National Military Park, 1933–2013* (Knoxville: University of Tennessee, 2014).

And on the memory and meaning of the Civil War more generally, a burgeoning field, readers should start with David Blight, *Race and Reunion: The Civil War in American Memory* (Cambridge, Mass.: Harvard University Press, 2001);

FURTHER READING

Nina Silber, *The Romance of Reunion, 1865–1900* (Chapel Hill: University of North Carolina Press, 1993); Caroline E. Janney, *Remembering the Civil War: Reunion and the Limits of Reconciliation* (Chapel Hill: University of North Carolina Press, 2013); and Robert Cook, *Civil War Memories: Contesting the Past in the United States Since 1865* (Baltimore: Johns Hopkins University Press, 2017).

PICTURE AND MAP ACKNOWLEDGMENTS

Fig. 2.1 https://www.loc.gov/resource/cph.3a47524/

Fig. 3.1 https://www.flickr.com/photos/britishlibrary/11289122496/

Fig. 4.1 https://www.gettysburgdaily.com/the-gettysburg-sketches-of-edwin-forbes/

Fig. 5.1 Hartford, Conn.: The War Photograph & Exhibition Company, No. 21 Linden Place, printed later. Photograph. https://www.loc.gov/item/2009630184/

Fig. 6.1 Engraving in public domain: https://commons.wikimedia.org/wiki/File:The_battle_of_Gettysburg_-_P.F._Rothermel_1870_;_P.F._Rothermel_pinx._;_John_Sartain_sculp._LCCN2006678602.jpg

Fig. 7.1 https://www.loc.gov/item/93517377/

Fig. 7.2 Author's photo

Fig. 7.3 Published in John W. Frazier, *Reunion of the Blue and Gray: Philadelphia Brigade and Pickett's Division* (Philadelphia: Ware Bros, 1906), 105.

Fig. 7.4 https://en.wikipedia.org/wiki/1913_Gettysburg_reunion#/media/File:Reunion_of_Confederate_and_Federal_veterans_at_Gettysburg.jpg

Fig. 7.5 O'Sullivan, Timothy H., photographer. *Gettysburg, PA. Dead Confederate soldier in Devil's Den.* United States Pennsylvania Gettysburg, 1863. July. Photograph. https://www.loc.gov/item/2018666313/

Fig. 8.1 Collections of the Boston Public Library. https://www.digitalcommonwealth.org/search/commonwealth:gx41nk00p

Fig. 8.2 https://www.nps.gov/Museum/exhibits/eise/Mamie/personal_interests/ENHS2453A-T.html

Map 2.1 https://upload.wikimedia.org/wikipedia/commons/7/77/Gettysburg_Campaign.png

Map 3.1 https://upload.wikimedia.org/wikipedia/commons/e/ea/Gettysburg_Battle_Map_Day1.png

Map 3.2 https://en.wikipedia.org/wiki/Battle_of_Gettysburg#/media/File:Gettysburg_Day2_Plan.png

Map 3.3 https://en.wikipedia.org/wiki/Battle_of_Gettysburg#/media/File:Gettysburg_Battle_Map_Day2.png

Map 4.1 https://upload.wikimedia.org/wikipedia/commons/9/9e/Gettysburg_Battle_Map_Day3.png

INDEX

For the benefit of digital users, indexed terms that span two pages (e.g., 52–53) may, on occasion, appear on only one of those pages.

Adams, Charles Francis, Jr. 52–4
Adams, John 23–4
Adams, John Quincy 23–4
African Americans (in 1863) 15–18, 77
Alabama Infantry Regiments: 4th 95–6; 44th 91; 48th 91, 93–4
Alexander, Edward Porter (Colonel, CSA) 48, 79, 100–1
Alfred Iverson (General, CSA) 72–3
American Colonization Society 20–1
American exceptionalism, concept of 143–7, 257–9
American Revolution 18–19, 24, 141, 143–4
Anderson, Marion 243–4
Anderson, Robert (Major, USA) 30–1
anti-war movement (in the North) 37–8, 43–4, 56–7
Archer, James (General, CSA) 64–5, 68–9
Arkansas Regiments: 3rd 91
Armistead, Lewis A. (General, CSA) 9–10, 110–11, 117–18, 251
Army of Northern Virginia 35, 37–8, 40–3, 47–8, 126–8 See also *individual Corps and Regiments*
Army of the Potomac 37–40, 61–2 see also *individual Corps and Regiments*
Arnold, Frederick 187–8
Arquette, Cliff 227
Artillery Bombardment (engagement on July 3) 112–15

Bachelder, John B. 24, 192–200, 206–8, 241
Barksdale, William (General, CSA) 101–2
Barlow, Francis C. (General, USA) 52–4, 74–5
Barnett, Ross 241–2
Begin, Menachem 246–7
Biden, Joe 258–9

Big Pipe Creek, MD 62–3, 79, 129–30
Bingham, Henry H. 206–7
Black Lives Matter 256–8
Black, John C. (Colonel, USA) 21–2
Blackford, W. W. 49
Blenker, Ludwig 70–2
Bragg, Braxton, (General, CSA) 41, 150
Brandy Station, Battle of (1863) 49–50
Brooks, David 254–5
Brown, Pat 243
Buchanan, James 27–9, 31
Buck, George Washington (Private, USA) 97–8
Buford, John (General, USA) 49–50, 63, 65–8
Bull Run, Battle of (1861) 129
Bureau of Military Intelligence 56–7, 107–8
Burns, Ken 249–50, 253–5

Calder, William (Private, CSA) 78–9
Carlisle, Pennsylvania 51–2
Carter, Jimmy 246–7
Cashtown, Pennsylvania 59–60, 64–5
casualties 118, 121
Catton, Bruce 20, 62–3, 245–6, 260
cavalry, role of in Pennsylvania campaign 49–50, 63–4, 66–7, 120–3, 128
Cemetery Hill 18–19, 72–3, 78–80, 105–6
Chamberlain, Joshua Lawrence (Colonel, USA) 21, 85–6, 94–100
Chambersburg, Pennsylvania 15, 31–2, 51–2, 60–1
Chancellorsville, Battle of (1863) 38–41, 61–2, 85, 88, 91–3
Chandler, Zachariah 129
Chickamauga, Battle of (1863) 150
Churchill, Winston 21, 224–5
Civil Rights Movement 235–45

INDEX

Civil War Centennial 235–45
Civil War Centennial Commission 235–9
Civil War, causes 15–31, 251–2
Civil War, reasons for Union victory 37–8, 150–6
Civilian Conservation Corps 221–2, 224
Clare, Lydia (Gettysburg resident) 64
Cleveland, Grover 166–7
Coates, Ta-Nahisi 254–5
Coddington, Edwin B. 122–3, 194–5
Cold War 235–6, 238–9, 248
Columbia-Wrightsville Bridge (engagement, June 28, 1863), 58–9
Conscription, Union 39–40
Cook, Clarence 160–1
Corinth, Battle of (1862) 34
Cormany, Rachel (Chambersburg resident) 31–2
Creasy, Edward Sir 21–2, 187–9
Crouch, Darius, (General, USA) 55
Culp, Wesley (Private, CSA) 33–4, 111
Culp's Hill 18–19, 72, 78, 103–6, 110–12
Curtin, Andrew 55–6, 136–9
Custer, George Armstrong 120–1
cyclorama, "Battle of Gettysburg" 212–14, 236–7, 252–3

Dailey, Denis Burke (Private, USA) 68–9
Daniels, Jeff 95, 249–50
Daughters of the Confederacy 215–17
Davis, Charles (Private, USA) 54–5
Davis, Jefferson 31–2, 36–7, 42–3, 45–8
De Lue, Donald 239–47
De Peyster, John Watts 188–9
Democratic Party 22–3, 87–8, 147–8, 155, 240–1
Desjardin, Thomas 172, 197
Devil's Den (engagement on July 2) 90–4
Dooley, John (Private, CSA) 52
Doubleday, Abner (General, USA) 69–70, 129–30, 195–6
Douglas-Fairhurst, Robert 186–7
Douglass, Frederick 163–5, 181, 183
Dred Scott Decision (1857) 25–6

Early, Jubal (General, CSA) 51–2, 58–9, 73–6, 78, 104–5, 170–3
Eastman, Mary Henderson 184–5
Eisenhower, Dwight 16, 231–6, 238–9, 243–4, 246–7
Ellis, Van Horne (Colonel, USA) 91–3
Ellison, James (Captain, USA) 97–8

Emancipation Proclamation 27, 40
Emory, Ambrose 135
Eternal Light Peace Memorial 221–3, 239, 243
Evans, Hiram Wesley 219–20
Everett, Edward 140–1
Ewell, Richard (General, CSA) 20–1, 47–8, 76–80, 103–4, 110–11, 126–7, 172
Ewell's Corps (Army of Northern Virginia) 59–60, 73

Faulkner, William 8
Fields, Barbara 249–50
Fisk, Wilbur (Private, USA) 123
Floyd, George 254–5
Foner, Eric 251–3
Foote, Shelby 246–7, 249–50, 254–5
Forbes, Edwin 124
Fort Sumter, Battle of (1861) 30–1
Foster, Catherine (Gettysburg resident) 57–8
Fourteenth Amendment to the US Constitution 162–3
Franklin D. Roosevelt 221–2
Franklin, Benjamin 18–19
Fredericksburg, Battle of (1862) 38–9
Freedman, Max 245–6
Freeman, Morgan 253–4
Fremantle, Arthur 44, 83–4, 123–4, 132–3
Fugitive Slave Act of 1850 23–4

Garnett, Richard B. (General, CSA) 110–11, 117
Garrison, William Lloyd 260
Gettysburg (1993 film) 21, 249–50
Gettysburg (town) 32–4, 57–8
Gettysburg Address (of Abraham Lincoln) 2–3, 10–11, 138–49, 224–6, 235–6, 244–7
Gettysburg Battlefield Memorial Association 134–5, 188–94, 199–200, 203–8
Gettysburg Battlefield Preservation Association 227–8
Gettysburg National Military Park 186–7, 206–8, 214, 221–2, 248–9
Gibbon, John (General, USA) 88–9
Gilbert, Emma (Gettysburg resident) 75–6
Gilsa, Leopold von (Colonel, USA) 74–5
Gladstone, William E. 151–2
Gordon, John B. (General, CSA) 170–1
Grand Army of the Republic 164–7, 191–2, 197, 206, 210–11
Grant, Ulysses (General, USA) 27, 41, 99–100, 150, 179

294

INDEX

Greeley, Horace 154–5, 179
Greene, George S. (General, USA) 104–5

Haggler, Joseph 239–40
Halleck, Henry (General-in-Chief) 61–2
Hamilton, Alexander 18–19
Hampton, Wade (General, CSA) 48, 203
Hancock, Winfield Scott (General,
 USA) 77, 85, 88, 102, 114–15
Harding, Warren 219, 256
Harman, Troy D. 65
Harrisburg, PA 58–9
Harrison, Henry Thomas 59
Harrison, Walter 196–7
Harsh, Joseph 30–1
Haskell, Frank (Lieutenant, USA) 17–18,
 61–2, 115–16
Hawthorne, Nathaniel 144
Hay, John 140
Hays, Harry T. (General, CSA) 105–6
Hesburgh, Theodore M. 243
Heth, Henry (General, CSA) 64–7, 74, 136
High Water Mark Monument
 196–200, 224
Hill, A. P. (General, CSA) 20–1, 47–8,
 64–5, 110–11
Hill's Corps (Army of Northern
 Virginia) 59–60, 73, 78, 102–3, 110–11
Hogg, Quintin 224–5
Hoke, Jacob 179–80, 183–4
Holmes, Richard 17–18
Hood, John B. (General, CSA) 86–7, 91–3
Hooker, Joseph (General, USA) 39–40, 48,
 50, 59, 61–2, 129
Howard, Oliver O. (General, USA) 35,
 70–2, 77, 105–6, 209–10
Hughes, Richard 243
Humiston, Amos 135–6
Humphreys, Andrew (General, USA) 101
Hunt, Henry (Colonel, USA) 89, 112, 114

I (First) Corps (Army of the Potomac) 72–3
II (Second) Corps (Army of the
 Potomac) 77, 88–9
III (Third) Corps (Army of the
 Potomac) 72–90, 101
Ingraham, William M. 218–19
Ireland, David (Colonel, USA) 104–5

Jackson, Thomas J. "Stonewall"
 (General, CSA) 40–1, 47–8, 74–5,
 151–2, 171–2, 181–2, 230

Jacobitism 141
Jenkins, Albert (General, CSA) 15
Johnson, Andrew 163–4
Johnson, Lyndon 240–1, 243
Johnson, Martin P. 142–3
Joint Congressional Committee on the
 Conduct of the War 129–31
Jomini, Antoine-Henri 35
Jones, John B. 150
Jones, Marcellus (Lieutenant, USA)
 65–6
Julian, George Washington 129

Kammen, Michael 227
Kemper, James L. (General, CSA)
 110–11, 118
Kennedy, John F. 240–1, 243–4
King, Louis 221–2
King, Martin Luther 235–6
Ku Klux Klan 219–20, 256

Ladies Memorial Associations 168–9
Lang, David (General, CSA) 110–11
Latimer, E. 184
Law, Evander M. (General, CSA) 91–4
Lee, Robert E. (General, CSA) 9, 31–2, 35;
 and strategy during the invasion of
 Pennsylvania 37–9, 43–8, 54, 58–60;
 and slavery 17–18; on July 1 73,
 78–80; leadership on July 2 80–5, 106;
 leadership on July 3 107–13, 122–5,
 131–3; loss of aura of invincibility 126;
 and end of the war 156; death 172,
 180–1; and postwar/posthumous
 reputation 171–7, 232–3, 239–40,
 249–50, 254–5 See also Virginia
 Monument
Lincoln, Abraham 10–11, 21–3, 259; rise to
 power of 25–6; and Union military
 strategy 39–40, 128–9 and
 slavery 25–6, 40, 145–7 See also
 Gettysburg Address
Little Round Top 4–5, 19–21, 72, 86,
 91–100, 190–1
Long, James T. (Captain, USA) 179–80,
 186–7
Longstreet, James (General, CSA)
 mentioned 17, 20–1, 35, 42–3, 59, 61, 82;
 disagreements with Lee 46, 84; alleged
 misjudgements 21, 47–8; leadership
 on July 2 86–7, 90; leadership on
 July 3 108–11; postwar reputation 172–7

295

INDEX

Longstreet's Corps (Army of Northern Virginia) 61, 73, 80, 102–3, 110–11
"Lost Cause", myth 18, 24, 51–4, 167–77, 182–4, 189–90, 202–3, 219–20, 234–5, 240–3, 245–7
Louisiana Monument 244
Lutheran Theological Seminary, Gettysburg 64, 75

Maine Regiments: 20th Infantry 85–6, 94–100
Makepeace, Clare 18
Maloney, Patrick (Private, USA) 68–9
Mann, Henry 157–8
Mann, William Hodges 215
Marshall, Charles 59–61
McAllister, Mary (Gettysburg resident) 68–9, 74
McClellan, George (General, USA) 35–6
McConaghie, James R. 222–3
McConaughy, David 134–5, 190–4
McCreary, Albertus (Gettysburg resident) 77
McCullough, David 249–50
McKaye, Percy 164–5
McPherson, James 78–9
McPherson, James 251–3
Mead, Chrisopher (Corporal, USA) 115–16
Meade, George (General, USA) 9, 35, 61–2; and strategy during the invasion of Pennsylvania 62–3; on July 1 77–8; on July 2 85, 88–9, 100–1, 103; on July 3 107–8, 124–5; failure to capture Lee's army after the battle 126–31; postwar 165–6
Mexican War 21–3
Military Strategy (Confederacy) 36–8
Military Strategy (Union) 30, 36
Miller, Francis Trevelyan 213
Minnesota Infantry Regiments: 1st 101–2
Mississippi Monument 244–5
Montgomery, Bernard Law (Viscount Montgomery of Alamein) 232–6
Moore, Ward 6
Morton, Oliver P. 165–6
Myers, Sallie (Gettysburg resident) 75–6

Nathan, Adela 238–9
National Cemetery (at Gettysburg) 25, 136–8, 165–6
National Park Service 221–3, 226–7, 229–32, 236–9, 241, 249–53, 257–8

New Deal 221–2
New York Infantry Regiments: 40th 93–4; 95th 69 76th 70 147th 70 124th 93–4 137th 104–5
Nixon, Richard 256

Oates, William C. (General, CSA) 95–6, 100
Olivier, Laurence 224–5

Peach Orchard (site of engagement on July 2) 88–9, 100–1
Pemberton, John C. (General, CSA) 41–2
Pendleton, William N. (General, CSA) 113–14, 172–3
Pennsylvania Regiments: 56th 70; 71st 104–5; 72nd 199–200
Pennsylvania State Centennial Commission 237
Pennsylvania, Confederate Invasion of 38–9
Pettigrew, James J. (General, CSA) 64–5, 110–11
Philippoteaux, Paul 212–14, 252–3
Pickett, George (General, CSA) 6–7, 17, 85–6, 109–11, 176–7
Pickett's Charge 2, 6–7, 9–10, 110, 115–21, 176–7, 210, 232–3, 237–8, 242–3
Pierce, Tillie (Gettysburg resident) 33, 58
Pollard, Edward 171–2, 189
Power, J. Tracy 152
Providentialism 171, 187–8
Public Works Administration 221–2

re-enactors 229–31, 242–3, 248, 250–1, 257–8
Reardon, Carol 3–4
reconstruction, postwar 161–3
redemption, concept of in relation to the battle 136, 140, 144–7, 183–5, 249–53
Republican Party 25–7, 161–5
reunions: 1887 203–6; 1913 208–14; 1938 221
Reynolds, John (General, USA) 62–3, 66–7, 69, 136, 142–3
Rhodes, E. Washington 243–4
Robertson, James I. 238–9
Robertson, Jerome Bonaparte (General, CSA) 91
Robinson, Leigh 218–19
Rodes, Robert (General, CSA) 70, 72–3, 172–3
Rosecrans, William (General, USA) 41
Rothermel, Peter F. 157–61, 177–8
Ruskin, John 181–2

INDEX

Russell, Lord John 151–2
Rutherford, Mildred 215–17

Sadat, Anwar 246–7
Sanford, Terry 237–8
Saunders, William 137
Scales, Alfred M. (General, CSA) 75
Schimmelfennig, Alexander (General, USA) 70–3, 113–14
Schurz, Carl (General, USA) 70–2, 79, 85–7, 116
Scott, Winfield (General, USA) 35–6
Sears, Stephen W. 50, 107–8
secession 26–30
Seddon, James 42–3
Sedgwick, John (General, USA) 35
Setser, Tom (Private, CSA) 74
Shaara, Michael 21, 99–100, 249–50
Sherman, William T. (General, USA) 154–5
Sickles, Dan (General, USA) 72–90, 100–1, 103, 129–31, 209–10
Sigel, Franz 70–2
Silber, Nina 251–3
slavery 15–32, 95, 140–1, 145–7, 155, 161–2, 165–6, 168, 183–5, 209–10, 215–19, 247, 260–1
Slocum, Henry (General, USA) 72
Smith, James E. (Captain, USA) 89, 94
Southern Historical Society 170
Speed, John Gilmer 7–8
Stanton, Edwin B. 87–8, 129–30
Staunton, VA 51–2
Steinwehr, Adolph (General, USA) 72
Stephens, Alexander 17–18
Stevens, Thaddeus 51–2, 163
Stockton, Thomas 140
Stowe, Calvin 95
Stowe, Harriet Beecher 23, 95
Stuart, Henry Carter 217–18
Stuart, J. E. B. (General, CSA) 20–1, 49–51, 59–61, 120–1, 128, 172, 234
Sumner, Charles 163–4
Swinton, William 176–7
Sykes, George (General, USA) 89

Tate, James 251–2
Texas Infantry Regiments: 1st 91; 4th 95–6; 5th 94–6
The Killer Angels 21, 99–100, 249–50
Thirteenth Amendment to the US Constitution 155, 161–2
Tilberg, Frederick 226
Tolkein, J. R. R. 12

Toombs Robert 31–3
tourism at Gettysburg 190–5, 212–14, 226–30, 239–42, 248, 250–1, 257–8
Tozier, Andrew (Sergeant, USA) 97–8
Trimble, Isaac Ridgeway (General, CSA) 54–5, 110–11, 116–17
Trump, Donald 254–9

United States Christian Commission 121

V (Fifth) Corps (Army of the Potomac) 89
V Corps (Army of the Potomac) 85–6, 89–90, 124–5
Vicksburg, Battle of 27–8, 41–2
Vincent, Strong (Colonel, USA) 90, 94–5, 99, 190–1
Virginia Infantry Regiments: 10th CeP71; 23rd 104–5
Virginia Monument 217–19, 232–3

Wade, Ben 129
Wade, Mary Virginia ("Jennie") 184–5
Walker, James 194–5
Wallace, George C. 242–3, 256
Wallace, Henry 224–5
Warren, Gouverneur K. (General, USA) 62–3, 90
Waterloo, Battle of 21–2, 27, 125–6, 187–90, 197, 209–10, 258
Webb, Alexander (General, USA) 118–20
Weeks, Jim 135
Wert, Jacob (Gettysburg resident) 183–4
West Point Military Academy 35–6, 104
Wheatfield (site of engagement on July 2) 100–1
Wilcox, Cadmus (General, CSA) 110–11
Willard, George L. (Colonel, USA) 101
Willis, David 136–9
Wills, Gary 143–4
Wilson, Woodrow 211–12, 218–19
Wisconsin Infantry Regiments: 2nd 68–9 6th 69; 7th 68–9
World War II 223–6, 232–3
Wright, Ambrose (General, CSA) 102–3

XI (Eleventh) Corps (Army of the Potomac) 63–4, 70–6, 105–6
XII (Twelfth) Corps (Army of the Potomac) 72

Young, Annie (Gettysburg resident) 75–7
Young, Louis (Lieutenant, CSA) 64–5

297